"Through Newton's words and Tony's w[...]
on the heart, so that we see Christ more ~~fully. And more fully~~ means seeing him
as *more precious*. And *more precious* means *more powerful to heal us and change us*.
Relentlessly focused on the sweetness and the greatness of Christ as the Savior
and Satisfier of our souls, over this book flies the banner of John Newton: 'None
but Jesus.'"

> **John Piper,** Founder, desiringGod.org; Chancellor, Bethlehem College and
> Seminary

"Here is mastery! As the Lord Jesus Christ, crucified and reigning, was the life-
giving focus of the Evangelical Revival, and as George Whitefield was its supreme
awakener, and John Wesley its brilliant discipler, so ex–slave trader John Newton
was its peerless pastoral counselor and perhaps the greatest Christian letter
writer of all time. In his 768-footnote digest of the spiritual wisdom in Newton's
thousand-plus published letters, along with his published sermons and hymns,
Reinke distills a vast flow of pure honey for the Christian heart. This is a book to
read over and over again."

> **J. I. Packer,** Board of Governors' Professor of Theology, Regent College

"Linger long here. The depths and riches within these pages are truly rare and answer what your soul most hungers for: life in Christ. I will be returning to this book
many, many times over."

> **Ann Voskamp,** author, *New York Times* best seller, *One Thousand Gifts*

"*Newton on the Christian Life* is a magnum opus (though Tony still has plenty of time
to surpass it)—a bold project, beautifully done. You know *about* John Newton; now
you can be pastored by him. You will feel known by him. You will be encouraged
that your struggles are like his and his congregants. And you will discover again
that huge helpings of the beauty and love of Jesus are the perfect antidote for our
self-consumed lives."

> **Ed Welch,** counselor and faculty member, The Christian Counseling and
> Educational Foundation

"The Christian life is *Christ*, as John Newton clarified so helpfully. If you are still
treating Christianity as a strategy for your own self-improvement, this book will not
satisfy you. But if you have despaired of yourself and are now clinging only to Christ,
this book will refresh you. Newton's practical counsel, brought vividly to life again
by Tony Reinke, will lead you into the green pastures and beside the still waters that
are, at this moment, awaiting you in your all-sufficient Savior. For some readers,
this book may just become the most important book, outside the Bible, they will
ever read."

> **Raymond C. Ortlund Jr.,** Lead Pastor, Immanuel Church, Nashville,
> Tennessee

"Best known for the iconic hymn 'Amazing Grace,' John Newton deserves to be equally known for his tremendous corpus of spiritual letters. In them, Newton's gifting as a pastoral cardiologist with few peers is on full display. Many of the main struggles and joys of the human heart have not changed. And, as Reinke ably shows, Newton's advice, given in a world somewhat different from ours, is still potent and relevant. Very highly recommended."

Michael A. G. Haykin, Professor of Church History and Biblical Spirituality, The Southern Baptist Theological Seminary

"Newton's pastoral letters are a unique and rich resource for Christians today, and both of us owe them a debt too great to describe. However, they constitute a notoriously difficult body of work in which to navigate. Many a time you can remember some gem you have read in these letters but now can't locate. Here we have a guide to Newton's main themes and topics, as well as considered treatments of many of his most valuable letters. This is a welcome tool for Christian growth and discipleship."

Tim and Kathy Keller, Redeemer Presbyterian Church, New York City

"This book is worth every minute of your time, whether or not you have any interest in John Newton. Reinke brings out Newton in all his cheer to minister to readers. The result is a Christ-exalting manual for growth into Christian joy, freedom, and fruitfulness. No, more than a manual, this is a work of beauty to be read again and again."

Michael Reeves, Director of Union and Senior Lecturer, Wales Evangelical School of Theology; author, *Delighting in the Trinity*, *The Unquenchable Flame*, and *Rejoicing in Christ*

"John Newton mentored his young friend William Wilberforce into politics, which eventually led to the abolition of the British slave trade. To this day, Newton's letters continue to disciple generations of Christians. This book draws together Newton's key life lessons in a way every Christian can apply. As a state governor, a former member of Congress, and a Christian in public service, I am reminded by Newton that we are never more valuable to our society than after we have been humbled by the amazing grace of God."

Mike Pence

"Reinke takes us well beyond the hymn 'Amazing Grace' to explore John Newton's stirring pastoral ministry and soaring vision of the believer's life in Christ. I am delighted to recommend this book."

Thomas S. Kidd, Professor of History, Baylor University; author, *The Great Awakening: The Roots of Evangelical Christianity in Colonial America*

"This book, by one of the brightest writers in contemporary evangelicalism, examines the life lessons of a hymn writer, a freedom fighter, and a gospel preacher. Even if you don't think you like church history, you will love this book. Reinke ties Newton's life and thought to practical applications for every believer. I encourage you to read and savor anew the grace that saved wretches like us."

Russell D. Moore, President, The Ethics & Religious Liberty Commission; author, *Tempted and Tried*

"You may think you are acquainted with John Newton: converted slave trader, pastor, writer of the hymn 'Amazing Grace.' Get ready to meet the man you only think you know. Reinke guides us on a tour of Newton's theology through his life and letters. This book is pastoral theology at its finest. Newton was a man captured by Christ, exalting Christ, and caring for God's people by pointing them to Christ and him crucified."

C. J. Mahaney, Senior Pastor, Sovereign Grace Church of Louisville, Louisville, Kentucky

"Although John Newton authored what would become America's best-loved hymn, his contemporaries thought his best gift was letter writing. Rarely, if ever, has so much wisdom, love, sanity, balance, genuine affection, and wonderfully down-to-earth-because-full-of-heaven practical counsel been expressed in letters written in the English language. Underneath them all runs knowledge of the Word of God, a devotion to the Son of God, and a love for the people of God. Newton makes us feel, even two centuries later, that he was writing for us, and that he knew us well. Reinke has done the whole church a service by recovering Newton's letters from obscurity. *Newton on the Christian Life* is a taste of spiritual manna that will make us want to read the letters of Newton for ourselves."

Sinclair B. Ferguson, Professor of Systematic Theology, Redeemer Seminary, Dallas, Texas

"This book presents valuable lessons from the ministry of John Newton. His perception of grace permeated his theology, his thinking, his experience, his hopes, his ministry, and even his dying. As Reinke writes, grace was 'the air he breathed.' Here we catch glimpses into the workings of Newton's heart as he focused unreservedly on living for and through the Lord Jesus Christ."

Marylynn Rouse, Director, The John Newton Project

NEWTON

on the Christian Life

THEOLOGIANS ON THE CHRISTIAN LIFE

EDITED BY STEPHEN J. NICHOLS AND JUSTIN TAYLOR

Bonhoeffer on the Christian Life:
From the Cross, for the World,
Stephen J. Nichols

Calvin on the Christian Life:
Glorifying and Enjoying God Forever,
Michael Horton

Edwards on the Christian Life:
Alive to the Beauty of God,
Dane C. Ortlund

Luther on the Christian Life:
Cross and Freedom,
Carl R. Trueman

Newton on the Christian Life:
To Live Is Christ,
Tony Reinke

Packer on the Christian Life:
Knowing God in Christ, Walking by the Spirit,
Sam Storms

Schaeffer on the Christian Life:
Countercultural Spirituality,
William Edgar

Warfield on the Christian Life:
Living in Light of the Gospel,
Fred G. Zaspel

Wesley on the Christian Life:
The Heart Renewed in Love,
Fred Sanders

NEWTON

on the Christian Life

TO LIVE IS CHRIST

TONY REINKE

FOREWORD BY JOHN PIPER

CROSSWAY

WHEATON, ILLINOIS

Newton on the Christian Life: To Live Is Christ

Copyright © 2015 by Tony S. Reinke

Published by Crossway
   1300 Crescent Street
   Wheaton, Illinois 60187

Cover design: Josh Dennis

Cover image: Richard Solomon Artists, Mark Summers

First printing 2015

Printed in the United States of America

The author's Scripture quotations are from the ESV® Bible (The Holy Bible, English Standard Version®), copyright © 2001 by Crossway, a publishing ministry of Good News Publishers. Used by permission. All rights reserved.

All emphases in Scripture quotations have been added by the author.

Trade paperback ISBN: 978-1-4335-3971-8
ePub ISBN: 978-1-4335-3974-9
PDF ISBN: 978-1-4335-3972-5
Mobipocket ISBN: 978-1-4335-3973-2

Library of Congress Cataloging-in-Publication Data

Reinke, Tony, 1977–
Newton on the Christian life: to live is Christ / Tony Reinke;
foreword by John Piper.
   pages cm. — (Theologians on the Christian life)
 Includes bibliographical references and index.
 ISBN 978-1-4335-3971-8 (tp)
1. Newton, John, 1725–1807. 2. Church of England—Clergy—
Biography. 3. Hymn writers—England—Biography. I. Title.
BX5199.N55R45   2015
248.4092—dc23   2014038068

Crossway is a publishing ministry of Good News Publishers.

VP		25	24	23	22	21	20	19	18	17	16	15
15	14	13	12	11	10	9	8	7	6	5	4	3	2	1

To Karalee

I thank the Lord if he makes my writings useful. I hope they contain some of his truths; and truth, like a torch, may be seen by its own light without reference to the hand that holds it.

JOHN NEWTON

CONTENTS

SERIES PREFACE

Some might call us spoiled. We live in an era of significant and substantial resources for Christians on living the Christian life. We have ready access to books, DVD series, online material, seminars—all in the interest of encouraging us in our daily walk with Christ. The laity, the people in the pew, have access to more information than scholars dreamed of having in previous centuries.

Yet for all our abundance of resources, we also lack something. We tend to lack the perspectives from the past, perspectives from a different time and place than our own. To put the matter differently, we have so many riches in our current horizon that we tend not to look to the horizons of the past.

That is unfortunate, especially when it comes to learning about and practicing discipleship. It's like owning a mansion and choosing to live in only one room. This series invites you to explore the other rooms.

As we go exploring, we will visit places and times different from our own. We will see different models, approaches, and emphases. This series does not intend for these models to be copied uncritically, and it certainly does not intend to put these figures from the past high upon a pedestal like some race of super-Christians. This series intends, however, to help us in the present listen to the past. We believe there is wisdom in the past twenty centuries of the church, wisdom for living the Christian life.

Stephen J. Nichols and Justin Taylor

FOREWORD

One of the most remarkable things about this book is that the voice of Tony Reinke and the voice of John Newton have become almost indistinguishable. This is not because Tony fails to cite Newton or give him credit. Quotations abound. It's because Tony has absorbed the spirit and mind of John Newton. This makes for an uninterrupted immersion into the soul of "the old African blasphemer."

There are few immersions that would be more valuable for your soul. J. I. Packer gives part of the reason: "Ex-slavetrader John Newton was the friendliest, wisest, humblest and least pushy of all the eighteenth-century evangelical leaders, and was perhaps the greatest pastoral letter-writer of all time." Tony has lived in those one thousand letters long enough to be the sweet aroma of this "least-pushy" of eighteenth-century giants.

True humility can take dramatically different forms from one clay pot to another. The form it took in Newton was Christ-exalting tenderness. His own experience of "amazing grace" (he wrote the song) worked its way so deeply into his soul that the log of self-justification was chopped up, and Newton became a delicate surgeon for taking specks out of many sin-sick eyes.

And since, as Tony demonstrates, "Newton is a master craftsman of metaphors for the Christian life," we may listen as he illustrates the way tenderness arises from the experience of grace.

> A company of travellers fall into a pit: one of them gets a passenger to draw him out. Now he should not be angry with the rest for falling in; nor because they are not yet out, as he is. He did not pull himself out: instead, therefore, of reproaching them, he should show them pity. . . . A

man, truly illuminated, will no more despise others, than Bartimaeus, after his own eyes were opened, would take a stick, and beat every blind man he met.[1]

So Newton is a double master: a master of tender pastoral surgery, and a master of metaphor. As Tony says, "a spiritual doctor" whose specialty is "cardiology," and whose scalpel and sutures are Bible-saturated, image-laden words.

It is not an inconsistency to say that Newton is "a delicate surgeon for taking specks out of sin-sick eyes," and to say his specialty is cardiology. In fact, this juxtaposition of eyes and heart points to the essence of Newton's spiritual method of healing. The heart has eyes (Eph. 1:18). They are made for seeing Christ. But they are blind. Only God can open them. And he uses words.

Through Newton's words and Tony's words—one voice—God does eye surgery on the heart, so that we see Christ more fully. And *more fully* means seeing him as *more precious*. And *more precious* means *more powerful to heal us and change us*.

This is how Newton saw the Christian life: "Every step along the path of life is a battle for the Christian to keep two eyes on Christ"—the eyes of the heart. "If I may speak my own experience," he said, "I find that to keep my eye simply upon Christ, as my *peace*, and my *life*, is by far the hardest part of my calling."[2] "I approach the throne of grace encumbered with a thousand distractions of thought, each of which seems to engage more of my attention than the business I have in hand."[3]

This is why Newton is such a good eye surgeon for us: he has done the work on himself first. With no formal theological education, he has studied his own soul, his own diseased eyes, until he knows us very well. As the Lord taught him how to see the Savior, he teaches us.

And that is the essence of Christian living. "To know him, is the shortest description of true grace; to know him better, is the surest mark of growth in grace; to know him perfectly, is eternal life."[4]

The reason most of us "live so far below our privileges, and are so often

---

[1] *W*, 1:105. (Direct quotes in this book from the works of Newton have been slightly modified to conform to current American standards of spelling, punctuation, and lowercase divine pronouns. Otherwise all quotes reflect the originals. Unless otherwise indicated, italics in quotations are original to the sources cited.—TR)
[2] *W*, 6:44–45.
[3] *W*, 6:179–80.
[4] *W*, 6:73–74.

heavy and sorrowful," is that the eyes of our hearts—the eyes of faith—
do not see that "we have in him grounds of continual joy."[5] "The greatest happiness we are capable of," Newton says, is our communion with
Christ.[6] "Hungering and thirsting for Christ is the central daily Christian
discipline"—to see him clearly and to depend "on him for hourly supplies
of wisdom, strength, and comfort."[7]

Newton was the tender, "least pushy" of the eighteenth-century giants
because this was his experience—a tender, nearby Jesus. "Jesus is always
near, about our path by day, and our bed by night; nearer than the light by
which we see, or the air we breathe; nearer than we are to ourselves; so that
not a thought, a sigh, or a tear, escapes his notice."[8]

But Newton does not sink into individualistic sentimentalism. Jesus
is too great for that.

> His treasury of life and salvation is inexhaustible . . . like the sun,
> which having cheered the successive generations of mankind with his
> beams, still shines with undiminished luster, is still the fountain of
> light, and has always a sufficiency to fill innumerable millions of eyes
> in the same instant.[9]

This is what we long for in our day—a great awakening in which the
glory of Christ fills innumerable millions of eyes. Newton was the fruit of
one of those awakenings. Perhaps God may be pleased to make him a bridge
from that one to the one we need.

If he blesses this book that way, it will be because of Newton's—and
Tony's—relentless focus on the sweetness and the greatness of Christ as
the Savior and Satisfier of our souls. Over this book flies the banner of John
Newton: "None but Jesus." I join Tony in praying that the readers will be
many, and the testimony of each will be Newton's own:

> Then let me boast with holy Paul,
> That I am nothing, Christ is all.[10]

John Piper

---

[5] W, 2:578.
[6] W, 2:213.
[7] W, 1:33.
[8] *Letters* (Taylor), 187.
[9] W, 4:78.
[10] W, 3:450.

ABBREVIATIONS

Aitken

Aitken, Jonathan. *John Newton: From Disgrace to Amazing Grace.* Wheaton, IL: Crossway, 2007.

Bull, *Life*

Bull, Josiah. *The Life of John Newton.* 1868. Edinburgh: Banner of Truth, 2007.

Eclectic

Pratt, Josiah, ed. *Eclectic Notes: Or Notes of Discussions on Religious Topics at the Meetings of the Eclectic Society, London, during the Years 1798–1814.* London, 1856.

Hindmarsh

Hindmarsh, Bruce. *John Newton and the English Evangelical Tradition: Between the Conversions of Wesley and Wilberforce.* Grand Rapids: Eerdmans; 2001.

Letters (Barlass)

Sermons on Practical Subjects by William Barlass, Minister of the Gospel, with the Correspondence between the Author and the Rev. John Newton. New York, 1818.

Letters (Bull 1847)

Bull, William, ed. *One Hundred and Twenty Nine Letters from the Rev. John Newton to Josiah Bull.* London, 1847.

Letters (Bull 1869)

Bull, William, ed. *Letters of John Newton.* Edinburgh: Banner of Truth, 2007. Previously published as *Letters of the Rev. John Newton of Olney and St. Mary Woolnoth, Including Several Never Before Published, by the Rev. Josiah Bull, M.A.* London, 1869.

Letters (Campbell)

Campbell, John, ed. *Letters and Conversational Remarks, by the Late Rev. John Newton.* New York, 1811.

Letters (Clunie)

The Christian Correspondent: Or a Series of Religious Letters Written by the Rev. John Newton to Alexander Clunie. Hull, 1790.

Letters (Coffin)

Coffin, John, ed. *Sixty-Six Letters from the Rev. John Newton to a Clergyman and His Family.* London, 1844.

Letters (Dartmouth)	*Historical Manuscripts Commission. XV Report, Appendix, Part 1, The Manuscripts of the Earl of Dartmouth. Vol. 3.* London, 1896.
Letters (Jay)	*The Autobiography of the Rev. William Jay.* New York, 1855.
Letters (Jones)	Jones, Robert, ed. *Twenty-Five Letters Hitherto Unpublished, of the Rev. John Newton.* Edinburgh, 1847.
Letters (More)	*Memoirs of the Life and Correspondence of Mrs. Hannah More. Vol. 3.* London, 1835.
Letters (Palmer)	*The Correspondence of the Late Rev. John Newton with a Dissenting Minister* [Samuel Palmer] *on Various Subjects and Occasions.* N.p., 1809.
Letters (Ryland)	Gordon, Grant, ed. *Wise Counsel: John Newton's Letters to John Ryland, Jr.* Edinburgh: Banner of Truth, 2009.
Letters (Scott)	*The Force of Truth: An Authentic Narrative by Rev. Thomas Scott, to Which Are Added Eight Letters to Dr. Scott by Rev. John Newton.* Philadelphia, 1841.
Letters (Taylor)	*The Aged Pilgrim's Triumph over Sin and the Grave, Illustrated in a Series of Letters* [to Walter Taylor et al.], *Never Before Published, by the Rev. John Newton.* New York, 1825.
Letters (Thornton)	Rinehart, John, ed. *Letters to a Gospel Patron: John Newton and John Thornton, 1770 to 1786.* Redmond, WA: Reclaimed, forthcoming.
Letters (Wilberforce)	*The Correspondence of William Wilberforce. Vol. 1.* Philadelphia, 1846.
W, 1–6	Newton, John. *The Works of John Newton.* 6 vols. London, 1824. Reprint, Edinburgh: Banner of Truth, 1985.

Other Newton sources, consulted but not cited directly:

Cecil, Richard, and Marylynn Rouse, eds. *John Newton.* Fearn, Ross-shire: Christian Focus, 2000.

The Life and Writings of Mrs. Dawson of Lancaster: With Nine Unpublished Letters from the Rev. John Newton. Kirkby Lonsdale, 1828.

Newton, John. *An Authentic Narrative.* In *The Life and Spirituality of John Newton.* Vancouver, BC: Regent College, 1998.

INTRODUCTION

In the spring of 1758, New England pastor and theologian Jonathan Edwards died from smallpox at the age of fifty-five. Three months later, and three thousand nautical miles away, a young man in England sunk to his knees in prayer. The young man was John Newton (1725–1807). Newton began an intense season of prayer, fasting, Bible reading, self-inquiry, and intense deliberation before the Lord concerning his burgeoning desire for pastoral ministry. The forty-two days of self-examination concluded on his thirty-third birthday, August 4, 1758. Newton wrote in his diary, "The day is now arrived when I propose to close all my deliberations on this subject with a solemn, unreserved, unconditional surrender of myself to the Lord."[1]

Ministry was an unlikely career path for the young man born with salt-water in his veins and with nearly two decades of sailing experience on his résumé. Newton's sailing days began at age eleven when he accompanied his father on the sea, but ended at age twenty-nine when he suffered a surprise epileptic seizure. A year later, in 1754, he became a land-based surveyor of the tides (a senior customs official) in Liverpool, the busiest slave-ship harbor in England, and, as a result, Europe's richest port.[2] With the position came significant authority, desirable comforts, and a solid paycheck.

Newton had everything. He was a young Christian, married to the woman of his dreams, shrewd in business, and settled in a secure job. But despite the securities, his heart remained restless for a very improbable calling. On his thirty-third birthday Newton was fully persuaded: the Lord

---

[1] Aitken, 149.
[2] William E. Phipps, *Amazing Grace in John Newton: Slave-Ship Captain, Hymnwriter, and Abolitionist* (Mercer, GA: Mercer University Press, 2001): "When a famous actor was booed on a Liverpool stage, he responded, 'I have not come here to be insulted by a set of wretches, every brick in whose infernal town is cemented with an African's blood'" (28–29).

had called him to pastoral ministry, and to a significant pay cut. The transition ahead was long and painful. Due to ecclesiastical hurdles, it would take six years and the help of the distinguished William Legge, the second earl of Dartmouth, to finally land Newton's first pastorate in 1764.

Newton's fruitful forty-three years as a shepherd, first in the village of Olney (1764–1779), then in the city of London (1779–1806), would not hallow his name in church history. He's mostly remembered for his hymn "Amazing Grace," for his radical spiritual transformation from a near-death shipwreck, and for his work with William Wilberforce (1759–1833) to end the "inhuman traffick" of the British slave trade, a trade in which he once sought his personal wealth and fortune. But spread out between Newton's dramatic conversion as a young man and his abolitionist efforts as an old man span over four decades of pastoral letter writing—a remarkable legacy of its own.

Providentially, Newton's placement in history opened to him the full potential of letter writing in England. First, the Post Office had developed to the point where letter delivery was more affordable and reliable than ever. Second, British society was embracing a new, flexible, abbreviated, and informal style of English, perfectly suited for the post. These two critical developments propelled the eighteenth century into "the great age of the personal letter."[3] And the best of these "personal letters" were written with the intent to be read aloud in households and shared with others (think blog, not e-mail). Trending in this direction, letter writing emerged as the popular social media of Newton's day, and religious leaders like Newton turned to writing pastoral letters that sometimes rivaled sermons in both substance and usefulness.[4] Personal letters from Newton were prized and were often collected as family heirlooms. Not so with his sermons. Though respectable, they were too simple to endure the ages. And his most substantive book, a fairly detailed work titled *A Review of Ecclesiastical History*, didn't sell well. So as other, superior church histories began appearing in print, and as pastoring required more of his time, Newton abandoned the future volumes he envisioned in the series. Early in his ministry, Newton became aware that his greatest gift to the church would emerge out of the time he spent alone, next to a fire, with single pages of blank paper, his pen in hand, his black ink close, and a lit pipe in his mouth as he sat and wrote pastoral letters.[5]

---

[3] Hindmarsh, 244.

[4] J. C. Ryle, *The Christian Leaders of the Last Century* (London, 1869), 291.

[5] Newton communicated this discovery to William Jay. Newton said: "[James] Hervey, who was so blessed as a writer, was hardly able to mention a single instance of conversion by his preaching, and nothing could exceed the lifelessness of his audience; and I rather reckoned upon doing more good by some of

His most popular letters proved to be his most extemporaneous, his utterances of the heart. Newton's skill in directing the attention of his readers to the glory of Jesus Christ made his letters admired.[6] And readers appreciated Newton's clear, simple, and direct communication style. Shaped during his first sixteen years of ministry in Olney, Newton's unpretentious style served the poor, ignorant, and illiterate adults who labored in confined quarters, lacked proper nourishment, and lived under widespread struggles like poverty, nervous disorders, alcoholism, and suicide. There Newton led popular children's meetings and entered the homes of his people to listen to and care for their various spiritual struggles. In Olney, Newton honed his skill to capture the attention of children and then applied that same skill to adults.[7]

Newton first penned his autobiography in a series of letters to a friend in 1762. These letters were passed around, celebrated, and then expanded into a second series of letters for another reader the following year. Those letters became so popular they were collected and published under the title *An Authentic Narrative* (1764). The fourteen-letter autobiography propelled his status as a local celebrity, adding weight to his local preaching ministry.[8] Newton later found success writing periodic public letters for print under the pseudonym of Omicron and Vigil (1771–1774), which he later collected, edited, and published as a book. With the positive response of that collection, he recalled some of his private letters written to his friends so they could be copied, collected, redacted of private details, and then published as the book *Cardiphonia* (1780).[9]

Today, Newton's pastoral legacy is preserved in five hundred letters written and published in his lifetime (or soon thereafter), and another five hundred letters collected and published by others after his death. Through all of these letters Newton still speaks. Modern-day pastor Timothy Keller claims John Newton as "the best pastor I've ever seen in my life," and cites Newton

---

my other works than by my 'Letters,' which I wrote without study, or any public design; but the Lord said, 'You shall be most useful by *them*'; and I learned to say, 'Thy will be done! Use me as Thou pleases, only *make* me useful'" (Letters [Jay], 317). Newton wrote about his extemporaneous letters, "I seldom know how I shall begin, or when I shall end, when I take up my pen; but, as John Bunyan says, 'still as I pull, it comes,' and so I write" (Letters [More], 23).

[6] Newton: "We should never be weary of writing and reading about Jesus. If his name sounds warm to your heart, you may call this a good letter, though I should not add a word more" (*Letters* [Clunie], 131).

[7] *Eclectic*, 6–7.

[8] Shortly after *An Authentic Narrative* was published, Newton wrote a friend (December 11, 1764): "I have reason to hope that the publication of my letters will give some additional weight to my ministry here. The people stare at me since reading them, and well they may. I am indeed a wonder to many—a wonder to myself. Especially I wonder that I wonder no more" (*Letters* [Clunie], 62).

[9] *Cardiphonia* was the title (given by Cowper) to Newton's most famous collection of letters. The title is a Greek compound that simply means "utterance of the heart." At 158 letters total in length it was, Newton claimed, his most useful book (W, 1:97). Why? "I ascribe the blessing the Lord has given to *Cardiphonia* chiefly to this circumstance, that there was not a line written with the least thought that it would ever appear in public" (*Letters* [Campbell], 31).

in more sermons than he does any other figure in church history except
C. S. Lewis, Jonathan Edwards, and Martin Luther.[10] In 2013, Keller credited
Newton's letters for this influence on his own ministry and explained why.

> John Newton was not known for his stirring preaching. His sermons are
> actually fairly stodgy and pedestrian. However, his letters, in which he
> dealt with a wide variety of pastoral issues, are pure gold. Newton was
> able to take the great theological doctrines of the faith and apply them to
> the needs of friends, parishioners, even strangers who wrote for advice.
> In his letters he is often blunt, yet always tender. He is remarkably humble
> and open about his own flaws, but never in a cloying or self-absorbed
> manner. He is therefore able to point others to the grace of Christ on
> which he himself clearly depends.
>
> Reading one of Newton's letters is like taking a hike along some path
> between high walls of rock or foliage that suddenly affords breathtaking
> views. In the midst of addressing some commonplace condition, usually
> with realistic detail, Newton will suddenly, almost as an aside, toss in
> several lines that blaze with glory.
>
> Newton's letters have influenced both my pastoral work and my
> preaching. Newton did not simply call people to holy living, but he also
> did close analysis of their motives and showed them the specific rea-
> sons they were failing to obey God. Decades of constantly reading and
> re-reading the letters have taught me how to do better analysis of under-
> lying motives, so that when the high doctrines of grace are preached and
> applied, they do not merely press on the will but change the heart.[11]

---

[10] Timothy Keller, sermon, "Passive Discipline" (January 21, 1990). Throughout his preaching ministry
in Manhattan (1989–present), Keller has frequently cited Newton by name in sermons (the most significant references will be noted in the footnotes of this book). In the years 1989–2004, Keller preached
985 sermons at Redeemer Presbyterian Church (Manhattan). He mentioned Newton in 75 different sermons (7.6 percent). In the first five years alone he mentioned Newton in 30 sermons (8.3 percent). Here's
where Newton fits among other top names mentioned by Keller (by number of sermons): C. S. Lewis (277),
Jonathan Edwards (129), Martin Luther (105), John Newton (75), Martyn Lloyd-Jones (59), Augustine (59),
Charles Spurgeon (52), J. R. R. Tolkien (41), John Stott (26), and J. I. Packer (20). These numbers are impres-
sive for their sheer quantity, and even more impressive for the specific examples where Keller translates
Newton's humble counsel for Christians living in a sophisticated city like Manhattan. For this reason,
Keller makes occasional cameo appearances in this book to serve as a prime example of a Christian communicator making use of Newton's pastoral wisdom today. All Keller sermon quotes taken from Timothy
J. Keller, *The Timothy Keller Sermon Archive* (New York: Redeemer Presbyterian Church, 2013). Keller's
wife, Kathy, has likewise been influenced by Newton. In June 2013 she was asked what books have most
profoundly shaped her ministry. She offered one title: "The letters of John Newton, mostly the collection
published under the name *Utterance of the Heart* (*Cardiphonia*). Nothing is more insightful about dealing
with people and pastoral issues. Tim and I take people through them whenever we're able. In fact, we're
both doing so now, with different groups" (accessed June 11, 2013, http://thegospelcoalition.org/blogs
/tgc/2013/06/11/on-my-shelf-life-and-books-with-kathy-keller/).

[11] Timothy Keller, e-mail message to the author, December 18, 2013. Richard Cecil (1748–1810), a note-
worthy preacher and friend to Newton, wrote of Newton's preaching ministry: "He appeared, perhaps, to
least advantage in the pulpit; as he did not generally aim at accuracy in the composition of his sermons,
nor at any address in the delivery of them. His utterance was far from clear, and his attitudes ungrace-

Keller is not alone in his praise of Newton the letter writer. J. I. Packer has written, "Ex-slave-trader John Newton was the friendliest, wisest, humblest and least pushy of all the eighteenth-century evangelical leaders, and was perhaps the greatest pastoral letter-writer of all time."[12]

Newton's superb letter-writing skills, marked with spiritual clarity, self-deprecating wit, vivid metaphor, motive-piercing acuity, and insights of blazing glory, all help to explain why Newton's pastoral influence spread far beyond the village of Olney, beyond the city of London, beyond the eighteenth century, and now guides modern-day pastors in culturally sophisticated places like Manhattan. If Keller and Packer are right, Newton should be named among the most skilled pastors in church history.

Newton the Theologian?

But was John Newton a theologian? He displayed an incredible memory, was an avid reader, was rigorously self-educated, was a clear thinker, and tried his hand at technical writing, but he was far more comfortable as a biblicist than as a defender of any theological tradition.[13] As he grew older, Newton grew less patient with the complex metaphysical theology of Edwards in favor of the simpler theology of Scottish Presbyterian Robert Riccaltoun (1691–1769),[14] British Baptist Andrew Fuller (1754–1815),[15] and Scottish Episcopalian Robert Leighton (1611–1684).[16]

---

ful. He possessed, however, so much affection for his people, and so much zeal for their best interests, that the defect of his manner was of little consideration with his constant hearers; at the same time, his capacity and habit of entering into their trials and experience gave the highest interest to his ministry among them. Besides which, he frequently interspersed the most brilliant allusions; and brought forward such happy illustrations of his subject, and those with so much unction on his own heart, as melted and enlarged theirs. The parent-like tenderness and affection which accompanied his instruction made them prefer him to preachers who, on other accounts, were much more generally popular" (*W*, 1:92–93; see also Aitken, 185–91).

[12] Quoted from Packer's endorsement of J. Todd Murray, *Beyond Amazing Grace: Timeless Pastoral Wisdom from the Letters, Sermons and Hymns of John Newton* (n.p.: EP, 2007).

[13] *W*, 5:85–86.

[14] Despite his limited time for reading, Newton claims to have read Robert Riccaltoun's three-volume *Works of the Late Reverend Mr. Robert Riccaltoun* (1771) three times through. When the volumes became scarce, Newton advocated for them to be reprinted. Writes Newton, "I admire him as the most original thinker I have met with. He has confirmed and enlarged my views of gospel truth" (*Letters* [Bull 1869], 329), and "I seldom meet with a human writer, to whose judgment I can implicitly subscribe in all points" (*Letters* [Campbell], 32). In another place he writes that Riccaltoun was "a man of a strong comprehensive mind, and if not an *elegant* he was a *masterly* writer. His metaphysics, I think, are a good besom [broom] to swap away the fine-spun cobweb, skeptical metaphysics, which at present are too much in fashion" (*Letters* [Campbell], 68).

[15] Of Andrew Fuller's work *The Calvinistic and Socinian Systems Examined and Compared as to Their Moral Tendency* (1794), Newton writes, "It is at once a beautiful summary of Christian doctrine, and the best conducted book of controversy that I ever met with" (*Letters* [Coffin], 84).

[16] Newton appreciated all of Leighton's writings, but was especially fond of his theological lectures, *Praelectiones Theologiae*. "I believe this book is scarce: I set the highest value upon it. He has wonderfully united the simplicity of the Gospel with all the captivating beauties of style and language" (*W*, 2:102).

If Newton hesitated to defend a theological system, it was out of his leading concern to center his theology on Christ crucified.[17] He was certainly not afraid to say, "I am an avowed Calvinist,"[18] and appears to have embraced five-point Calvinism from before he ever pastored, but he also befriended Arminian leaders who shared his love for Christ.[19] Without question, the doctrines of grace seeped deep into Newton's ministry. Once asked if he was a Calvinist, Newton plunked a lump of sugar into his tea, stirred the hot liquid, and said, "I am more of a Calvinist than anything else; but I use my Calvinism in my writing and preaching as I use this sugar. I do not give it alone, and whole; but mixed, and diluted."[20] Diluted—not weakened—in a holistic and permeating way. "I think these doctrines should be in a sermon like sugar in a dish of tea, which sweetens every drop, but is no where to be found in a lump";[21] they should be "tasted everywhere, though prominent nowhere."[22] Convincing others to embrace Calvinism was decisively accomplished not by teaching, he said, but by experience. Often it was only after a Christian was hit by a personal trial (a "pinch") that he or she would be finally driven to embrace the comforting truths of Calvinism. Thus, from the pulpit, Newton felt no pressure to force-feed the doctrines of Calvinism.[23] But neither was

---

Newton's desire to see *Praelectiones Theologiae* translated from Latin into English was materialized. See *Theological and Expository Lectures by Robert Leighton, D.D., Archbishop of Glasgow* (London, 1828), 3–144.
[17] *W*, 3:20; 4:106, 358–59; *Letters* (Coffin), 62.
[18] *W*, 6:278.
[19] Wrote Newton to a minister in a letter: "My part is only to say with the Apostle, 'Grace be with all that love the Lord Jesus Christ in sincerity' (Eph. 6:24). I hope my heart is with them all, whether Episcopalians, Presbyterians, Independents, Baptists, Methodists, Seceders, Relief-Men, Moravians, etc. etc.; Nay if a Papist gave me good evidence that he loved my Savior, I would beg leave of men, and ask grace of the Lord, that I might love such Papists likewise, with a pure heart fervently. We shall be known by none of these names of party and prejudice when we meet in the kingdom of glory" (*Letters* [Ryland], 345).
[20] *Letters* (Jay), 308.
[21] *Letters* (Campbell), 64.
[22] *Eclectic*, 284.
[23] Newton: "I am an avowed Calvinist: the points which are usually comprised in that term, seem to me so consonant to scripture, reason, (when enlightened,) and experience, that I have not the shadow of a doubt about them. But I cannot dispute, I dare not speculate. What is by some called high Calvinism, I dread. I feel much more union of spirit with some Arminians, than I could with some Calvinists; and, if I thought a person feared sin, loved the word of God, and was seeking after Jesus, I would not walk the length of my study to proselyte him to the Calvinistic doctrines. Not because I think them mere opinions, or of little importance to a believer—I think the contrary; but because I believe these doctrines will do no one any good till he is taught them of God. I believe a too hasty assent to Calvinistic principles, before a person is duly acquainted with the plague of his own heart, is one principal cause of that lightness of profession which so lamentably abounds in this day, a chief reason why many professors are rash, heady, high-minded, contentious about words, and sadly remiss as to the means of divine appointment. For this reason, I suppose, though I never preach a sermon in which the tincture of Calvinism may not be easily discerned by a judicious hearer, yet I very seldom insist expressly upon those points, unless they fairly and necessarily lie in my way. I believe most persons who are truly alive to God, sooner or later meet with some pinches in their experience which constrain them to flee to those doctrines for relief, which perhaps they had formerly dreaded, if not abhorred, because they knew not how to get over some harsh consequences they thought necessarily resulting from them, or because they were stumbled by the miscarriages

Calvinism a relative matter for Newton; it was sweetness for the weary
soul. "The views I have received of the doctrines of grace are essential to
my peace," he wrote. "I could not live comfortably a day, or an hour, without them."[24] In this way Newton's life was driven theologically. Rooted
deep in personal experience, theology was the stuff of life, the stuff of
Newton's life, the stuff of the Christian life.

Still others would say, no, he was not a theologian because he did not
produce large theological tomes to be churned off presses, but merely com-
piled single sheets of paper mailed through the post to address the immediate spiritual needs of his correspondents. This may be true, but whatever
truth we find in this claim must also be applied to the Epistles of the New
Testament. Newton wrote with the awareness that his best and most enduring letters could be collected later (and would be). Had he written a full-
bodied theology of the Christian life, this may have actually limited him
from addressing the spectrum of Christian experiences he could address
by letter.

As I hope to demonstrate in this book, Newton was a theologian. When
read together, his collected epistles show the extraordinary skill of a mentor
who wisely fused doctrine, experience, and practice.[25] But he bonded these
services with a unique emphasis. Newton was a spiritual doctor, and his chosen specialty, as he called it, was *cardiology*, the careful and exhaustive study
of the human heart's response to every conceivable situation and condition
in this life.[26] From his experience as a diagnostician of the heart, Newton
labored to apply the treasures of divine truth to each of the manifold circumstances faced in the Christian life. As the cover image of this book reflects,
Newton was a keen-eyed student of the human heart who eagerly leaned into
the human experience. In this sense he was, and remains, one of the church's
most perceptive and practical theologians on the Christian life.

Pilgrim's Progress

Newton's theology best works itself out in letters because Newton understood the Christian life to be a journey between two worlds (Phil. 3:12–4:1).

---

of those who professed them. In this way I was made a Calvinist myself; and I am content to let the
Lord take his own way, and his own time, with others" (W, 6:278–79).
[24] W, 3:303.
[25] Letters (Jay), 316. Charles Spurgeon reportedly said of Newton, "In few writers are Christian doctrine,
experience and practice more happily balanced than in the author of these *Letters*, and few write with
more simplicity, piety and force" (source unknown).
[26] W, 1:477.

The journey has a dark past, a setting-out, snares and dangers along the way, and then a glorious end. Because the Pilgrim has not yet reached home, his focus remains set on the daily steps of progress. This explains Newton's deep concern with the stuff of the daily Christian life and his attraction to John Bunyan's classic allegory *The Pilgrim's Progress*. Newton read the allegory so frequently he claims to have nearly memorized it.[27] And for over six years, he delivered weekly lectures to the meager farmers and dejected lace makers of Olney through the text of *The Pilgrim's Progress*.[28] Newton believed that explaining the storyline of Bunyan's classic was essential for preparing youth for life.[29] As he lectured on the allegory, he traveled slowly, once writing to a friend of these lectures, "I find this book so full of matter, that I can seldom go through more than a page, or half a page at a time."[30] Newton's love for the allegory, and his careful study of it, became known, and he was approached by an editor to write a preface to a 1776 edition, which he did. *The Pilgrim's Progress* was a comprehensive map, Newton wrote in the preface, "a map, so exactly drawn, that we can hardly meet with a case or character, amidst the vast variety of persons and incidents, that daily occur to our observation, to which we cannot easily point out a counterpart in the pilgrim."[31]

In Bunyan, Newton finds a like-minded model for the application of theology to various and comprehensive life situations, stages of maturity, and personality types. And while no Christian life experience is exactly like any other, all Christian journeys share certain similarities. This explains why *The Pilgrim's Progress* is perhaps the best-selling book in church history, behind only the Bible. Newton published his personal letters from a similar conviction. In Bunyan's classic we find the allegorical counterpart to Newton's letter-writing ministry.

Biographically, Bunyan and Newton share other traits. Newton, "the African blasphemer," was a monster of sin, whose debaucheries made even sailors blush. Bunyan, "the village rebel," was a man who breathed obscenities and once was rebuked by a prostitute for his swearing. Said Spurgeon of

---

[27] *Letters* (Clunie), 129.
[28] Newton: "I am sure Mr. Bunyan was a plain writer. I expounded or explained the first part of his *Pilgrim*, twice during my residence at Olney; each time it employed one evening in a week for more than three years. And perhaps in those lectures I came nearer to the apprehension of the poor lace-makers, and engaged their attention more, than when I spoke from the pulpit" (Letters [More], 6). It appears after his pastoral transition to London, he was invited to lecture through the allegory in the Wilberforce home in a setting he called "parlor preaching."
[29] *Eclectic*, 263.
[30] *W*, 6:38.
[31] John Bunyan, *The Pilgrim's Progress from This World to That Which Is to Come* (London, 1776), preface.

Bunyan and Newton, "Both of them had been ringleaders in sin before they became leaders in the army of the Redeemed," and "no man in his senses will venture to assert that there was anything in Newton or Bunyan why they should engross the regard of the Most High."[32] Each was converted by free grace. Neither forgot it. Both were later called to ministry, but neither man was afforded academic training in theology. Both took pastorates, and each relied heavily on the experience of his dramatic conversion, a careful (but fairly simple) understanding of Scripture, a vivid imagination, and street smarts, to help lead others along this journey of the Christian life.

With everything else Bunyan and Newton are remembered for, they both expressed pastoral skill creatively via popular cultural mediums to help fellow believers reach Zion. Newton's letters were written to pilgrims on the road because Newton thought of the Christian life in terms of progressive growth. Even with all the setbacks and disappointments along the way, the true believer matures from spiritual child to adolescent to adult, or from acorn to sapling to large oak. Newton's letters are filled with spiritual progress because Newton kept the end goal of the Christian life in view. While letters of gossip are *aimless*, Newton's letters are always *aimed*, and they are aimed because Newton was self-consciously theologically driven. Because his theology was cohesive, he was able to point other Christians forward and able to help them move away from spiritual immaturity and toward spiritual adulthood.[33]

Like Bunyan, Newton never lost sight of the pilgrim's progress or the pilgrim's end.

The Core of Newton's Counsel

But is it possible to locate a unity in Newton's letters? Because his greatest written legacy on the Christian life is his mail, we are faced with this daunting challenge from the outset. Bruce Hindmarsh, in his valuable study of Newton, wrote of the letters, "It is difficult to extract a unified core of teaching on the spiritual life" because "most of Newton's letters were by definition *ad hoc* compositions reflecting the particular concerns

---

[32] All details and points from C. H. Spurgeon: *The New Park Street Pulpit Sermons*, vol. 6 (London, 1860), 73; *The Metropolitan Tabernacle Pulpit Sermons*, vol. 22 (London, 1876), 102; *C. H. Spurgeon's Sermons Beyond: An Authentic Supplement to the Metropolitan Tabernacle Pulpit*, vol. 63 (Leominster, UK: Day One, 2009), 195; *The Metropolitan Tabernacle Pulpit Sermons*, vol. 10 (London, 1864), 76, 639–40.

[33] For the points in this paragraph, I owe a debt to J. I. Packer (personal conversation, June 2, 2012, Vancouver).

of the correspondents, an occasion within Newton's personal milieu, or a theme of immediate topical relevance."[34] Hindmarsh is right; each letter was situated within a particular context. At best, Newton's most pastoral letters are one-sided fragments of a conversation canvasing a broad range of themes. But again, this is true of the New Testament Epistles, and it does not prevent theologians from identifying prominent themes in the letters of Paul.

Yet because personal visitors frequently interrupted Pastor Newton's solitude, his letters are filled with a variety of "desultory" thoughts, and many of those thoughts seem to break off prematurely. However unfortunate, this fact of pastoral life in eighteenth-century England does not hinder us from identifying a single core theme (or a cluster of themes) in those letters. I believe Newton's letters are bound together by a cohesive theology of the Christian life, and as a result I believe it is possible to synthesize his pastoral counsel and discover his core message on the aim of the Christian life. This is my attempt:

> John Newton's vision for the Christian life centers on the all-sufficiency of Jesus Christ. Awakened to Christ by the new birth, and united to Christ by faith, the Christian passes through various stages of maturity in this life as he/she beholds and delights in Christ's glory in Scripture. All along the pilgrimage of the Christian life—through the darkest personal trials, and despite indwelling sin and various character flaws—Christ's glory is beheld and treasured, resulting in tastes of eternal joy, in growing security, and in progressive victory over the self, the world, and the devil—a victory manifested in self-emptying and other-loving obedience, and ultimately in a life aimed to please God alone.[35]

To corroborate this thesis, I have combed through Newton's thousand published letters, complementing them with his sermons and hymns. What I have found is that at the core of his pastoral theology radiates the all-sufficiency of Christ. Christ is the comprehensive vision that unifies Newton's pastoral letters, his sermons, and the many hymns written out of his own spiritual experience and personal devotional life.[36] The glory of the ascended Jesus Christ is the North Pole magnet which fixes the

---

[34] Hindmarsh, 250.

[35] I wrote this thesis after studying Newton's published letters and was pleasantly surprised to later find it echoed by Newton in his summary of the Christian life in *A Review of Ecclesiastical History* (*W*, 3:295–96).

[36] Letters (Dartmouth), 248.

compass of the Christian life (Heb. 12:1–2). Newton's Christ-centered vision of the Christian life embraces all the ultimate aims of the spiritual disciplines lived out in the local church, the family, and the marketplace, whether in rightly handling religious controversy, developing friendships, winning the battle over insecurity, overcoming weariness, finding delight in God, or enduring all seasons of suffering. Every dilemma faced and every joy embraced and every hope anticipated in the Christian life is bound up with the glory of Christ. This is the driving theme of Newton's ministry.

Into Newton's Heart

John Newton's life "was stranger than the most improbable fiction."[37] But this book is not a biography. Jonathan Aitken has skillfully crafted a captivating narrative of Newton's dramatic life under the title *John Newton: From Disgrace to Amazing Grace* (Wheaton, IL: Crossway, 2007). In my debt to Aitken's masterful storytelling, I feel no need to duplicate Newton's life story (though I will rehearse some key moments from it).

And although this book is not a formal biography, we will pick up on Newton's phrasing, his writing style, his wit, and some of his mannerisms. As we listen to Newton through the words he wrote, we will *meet* Newton in a very intimate way because, as Spurgeon once said, "A man's private letters often let you into the secrets of his heart."[38] This is true of Newton. In this book I've sought to get into his heart and mind through the doorway of his published letters. I have read and reread every letter with the goal of condensing his core message and collecting his most distinct contributions on the Christian life into one book, in his own words, to serve readers who are not inclined to labor through all the letters for themselves. And for those readers who are so inclined, I have used extensive footnotes to cite (when possible) primary sources in the public domain and editions you can find online and download and read for free.

Finally, fitting to the legacy of Newton's pastoral heart, this book is not intended to be a laboratory specimen of his mind, sliced off to be archived or filed away in a library. Newton was a man of utility, and

---

[37] Grace Irwin, *Servant of Slaves: A Biographical Novel of John Newton* (Grand Rapids: Eerdmans, 1961), 7. Irwin goes on to write of her novel, "The reader may be assured that if he finds anything unbelievable of adventure or coincidence, anything excessive, either sensual or spiritual, anything improbable in emotion or devotion, that part of the book is provably factual, even understated" (ibid.).
[38] C. H. Spurgeon, *The Sword and Trowel: 1868* (London, 1868), 108.

he showed little patience for theorizing about the Christian life.[39] We would fail to honor his pastoral legacy if this study of Newton's letters were nothing more than academic analysis. With two eyes fixed on Christ, Newton was a man of purpose and action. To honor his legacy, I will adopt his aim as my aim for this project. Think of this book as a field guide meant to get dirty, dog-eared, and faded in the clenched hands of a Christian pilgrim.

---

[39] Josiah Bull: "Were we to seek, in one word, to characterize the whole of Mr. Newton's life-work, we should say its whole aim was utility" (Bull, *Life*, 322).

CHAPTER I

AMAZING GRACE

A savage ocean storm awoke the crew of the *Greyhound*, a cargo ship crammed with merchandise collected from the west coast of Africa. From port to port, the ship had been slowly filled with African gold, ivory, beeswax, and camwood (lumber). But now, late in the dark night of March 21, 1748, a twenty-two-year-old sailor named John was awakened by gale-force winds battering the ship. Waves slammed into her and ripped away the upper timbers on one side, sending water through a gaping hole into John's room. Awakened by the chaos, he jumped half naked from his bed to furiously hand pump water back into the swaying ocean.[1] With the cold saltwater pouring into the aging and broken vessel, crewmates grabbed buckets and began tossing the water back into the dark sea. Newton cranked for his life while waves broke over his head. Desperation overwhelmed the doomed crew, and John's heart pounded furiously with adrenaline-charged fears of being dumped overboard in the middle of a dark sea, weeks away from the nearest coastline. Like many sailors of his time, he couldn't swim.

As John Newton later reflected, he was unfit to live and unfit to die. The fear of death strained his energies at the water pump, but it was a battle he could not win. Saltwater waves continued crashing against the ship, and the endless ocean of water rushed over the deck faster than the men could spit it back out. The ship creaked and groaned under the assault as the crew frantically battled the angry forces of the sea.

Newton's moral life had already sunk. He was a wicked and insubordinate

---

[1] For a detailed account, see Aitken, 69–84.

young man with a profane tongue, flesh-driven appetites, and stone-cold heart. He had gambled his way into debt and dabbled in witchcraft. And as a young man in foreign lands, he had become sexually promiscuous. Later, as a young captain of a slave-trading ship, he may have indulged his lusts further by raping captive African women in the "sexual free-for-alls on board ship that most captains in the trade regarded as theirs by right."[2] He didn't particularly enjoy alcohol, but he drank to prompt drunkenness in others and to entertain himself by the follies the liquor encouraged in them. What is clear: Newton was immune from no sin. He delighted to lead others into temptation, later calling himself "a ringleader in blasphemy and wickedness."[3]

> Not content with running the broad way myself, I was indefatigable in enticing others; and, had my influence been equal to my wishes, I would have carried all the human race with me. I had the ambition of a Caesar or an Alexander, and wanted to rank in wickedness among the foremost of the human race.[4]

Life on the sea only amplified Newton's wretched tendencies.[5] He sailed for months in a bubble of unchecked sin, estranged from godly examples, cut off from the gospel, hardened by the dangers of sea life, and entrenched among a group of men who incited one another to sin. Life on an eighteenth-century merchant ship was the spiritually deadening climate his soul least needed.

The Wretch

If any man was unworthy of deliverance from the raging sea, it was the twenty-two-year-old sailor John Newton. In this moment Newton was focused on

---

[2] Aitken, 111. Phipps will only say Newton "probably raped slaves" (William E. Phipps, *Amazing Grace in John Newton: Slave-Ship Captain, Hymnwriter, and Abolitionist* [Mercer, GA: Mercer University Press, 2001], 33). Aitken is convinced of it (see Aitken, 64, 93, 107, 111, 116, 169, 320). But the evidence is lacking and this conclusion is disputed. The cash value of a female slave swelled if she was carrying the child of a white man, a prospect that only incited further sexual misuse by sailors at sea (Phipps, *Amazing Grace in John Newton*, 33).
[3] *Letters* (Taylor), 209.
[4] *W*, 2:246.
[5] In a preface he wrote for a book meant to reach sailors with the gospel, Newton said: "I traversed the ocean, in a great variety of situations and circumstances, near twenty years. But long, too long, I was a careless inattentive spectator of the wonders of the Lord in the great deep. My heart was hard, my language profane, my conduct most profligate and licentious. Thus I know, not only from observation, but from sorrowful experience, the disadvantages sea-men are in general under, with respect to the concernments of their precious souls. They usually pass the greatest part of their lives upon the sea, and therefore can derive little benefit either from instruction or example. Rather, they too recently strengthen and confirm each other in habits of wickedness. The frequency of their deliverances from the dangers to which they are exposed, often harden them into fearless insensibility. Thus they go on from bad to worse, strangers to God, and thoughtless of eternity" (John Ryther, *The Sea-Man's Preacher* [London: 1803], vii–viii).

survival and frightened by the nearness of death that knocked on the door with each crashing wave. Desperate and fully expecting to die, Newton finally blurted aloud, "If this will not do, the Lord have mercy on us." The Lord's name from his mouth—that word he only spouted in vain—now struck his heart like an arrow, humbling and breaking him. "I was instantly struck by my own words. This was the first desire I had breathed for mercy for many years."[6]

As with the thief on the cross facing death, the Lord ignited a marvelous work in John Newton's heart here in this "great day of turning." Although the precise time of his conversion is unknown,[7] his plea for mercy on the sea was immediately answered. And Newton's heart, which once spewed wickedness and blasphemy, would soon become a heart gushing beloved hymns of praise to God. The same tongue that spit curses at the name of God and made sailors blush would become the tongue that steered the corporate worship of God's people in honoring God's holy name. This drowning wretch of a sailor would pen a hymn that endures in the minds and hearts of people to this day, a hymn so popular that its lyrics are as recognizable throughout the English-speaking world as any national anthem. On top of this, the lucrative African slave trade that he participated in would be ended, in part because of his abolitionist work. Newton would become a pastor, no longer leading sinners into sin but now enticing sinners away from it. In time, hundreds of souls would gather weekly on Sundays to listen to his sermons. Only God himself could have imagined what was in store for John Newton. Like Jonah running away from God, Newton was delivered from death at sea in order to preach the good news.

Though never formally trained, Newton would become a prominent pastor in two churches in England for forty-three years. He would befriend George Whitefield and John Wesley. As Newton frantically churned the water pump on March 21, 1748, he could not have imagined his life physically *continuing*; still less could he have imagined his life spiritually *thriving* under the incredible plans foreordained by God.[8]

---

[6] Aitken, 76.

[7] Newton: "I have still some faint remembrance of my pious mother, and the care she took of my education, and the impression it made upon me when I was a child, for she died when I was in my seventh year. I had even then frequent intervals of serious thoughts. But evil and folly were bound up in my heart; my repeated wanderings from the good way became wider and wider; I increased in wickedness as in years: But you have my *Narrative*, and I need not tell you how vile and how miserable I was, and how presumptuously I sat in the chair of the scorner, before I was twenty years old. My deliverance from Africa [1747], and afterwards from sinking in the ocean [1748], were almost miraculous; but about the year 1749 (I cannot exactly fix the date) the Lord, to whom all things are possible, began to soften my obdurate heart" (*Letters* [Taylor], 125).

[8] The actual date of the storm as recorded by Newton was March 11 (OS), but due to an eleven-day shift in the calendar that occurred in 1752, the successive anniversary was celebrated by Newton on

Leading with a Limp

During that frantic night in 1748, one sailor was swept overboard and died, but Newton and his other crewmates miraculously survived the storm. They endured intense starvation for weeks as the ship limped to shore, staying afloat thanks to the buoyant cargo of beeswax and lumber. For the remainder of his life, Newton would celebrate March 21 as the annual reminder of God's gracious deliverance of his fragile life. The smashed and sinking ship provided a fitting metaphor for his spiritual state; the churning abyss clawing at him was a fitting metaphor for the flames of hell. He had been to the edge of human existence. In desperation, Newton had turned to the God he despised, grasped the hope of the gospel, and never let go.

From that day until the end of his life, Newton walked with a spiritual limp. John Newton was the chief of sinners, and if he could be saved by God's unmerited favor, no person on planet Earth was too wicked or too far beyond the reach of God's grace to be saved. If there is one point of self-understanding Newton lived with, it is that his salvation could never have originated within himself. Grace broke his life just as powerfully as an unexpected ocean storm broke his security. Out of his humble self-awareness, Newton wrote hymns as if he were composing words for himself; he preached sermons as a hungry sheep himself telling other sheep where to find food; he wrote pastoral letters as a fellow traveler with dusty feet on his own journey to the Celestial City, and as a friend with a second crutch he was willing to lend to fellow travelers. John Newton lived with a deep and abiding awareness of God's amazing grace that broke into his wicked life. And out of that redemption flowed decades of merciful pastoral care for fellow sinners.

How Sweet the Sound

For all the many themes Newton addresses in his ministry, his sermons, his hymns, and his letters, one word provides a summary of his life and testimony—*grace*. From start to finish, Newton's life in Christ was lived in grace. Grace was not only a defibrillator jolt at the beginning of his Christian life; grace was the saving and restraining power of God at every stage. "If the Lord were to leave me one hour, I should fall into gross evil. I am like a child, who dares not go across Cheapside [a bustling downtown Lon-

---

March 21 (NS). To avoid confusion I have chosen to use only the memorial date Newton celebrated throughout most his life, March 21.

don street], unless someone holds his hand."[9] For Newton, the Christian life could only be explained by God's sustaining grace. Grace saved his wretched soul. Grace sought him out. Grace removed his spiritual blindness and opened his spiritual eyes. Grace taught him to fear God. Grace relieved his fears. Grace led him to hope. The life and ministry of Newton can all fit under the banner of grace—God's abundant, all-sufficient, infinite, sovereign, unceasing, and amazing grace.

Fittingly, we begin this study with Newton's most famous and most often recited words, a New Year's Day hymn inspired by 1 Chronicles 17, a chapter that speaks of King David's past, present, and future. Newton aptly titled the hymn "Faith's Review and Expectation," but today it is more widely remembered by its first two words: "Amazing Grace." The language and biblical theology of 1 Chronicles 17 drench Newton's hymn.[10] But it's more than instructive. Reflecting his personal practice on New Year's, the hymn itself provides a doxological moment in time to stop to thank God for his past mercies, his present mercies, and his future mercies.

The brief hymn summarizes grace as one of the essential themes in the Christian life, from beginning to end. It originally appeared in published form like this:

[1] Amazing grace! (how sweet the sound)
  That sav'd a wretch like me!
I once was lost, but now am found,
  Was blind, but now I see.

[2] 'Twas grace that taught my heart to fear,
  And grace my fears reliev'd;
How precious did that grace appear
  The hour I first believ'd!

[3] Through many dangers, toils, and snares,
  I have already come;
'Tis grace has brought me safe thus far,
  And grace will lead me home.

---

[9] *Eclectic*, 272.
[10] Marylynn Rouse makes this perceptive connection in her resources at www.johnnewton.org. Setting the text of "Amazing Grace" alongside 1 Chronicles 17 will show just how deeply Newton's hymn soaked up the rich biblical theology of this chapter of Scripture. Direct lines of contact are made by the terms *house/home*, *word*, and *forever*. Also notice the corresponding tenses of the hymn echoed in 1 Chronicles 17: *past* (v. 7, "I took you from the pasture"), *present* (v. 16, "Who am I, O LORD God, and what is my house, that you have brought me thus far?"), and *future* (v. 26, "O LORD, you are God, and you have promised this good thing to your servant").

[4] The Lord has promis'd good to me,
    His word my hope secures:
He will my shield and portion be,
    As long as life endures.

[5] Yes, when this flesh and heart shall fail,
    And mortal life shall cease,
I shall possess, within the vail,
    A life of joy and peace.

[6] The earth shall soon dissolve like snow,
    The sun forbear to shine;
But God, who call'd me here below,
    Will be for ever mine.[11]

Although this book will mostly focus on Newton's letters, hymns like "Amazing Grace" are a fitting big-picture introduction into his understanding of the Christian life. The entire Christian life is here: from salvation ("sav'd a wretch like me"), through trials ("many dangers, toils, and snares"), struggles with doubts and need for divine promises ("his word my hope secures"), protection in spiritual battle ("he will my shield and portion be"), and aging and facing death ("when this flesh and heart shall fail"), to hopes for re-creation ("earth shall soon dissolve like snow"), anticipation for the beatific vision ("A life of joy and peace"), and on into eternity ("But God, who call'd me here below, / will be for ever mine"). From the beginning to the end of this autobiographical hymn, we are introduced to the unwavering grace of God throughout the Christian's immortal, eternal existence. Newton communicates this vision of the Christian life in catchy language very easily read and sung. Most of the words he uses (about 85 percent of the hymn) are one syllable, and that reveals much about Newton's commitment to clarity and simplicity, traits that spill over into all his pastoral work and explain his enduring place as a spiritual luminary so many centuries after his death.

Of course, nothing from the pen of Newton endures like this hymn. Amazon.com currently sells the song in 12,700 different versions. It has been recorded in every genre, including jazz, country, folk, classical, R&B, hip-hop—even heavy metal! The popularity of the hymn is obvious at

---

[11] W, 3:353.

sporting events and political rallies, among other settings. It endures as one of few religious songs that can be sung impromptu in public because many people (if not most people) can recite at least the first verse by heart.

The hymn is, first, brilliant biography (of David) and, second, brilliant autobiography (of Newton). Newton is the *wretch*, a term he often used to allude to his own sin and to a period of captivity he endured before his conversion. But most brilliantly of all, the hymn functions as a collective autobiography for every Christian. "Amazing Grace" is perceptive biblical theology, embraced by one man deeply moved by his own redemption, articulated for corporate worship.

Amazing Theology

In a song reaching such heights of cultural popularity, it's easy to miss the radical claims of the lyrics. "Amazing Grace" is profoundly theological, and Reformed theology gleams like a diamond in the first two verses. The hymn is rooted in the sovereign initiative of God. It is a song about spiritually dead and spiritually blind sinners finding new life, or, rather, *being found* by God. We were lost, and grace found us. We were blind, and grace gave us sight. We were wretched, and grace initiated its saving work on us. To find grace so amazing, human boasting must be silenced, and that is essentially what the hymn accomplishes. Human boasting is excluded (Rom. 3:27).

According to records, the hymn was unveiled and first sung by Newton's congregation in Olney on January 1, 1773. Newton had spent weeks getting it ready to kick off the New Year. On hand that Friday morning was his friend the poet William Cowper (1731–1800). But just a few hours after singing the new hymn, Cowper, who was depression-prone, was suddenly seized with a sense of despair about his relationship with God. That afternoon Cowper penned a famous hymn of his own: "God Moves in a Mysterious Way." And later that night, overcome by nightmares and hallucinations, and believing God was now calling him to sacrifice himself in the same way he called Abraham to sacrifice his son Isaac, he rose from his bed, found a knife, and slashed himself.[12] He would be found before he bled to death, but Cowper would never again attend church, and the suicide attempt would be catalogued as one episode of many in his long bout with despair.

---

[12] Aitken, 218.

With his counsel and his hymn "Amazing Grace," Newton "had tried hard to persuade Cowper that God's grace is universal and never withheld from a believer, but depression closed the poet's mind to this truth."[13] Cowper was convinced God had become angry with him, and Newton would spend years—decades—serving his friend's physical needs and laboring to convince him of God's abundant and amazing grace. Amazing grace can be a hard sell. Even today, some professing Christians find the bold message of "Amazing Grace" tough to stomach. Yet this radical message of God's sovereign, life-transforming grace was the keynote of Newton's ministry.

Grace is amazing, as Newton discovered firsthand on the sinking *Greyhound*. Grace is free, sovereign, and sufficient. And yet, convincing sinners of God's free grace, as Newton would discover, was a laborious full-time task. He became an apologist of God's free and unmerited favor and devoted his life to confirming God's grace and applying the promises of Scripture to the lives of his parishioners, his acquaintances, and his friends; and he did so through songs, sermons, and personal letters. From the hard lessons learned at his friend's bedside, Newton would never make the mistake of assuming grace.

Sovereign Grace

One of the most beautiful paradoxes in God's wisdom is *sovereign grace*. The same grace that is *unmerited* is also *unstoppable*. Grace is a battering ram. Grace is forced entry. And Newton's famous hymn is filled with this sovereign grace. In another hymn he opens with this verse:

> Sovereign grace has pow'r alone
> To subdue a heart of stone;
> And the moment grace is felt,
> Then the hardest heart will melt.[14]

Grace alone is powerful enough to break the sinner's bondage to wickedness. "His grace can overcome the most obstinate habits."[15] Grace breaks in to free and unshackle souls. Grace takes away the guilt of sin, the love of sin, and the dominion of sin, even hard sins like drunkenness.[16]

---

[13] Aitken, 229.
[14] W, 3:428.
[15] W, 4:328.
[16] W, 4:189–90, 328.

Newton speaks firsthand of sin's self-destructive power, and firsthand of the power of grace to liberate the soul. "The mercy of God is infinite, and the power of his grace is invincible" (see Rom. 11:29).[17] And the same invincible grace that brings salvation is the same grace that is "training us to renounce ungodliness and worldly passions, and to live self-controlled, upright, and godly lives in the present age" (Titus 2:12). Only grace breaks us free from the power of self-destructive sins and empowers the true freedom of obedience (Rom. 6:14).

Understanding God's sovereign grace at the front end of the Christian life is critical for understanding the rest of the Christian life, because we are certain to face personal sin and insufficiency all throughout the Christian journey. What hope is there for a redeemed Christian who sees indwelling sin still lurking in his heart? If justification can be explained only by the sovereign grace of God, then sanctification can be rooted only in the same cause. God's sovereign grace stabilizes the Christian life. Newton explains, "That I am still preserved in the way, in defiance of all that has arisen from within and from without to turn me aside, must be wholly ascribed to the same sovereignty," that is, the same sovereignty that saved him.[18]

Grace Builds off a Blueprint

As we will see many times, Newton is a master craftsman of metaphor, and he employs every image at his disposal to explain the Christian life.[19] In one place, he explains the Christian life with a building metaphor framed by Paul's words in Philippians: "And I am sure of this, that he who began a good work in you will bring it to completion at the day of Jesus Christ" (1:6). Paul's "good work" was the Christian life in its complete form.

In a large building project the foundations are laid deep. Metaphorically, grace works below the soil and out of view to lay the sturdy foundations of the Christian life. Down under the soil the work seems slow, and then the walls begin to go up. But so does the scaffolding. The building progresses behind this scaffolding, and in broad daylight the mess and trash and broken stones and building materials lying around the site cloud the progress from many bystanders. The progress is obscured by the rubble. This is the perspective we often have of ourselves and other Christians. The

---

[17] Letters (Palmer), 129.
[18] W, 2:108.
[19] See Newton's poem "A Thought on the Sea Shore" (W, 3:670).

Christian life is a hard-hat area, and we struggle to see God's "good work" coming together in the mess of our lives.

How different is the view of the architect. The architect has done this many times before, and he perceives the end of the project from the first stone to the final shrub. He can steer the progress along to the end he designed. He may need to adjust the materials or change the schedule, but even in the jobsite mess, the end product is clear in his imagination. In time, the project will be finished: the scaffolding will be removed, the debris cleaned up, the discarded building supplies taken away, the windows and floors polished, and the project delightful in its completion. Writes Newton:

> Men, indeed, often plan what, for want of skill or ability, or from unforeseen disappointments, they are unable to execute: but nothing can disappoint the heavenly Builder; nor will he ever be reproached with forsaking the work of his own hands, or beginning that which he could not or would not accomplish (Phil. 1:6). Let us therefore be thankful for beginnings, and patiently wait the event.[20]

Grace finishes what the divine Architect planned. As the builder, grace never walks off the job or leaves the project unfinished. The Christian life is always progressing behind scaffolding and debris that clouds our vision and makes it difficult for us to gauge the work of grace in our lives and the lives of other Christians. Yet we are confident that grace executes the Architect's blueprint. Newton is confident that even when it feels like the construction has stopped, grace continues to labor. This trust in the active work of grace in the Christian life helped Newton keep his trust in God when his spirits were low or when progress was obscured. The work of grace progresses from behind the scaffold, until the great unveiling (1 John 3:2). This event is on schedule and the infallible Architect will deliver the end product, all by grace.

All-Sufficient, Red-Letter Grace

While Newton is most famous for the phrase *amazing grace*, he much preferred the phrase *sufficient grace*. The two are not unrelated, but *sufficient grace* was more common in his vernacular because few (if any) Bible pas-

---

sages more clearly shaped his thinking of the Christian life than Paul's testimony of grace in the Christian life in 2 Corinthians 12:7–10.

> A thorn was given me in the flesh, a messenger of Satan to harass me, to keep me from becoming conceited. Three times I pleaded with the Lord about this, that it should leave me. But he said to me, "*My grace is sufficient for you*, for my power is made perfect in weakness." Therefore I will boast all the more gladly of my weaknesses, so that the power of Christ may rest upon me. For the sake of Christ, then, I am content with weaknesses, insults, hardships, persecutions, and calamities. For when I am weak, then I am strong.

The Christian life is not comfortable. God makes us no promises to remove difficult circumstances, or alleviate our pains, or protect us from suffering, but he does promise *sufficient grace* for all our wants and needs. In his pain, Paul learned there is a full supply of grace for all God's children. This is not merely *adequate grace*, but *all-sufficient grace*. No matter how large and daunting the circumstance or need, grace is always larger and stronger and more fully sufficient to meet each battle or trial in the Christian life.

Deeply moved by Paul's words, Newton not surprisingly wrote multiple hymns on grace, including one titled "My Grace Is Sufficient for Thee." In it he elaborates further on the perspective-altering power of God's sufficient grace in light of the pains and struggles of the Christian life. The hymn opens with two verses of violent, descriptive words to recreate Paul's desperation. If "Amazing Grace" gives us a macro-look at grace and the Christian life, "My Grace Is Sufficient for Thee" is a micro-look into how grace gets applied to the warfare in the Christian life.

> Oppress'd with unbelief and sin,
> Fightings without, and fears within;
> While earth and hell, with force combin'd,
> Assault and terrify my mind:
>
> What strength have I against such foes,
> Such hosts and legions to oppose?
> Alas! I tremble, faint, and fall;
> Lord, save me, or I give up all.

Paul faced physical pain and outward oppression in his ministry, but here Newton applies the passage to the violent spiritual assaults against temptations, indwelling sin, the flesh, unbelief, the world, and a host of demonic foes. All the Christian's allied enemies crash on him at once. He trembles, he faints, and he falls to his knees. The combined force of the enemies quickly overwhelms the internal supplies of the Christian. In desperation, Newton cries out for deliverance.

> Thus sorely prest, I sought the Lord,
> To give me some sweet, cheering word;
> Again I sought, and yet again;
> I waited long, but not in vain.
>
> Oh! 'twas a cheering word indeed!
> Exactly suited to my need;
> "Sufficient for thee is my grace,
> Thy weakness my great pow'r displays."

The answer comes, but not immediately. And when it does arrive, the answer is not an alleviation of suffering, but the promise of all-sufficient grace to endure with joy. When sufficient grace breaks in, the entire mood of the hymn changes, even as the battles rage on. Notice how the hymn concludes with the mood-altering effect of this "awakening" to the sufficiency of God's grace.

> Now I despond and mourn no more,
> I welcome all I fear'd before;
> Though weak, I'm strong; though troubled, blest;
> For Christ's own pow'r shall on me rest.
>
> My grace would soon exhausted be,
> But his is boundless as the sea;
> Then let me boast with holy Paul,
> That I am nothing, Christ is all.[21]

Only all-sufficient grace can account for the change of tone in this hymn. Grace alone is powerful enough to comfort Newton in his darkest trial, under the most persistent pain, and under attack on all fronts. God's

---

[21] W, 3:449–50.

solution to trials may not always be an escape from circumstances, but may be a stable and ever-present response from God to those who ask. *My grace is sufficient for you.* "Such an assurance was more valuable than the deliverance he sought could be."[22]

"I am nothing, Christ is all." The all-sufficient grace of God provides us the context for discovering our insufficiencies. Grace welcomes us to look into our emptiness and personal weakness because our strength and security is outside of us, in God's all-sufficient grace. Our owning of personal weakness is one of the results of the active presence of grace. And our weakness is how we broadcast the grace of God to others.

Look closely and you'll notice something curious in 2 Corinthians 12:9. Red-letter Bibles print this verse in blood-red text. "My grace is sufficient for you, for my power is made perfect in weakness," is a phrase from the lips of the Savior to Paul, pushing us closer to the heart of Newton's theology, and closer to the heart of this book.

No Such "Thing" as Grace

The absence of the word *grace* from my book title and subtitle is not accidental. By personifying grace, "Amazing Grace" can be somewhat misleading to modern readers. It is certainly not wrong to put verbs after grace (e.g., Titus 2:11). Grace *saves* wretches. Grace *searches out* lost sinners. Grace *removes* spiritual blindness and *gives* spiritual sight. Grace *teaches* us to fear God. Grace *relieves* fear. But in our modern culture, where *grace* has become a synonym for *kindness*, "Amazing Grace" becomes a sort of hymn to the transforming power of niceness or, a little better, grace becomes abstracted divine benevolence. In either case, grace is depersonalized.

This misunderstanding of grace has led Sinclair Ferguson to go so far as to say there actually is no such *thing* as grace.[23] It has led Michael Horton to declare that grace is "not a third thing or substance mediating between God and sinners, but is Jesus Christ in redeeming action."[24] Their point is the same. We must resist the temptation to morph grace into spiritual currency or some abstracted spiritual power that mysteriously ebbs and

---

[22] W, 2:316.
[23] "Grace is not a 'thing.' It is not a substance that can be measured or a commodity to be distributed. It is 'the grace of the Lord Jesus Christ' (2 Cor. 13:14). In essence, it is Jesus Himself" (Sinclair B. Ferguson, *By Grace Alone: How the Grace of God Amazes Me* [Orlando, FL: Reformation Trust, 2010], xv).
[24] Michael Horton, *The Christian Faith: A Systematic Theology for Pilgrims on the Way* (Grand Rapids: Zondervan, 2011), 267–68.

flows. Grace is not dished out in spiritual gold coins of merit (a serious medieval Roman Catholic error confronted in the Reformation). No. Thinking of grace as spiritual currency is mistaken. To say there is no such *thing* as grace means that all the grace we have and can ever hope to have—all the sovereign grace, all the all-sufficient grace—is bound up in the favor of the Father and in our union with the Son.

If you have Christ, you have all of Christ, and to have all of Christ is to have free access to Christ's all-sufficient grace. Grace is not a gate to fence us back from Christ. Grace is not a substitute for Christ. Grace does not stand between me and Christ. Rather, says Calvin, "All graces are bestowed on us through Christ."[25] *Grace* is shorthand for the full and free access we have to all the merits and power and promises to be found *in the person of our Savior* (John 1:16–17; Eph. 2:7; 1 Cor. 1:4; 2 Cor. 8:9; 2 Tim. 2:1). Repeatedly, Newton accents "the grace *that is in Christ Jesus*." Grace is a stream from Christ, the fountain of all grace, he writes.[26] The "water of life" (Rev. 22:17) "stands for the communication of every grace from Jesus Christ. He is the fountain (John 7:37–39). [The outpouring of grace] is compared to water, for it is plenty. There is abundance of grace—a fountain, a river, an ocean (Isa. 44:3)."[27] "For from his fullness we have all received, grace upon grace," writes the apostle John (John 1:16). "All the streams of grace flow from Christ, the fountain," Newton concludes.[28]

In a letter to his eminent friend Hannah More, Newton wrote:

> When we understand what the Scripture teaches of the person, love, and offices of Christ, the necessity and final causes of his humiliation unto death, and feel our own need of such a Savior, we then know him to be the light, the sun of the world and of the soul, the source of all spiritual light, life, comfort and influence; having access to God by him, *and receiving out of his fullness grace for grace.*[29]

And thus, "we are gradually prepared to live more out of ourselves, and to

---

[25] John Calvin, *Commentaries on the Epistle of Paul the Apostle to the Hebrews*, trans. John Owen (Edinburgh: Calvin Translation Society, 1853), 357.

[26] *W*, 1:417; 2:574; 3:20; 6:253.

[27] John Newton, *365 Days with Newton*, ed. Marylynn Rouse (Leominster, UK: Day One, 2006), 122. Here I use the Logos software pagination.

[28] *W*, 1:417. To be fair, Paul sometimes speaks of grace (χάρις) without mentioning Christ. In these cases he appears to be speaking of grace as a mobilizing force or a spiritual gift for certain tasks (see Rom. 1:5; 12:3; 15:15; 1 Cor. 3:10; 15:10; 2 Cor. 9:8; Gal. 2:9; Eph. 3:7–8; Phil. 1:7). But ultimately, all the grace that gifts or mobilizes is a grace purchased in Christ and distributed by him (Eph. 4:7–8).

[29] *Letters* (Bull 1869), 350.

derive all our sufficiency of every kind from Jesus, the fountain of grace."[30] Such dependence on Christ empowers us: "Oh, it is a great thing to be strong in the grace that is in Christ Jesus!" (2 Tim. 2:1).[31]

In whatever ways our modern culture hears Newton's hymn as an abstracted and depersonalized divine blessing, his intent is clear. Christ "is the Fountain, the Sun, the Treasury of all grace."[32] When Newton speaks of grace, he is speaking of Christ in union with the believer. Newton's *grace* is ever "*My grace*," a sovereign grace, all-sufficient grace, alone-sufficient grace that flows freely and fully from the person of Jesus Christ. "By nature we are separated from the divine life, as branches broken off, withered and fruitless," Newton writes. "But grace, through faith, unites us to Christ the living Vine, from whom, as the root of all fullness, a constant supply of sap and influence is derived into each of his mystical branches, enabling them to bring forth fruit unto God, and to persevere and abound therein."[33] A life in union with Christ is "the life of grace."[34]

In our abiding union with Christ we find the context of the Christian life. Grace not only connects us to Christ; grace is the daily motivation for us to press closer toward Christ, to "be daily hungering and thirsting after him, and daily receiving from his fullness, even grace for grace; that you may rejoice in his all-sufficiency, may taste his love in every dispensation."[35] We seek *more grace* by seeking to experience *more Christ*.

Amazing Grace, Amazing Christ, Smoking Flax

Discovering the amazingness of grace requires that we focus on the amazingness of Christ in the theology and life of Newton. All we have is Christ. Separated from him, there is no saving or sanctifying grace for the Christian life. United to Christ, there is full and free access to the full riches of Christ, who is the fountain of all grace. Newton expressed this union perhaps most fully and beautifully in his sermon on Matthew 11:27.

> The great God is pleased to manifest himself in Christ, as the God of grace. This grace is manifold, pardoning, converting, restoring, persevering grace, bestowed upon the miserable and worthless. Grace finds the

---

[30] *W*, 1:430–31.
[31] *W*, 2:105.
[32] *365 Days with Newton*, 236.
[33] *W*, 1:322.
[34] *W*, 4:333.
[35] *W*, 6:47.

sinner in a hopeless, helpless state, sitting in darkness, and in the shadow of death. Grace pardons the guilt, cleanses the pollution, and subdues the power of sin. Grace sustains the bruised reed, binds up the broken heart, and cherishes the smoking flax into a flame. Grace restores the soul when wandering, revives it when fainting, heals it when wounded, upholds it when ready to fall, teaches it to fight, goes before it in the battle, and at last makes it more than conqueror over all opposition, and then bestows a crown of everlasting life. But all this grace is established and displayed by covenant in the man Christ Jesus, and without respect to him as living, dying, rising, reigning, and interceding in the behalf of sinners, would never have been known.[36]

Grace is not currency dispensed from an impersonal, computerized ATM. Grace is deeply personal, it is glue, securing the branch of our Christian life into the trunk of Christ's all-sufficiency. Grace binds us to the person of Christ, to his vital life, and to the full spectrum of his all-sufficient benefits. Before we learn from Newton about the common challenges of the Christian life, before we study the particular blemishes of Christian character, before we study his instructions to those who are discouraged and depressed, before we see his balm for the pain and trials and the insecurities Christians face, and before we can learn from him about trying to do business in the world, or about how to honor God in our marriages, or about how to deal with particular indwelling sins—before we look at any of these particulars, we must understand the root of all grace, Jesus Christ.

[36] W, 2:442.

CHAPTER 2

CHRIST ALL-SUFFICIENT

William Jay was a young pastor in London whose career was beginning to ascend just as John Newton's ministry was coming to an end. Like Newton, Jay was a gifted pastor with no formal theological training. In the fall of 1807, the thirty-eight-year-old brought along a notebook and pencil for what would prove to be his final visit to his old friend. Newton was in his eighties, bedridden, and confined to an upstairs bedroom in the London home of his adopted daughter and son-in-law. While Newton's health and eyesight and memory were all failing, Jay had his notebook at his side in anticipation of carrying away a piece of advice—anything—from his pastoral mentor.

After a brief meeting, Jay walked downstairs and reentered the bustle and clatter of London's cobblestone streets, not yet contemplating the lines he had scratched in his notebook. Later, he discovered the richness of the single line he jotted down, a line now etched into history as John Newton's final recorded words: "My memory is nearly gone, but I remember two things: that I am a great sinner and that Christ is a great Savior."[1] Newton died a few weeks later, on December 21, 1807. The words transcribed by Jay are a simple and profound summary of John Newton's life.

Newton's dying words summarize the message he preached and wrote about throughout his Christian life. Four decades earlier, in the prime of his health, Newton had written to a friend, "Our sins are many, but his mercies

---

[1] Aitken, 347.

are more: our sins are great, but his righteousness is greater."[2] At another point he wrote, "We cannot be so evil as he is good."[3] Newton was governed by the abiding hope that where sin increases, grace abounds all the more (Rom. 5:20). In one letter early in his pastorate he wrote, "Though our sins have been deep-dyed, like scarlet and crimson, enormous as mountains, and countless as the sands, the sum total is, but, *Sin has abounded*; but where sin hath abounded, *grace has much more abounded*."[4] Yes, sin is a monstrous, condemning force—but Christ is greater. Grace *abounds* because the Savior *superabounds*. This biblical truth worked itself deeply into Newton's heart very early in his Christian walk, and it was a conviction that drove him toward pastoral ministry and to preaching "the unsearchable riches of Christ" (Eph. 3:8).

Like an unceasing echo, the theme of Christ's superabundant grace is heard in everything Newton writes—in his hymns, his sermons, his letters—and in his weak and feeble dying words. In the profoundly sin-swallowing sufficiency of the Savior, we discover the heart and soul of Newton's theology. From his first spiritual breath to his final words, Newton held firm these two realities learned from his own experience: our sin is dark and ugly and damning and destructive, but Christ superabounds our sin with unassailable light and beauty and redemption and restoration.

All in All

Newton's christology not only comforts; it confronts. The greatest decision any human ever makes concerns the nature of Christ. Jesus inquired of the Pharisees, "What do you think about the Christ?" and the same question is pushed before every one of us (Matt. 22:42). What are we going to do with Christ? Everything hinges on that decision, with eternity in the balance. On the basis of how we respond to the Bible's truth about Christ, "so God is disposed to you, and mercy or wrath are your lot."[5] The stakes could not be higher.

This is why the Christian life is about Christ. Or to say it more starkly, "to live *is* Christ" (Phil. 1:21). The Christian's life *is* Christ. John Newton was committed to living the Christian life daily in this truth, and this struggle appears throughout his letters, his hymns, his sermons, and his final words. Christ was his life, his hope, and his "motto."

---

[2] W, 2:140–41.
[3] W, 6:195.
[4] W, 1:686.
[5] W, 3:403.

Christ is the motto of the Christian life because Christ is the substance of the Christian life. In highlighting Christ's all-sufficiency, Newton often returns to one of his favorite biblical phrases from Paul: *Christ is all in all* (Eph. 1:23; Col. 3:11). To have the faith to find Christ as "all in all in himself" and to see Christ as "all in all for us" has the power to cheer our sorrowing hearts, strengthen our spiritual eagerness, make hard duties easy, and make bitter experiences sweet.[6] The love of Christ controls our lives (2 Cor. 5:14). True faith in Christ changes everything about *how* the Christian life is lived, which is why Newton's own prayer for his friends is a fitting prayer for us as we continue our study: "This includes all I can wish for my dear friends, that you may grow in grace, and in the knowledge of Jesus. To know him, is the shortest description of true grace; to know him better, is the surest mark of growth in grace; to know him perfectly, is eternal life" (John 17:3).[7]

Newton's prayer is a keystone statement we will return to throughout this study because maintaining this Christ-centered outlook in his daily life, Newton admitted, was the supreme goal (and challenge) for the Christian. But before we address the struggle of Christ-centered Christian living, we must first look at the substance—the *all-in-all-ness*—of Christ.

Christ All-Sufficient

Newton frequently reminds his friends of the gospel. The gospel is free, full, and complete, and Christ invites all sinners to come to him "without exception, condition, or limitation."[8] In his all-sufficiency, Christ is precious (1 Pet. 2:4–7). Nothing can be added to his perfections and his completed work. In him, all our guilt is cancelled and blotted and swallowed up, and all our sins are "sunk in his precious blood as in a deep sea, so that, even if sought for, they can no more be found."[9]

While Newton was fully convinced of the importance of the Trinitarian nature of God (the "adorable Trinity" as he calls it, or worthy of all adoration[10]), he believed that the divinity of Christ is "the great foundation-stone upon which all true religion is built."[11] Perhaps Newton could have placed greater emphasis on the Holy Spirit in his ministry, but he operated with

[6] *W*, 1:296, 314, 393, 649; 2:472–73, 495; 4:239–40, 268; 6:73, 128–29.
[7] *W*, 6:73–74.
[8] *W*, 6:465.
[9] *W*, 4:483.
[10] *W*, 1:197–98.
[11] *W*, 2:10.

this conviction: since there is no jealousy within the triune God, it is impossible to overpraise the Son or to dishonor the Father or Spirit in the adoration of Christ.[12] Christ incarnate is the full revelation of God in the flesh. This truth is so important that no matter how religious you are, if you are without Christ, you are without God—an atheist (Eph. 2:12).[13] Only in Christ are the attributes of God rendered familiar to us in a human form as he relates to us as God our Friend, Brother, and Husband, thereby positioning Christ as the supreme object of our deepest longings and affections.[14]

Another of Newton's famous hymns opens affectionately:

How sweet the name of Jesus sounds
In a believer's ear!
It soothes his sorrows, heals his wounds,
And drives away his fear.

Near the end of the hymn, while singing about the many roles Christ fills, the worshiper discovers why Christ's name is precious.

Jesus! My Shepherd, Husband, Friend,
My Prophet, Priest, and King;
My Lord, my Life, my Way, my End.[15]

Such precious names for Christ's all-sufficiency must have filled the hearts and lips of Olney worshipers with joy. To find Christ is to find a priceless treasure in a field, an all-sufficient treasure to meet every need of every sinner. "Oh, may his precious name be engraven upon our hearts, and sound sweeter than music to our ears, for he has loved us, and washed us from our sins in his own blood, and will save to the uttermost in defiance of all our sins, fears, and enemies!"[16]

This all-sufficiency in Christ is substantiated in his relationships to the Christian, particularly in six names—Shepherd, Husband, Prophet, Priest, King, and Friend. As we examine later, these roles are certainly not comprehensive, but they do offer a sampling of how Newton framed his (very personal) relationship with Christ.

---

[12] W, 6:439–40.
[13] W, 4:575–76.
[14] W, 1:307.
[15] W, 3:370.
[16] W, 6:147.

Shepherd

Christ is the all-sufficient Shepherd who delivers his sheep (Heb. 13:20). Newton caught the shepherding language embedded in the Old Testament exodus of God's people out of Egypt (Isa. 63:11). The exodus offers him a typological picture of the entire Christian life, and he once called Deuteronomy 32:9–14 a "history of a believer in miniature, an Iliad in a nutshell."[17] The sinner, fast bound in slavery to his own sin, is delivered by miracle and shed blood, freed to walk for forty years—sustained by God—along a path toward the eternal rest of the Promised Land. The Christian life is exodus and exile.[18] But the redeemed never walk this path alone. Christians walk together, never far from our Good Shepherd who leads and guides us in even the darkest nights in the desert. Left to ourselves we wander off into thistles and danger. In the wilderness of these years on earth, our Good Shepherd sustains us, tames the ravens (provides necessities), and tames the lions (protects from dangers).[19]

Yet this exodus metaphor is frightening because sheep are defenseless: they cannot fight, they cannot run with much speed, and they have little foresight or sense of danger.[20] Little do we appreciate the danger we face at every moment of life. All our attempts at self-preservation are laughably insufficient. We are poor and silly sheep, unable to add one inch to our statures by all our worry. The fortresses we build around our souls for protection are castles of cardboard. The dangers we face far exceed our frail powers to defend ourselves. Our vulnerability and weakness draw out God's compassionate love and care.

The Good Shepherd promises to watch over us, and nothing less can tame our anxieties and insecurities. "I am prone to puzzle myself about twenty things," said Newton, "which are equally out of my power, and equally unnecessary, if the Lord be my Shepherd."[21] Christ's all-sufficiency as our Shepherd is the substance behind the command to be anxious about nothing (Phil. 4:6).

This trust in the Shepherd makes it possible to praise God for what is behind us and to "cheerfully trust him for what is to come."[22] The Christian

---

[17] *W*, 6:145–46. See also *Letters* (Taylor), 33, 75–76. Newton once wrote: "You will find an abridgment of my life thus far in Deut. 32:10–14. I have but too much reason to take the 15th verse into the account" (*Letters* [Bull 1869], 242).
[18] See G. K. Beale, *A New Testament Biblical Theology: The Unfolding of the Old Testament in the New* (Grand Rapids: Baker Academic, 2011), 856–63.
[19] *W*, 3:347.
[20] *W*, 3:560–61; 4:152–53.
[21] *W*, 6:191–92.
[22] *W*, 6:345.

path does not cut through many rose gardens, but it will always be the right path. Along the way, the Good Shepherd will bring trials that "are medicinal, designed to correct, or to restrain, or to cure" the maladies of our souls.[23] Trials serve our ultimate and eternal prosperity, and as we will discover later, the Shepherd brings no fiercer trial than he sustains us to face, and no heavier burden than he strengthens us to carry.

The Christian life is an exodus, with a Shepherd guiding the way. In order to be our Shepherd, Christ became a man, and he has now become the Chief Shepherd. All pastors are under-shepherds employed by him and serve a similar role of care in the church (1 Pet. 5:1–4). Christ intends for his sheep to be fed in the green pastures of local churches. Together, as a flock led by under-shepherds, we walk through this life with eternity at stake, and we are guided by the Chief Shepherd's voice along a path, across the wilderness, to the porch of the house of the Lord, and into the presence of the Good Shepherd forever (Ps. 23:6). Christ is our Good Shepherd. He died to protect our souls (John 10:1–18).[24] We follow his all-sufficient *voice* until we arrive at his all-sufficient *face*.

Husband

Christ is the all-sufficient Husband who willingly weds himself to us. On the one hand, he has taken full responsibility for all our debts, and on the other hand, his honor and riches and the inestimable value of his eternal estate are now all ours—"our debts are paid, our settlements secured, and our names changed."[25] He now deals with us with great affection, as is proper toward his bride, and we are given his "great love, tenderness, and sympathy." In the coming wedding of the church to Christ we are brought face-to-face with the divine affections. "The gospel is not designed to make us stoics: it allows full room for those social feelings which are so necessary and beneficial in our present state," writes Newton, and the affections and beauty and mutual love in the greatest marriage on earth are but an echo of the beauty in the gospel.[26] The beauty John Newton saw and was drawn toward in his precious wife, Polly, was a mere shadow of a greater reality and a greater marriage. That is to say, the most beautiful human mar-

---

[23] W, 4:156; 6:338.
[24] W, 6:179, 191–92.
[25] W, 1:323.
[26] W, 6:486.

riage is but a temporal taste of the full light and beauty and all-sufficiency of marriage to our Husband, Christ.

Faith in Christ is far more than intellectual ascent and stoic rationalism. As the Husband of the church, Christ weds the church. In our participation with him, we now experience "an intimate, vital, and inseparable union."[27] And one day history will be consummated when the Husband (Lamb) enters into an eternal marriage with his bride (the church) at the end of the age (Rev. 19:6–10).[28] The great end of the gospel is holiness and happiness. It is the complete restoration of the soul to the image of God. It sets aright all the evil in this world. The plan has been put in motion, the payment price of the cross has been made. The wedding feast has been planned. The all-sufficient Husband is in place.[29]

Prophet

In sin, humankind suppresses the truth, becomes futile and foolish in its thinking, forgets God, and worships its own crafts. "His life became vain and miserable; in prosperity, without security or satisfaction; in adversity, without support or resource; his death dark and hopeless; no pleasing reflection on the past, no ray of light on the future."[30] This was the state of humanity when Christ became a Prophet, writes Newton. Christ is the all-sufficient Prophet who has disclosed the invisible God to us (John 1:9, 18). Newton thus likens the "riches of Divine grace" of Scripture to precious jewels that are locked away in a thick safe. The door must be unlocked and opened for the true value to be discovered. This is the work of Christ. As the Prophet, he is the door that opens the riches of divine truth in Scripture to the eyes and the heart of the Christian.[31]

Divine truth cannot be perceived and received into the heart merely by opening a book and reading the words off the page.[32] Spiritual and relational dynamics must occur. By his work and through the gospel, Christ opens our eyes through the power of the Holy Spirit. In his work on the sinner's soul, Christ remakes the heart of stone into a heart of flesh, and he opens the sinner's eyes to the incredible riches of God's Word. This divine illumination

---

[27] *W*, 1:323.
[28] *W*, 1:323; 6:486.
[29] *W*, 3:32.
[30] *W*, 2:345.
[31] *W*, 2:375.
[32] I develop this point in Tony Reinke, *Lit! A Christian Guide to Reading Books* (Wheaton, IL: Crossway, 2011), 29–38.

comes from Christ alone as the Logos, or Word. Christ is our all-sufficient Prophet, our teacher, and the self-disclosure of the invisible God (John 8:26; 14:9; 17:8). Christ is the telescope by which we see God in creation, and the clue that leads us through the history of divine providence. Through Christ the Bible is applied to the hearts and lives of Christians. In Scripture, in creation, and in providence, Christ is our illuminating Prophet.

Priest

Christ is the pure and all-sufficient Priest who died the criminal's death. Although he was innocent, his death surpassed the inhuman death of an obnoxious and hardened criminal. None would dare mock that criminal in his death, "But when Jesus suffers, all that see him, laugh him to scorn; they shoot out the lip, they shake the head; they insult his character, and his hope."[33] He is the despised Priest; rejected by men, rejected by God. He is the holy sacrifice, his blood is holy blood, and he is at the same time the holy Priest transacting with a holy God on our behalf, on the basis of his own blood (Heb. 7:23–28, 10:11–14). Thus, there is one ultimate and final Mediator who acts between God and men—Christ Jesus (1 Tim. 2:5, a passage in which, Newton writes, "is summed up all that Christ has done, now does, or will do hereafter, either on the part of God or man").[34] Christ is our one Mediator on whom everything else hinges.

This is the wisdom of God that befuddles the wisdom of man. "It seems impossible to believe that the title of the true God and eternal life should properly belong to that despised Man who hung dead upon the cross."[35] And yet it does. Christ is the Lamb who absorbed the full wrath of God. He is the eternal focal point of all worship (Revelation 5). The Lamb that was slain "will ever be the head and Lord of the creation, the medium of communication of the light and love of God to his people; and God in him, the object of their eternal adoration and praise."[36]

The substitutionary atonement of Jesus Christ is the epicenter of ministry, Newton reminded a pastor friend. "I advise you by all means to keep close to the *atonement*," he wrote.

[33] W, 4:242.
[34] W, 2:344.
[35] W, 2:10.
[36] W, 4:580.

The doctrine of the cross is the sun in the system of truth. It is seen by its own light, and throws light upon every other subject. This will soften hearts that withstand threatenings. This opens a door of hope to the vilest—to despairing sinners. The strictness and sanction of the law must be preached, to show sinners their danger; but the gospel is the only remedy, and suggests those motives, which are alone able to break off the sinner from the love of his sins, and to enable him to overcome the world.[37]

Only the full and sufficient atonement of Jesus Christ has such power: to illuminate all other divine truth, to order all doctrines, to be the one thing needful, and the only thing sufficient to silence unbelief and pride, and provide us solid ground for hope and assurance.[38] Only the atonement of Christ is capable of these victories, and this conviction grew with Newton over time. At age sixty-five, he wrote to another minister: "The older I grow, the more I am drawn to preach much concerning the person, the atonement, the glory of the Savior, and the influences of the Holy Spirit. There are other truths, important in their places, but unless beheld through the medium of the cross, they have but a faint effect."[39] With the passing years, Newton found himself cherishing Christ's priesthood and atoning sacrifice more and more.

But Christ's priesthood does not end with atonement; it extends to his ascension and enthronement into heaven (Eph. 4:8). Our High Priest knows our temptations, and he pities us with "an experimental sympathy."[40] The ascended Christ in heaven is

the foundation of our hopes, the source of our sublimest joys, and the sufficient, the only sufficient, answer to all the suggestions by which guilt, fear, unbelief, and Satan, fight against our peace. Surrounded as we are with enemies and difficulties, we plead, against every accusation and threatening, that our Head is in heaven; we have an Advocate with the Father, a High Priest upon the throne, who, because he ever liveth to make intercession, is able to save to the uttermost [Heb. 7:25].[41]

That is to say, Christ our all-sufficient Priest is able to save to the uttermost and holds ultimate power over all our sins, temptations, difficulties,

---

[37] *Letters* (Coffin), 62.
[38] *W*, 6:470.
[39] *Letters* (Ryland), 232.
[40] *Letters* (Taylor), 189.
[41] *W*, 4:326–27.

fears, and backsliding. "Our Savior is now absent, but absent on our behalf."[42] Such an all-sufficient Priest is Christ.

King

Christ now reigns as the all-sufficient King.

> He fought, he bled, he died; but in dying, he conquered. . . . He destroyed death, and disarmed it of its sting. He destroyed him that hath the power of death, Satan. He shook, he overturned, the foundations of his kingdom, broke open his prison-doors, released his prisoners, delivered the prey out of the hand of the mighty.[43]

Through the cross, the King has won.

He is the King of Glory. Yes, the whole earth is full of God's glory, but most of that glory is "but scattered rays and emanations of light." In Jesus, "the glory of God resides in its source and fullness, as light in the sun. He is therefore the King of glory." As the all-sufficient King, Christ is the focal point of God's emanating glory.[44]

Christ is the King over the cosmos, bringing all things under his control (Eph. 1:10; Col. 1:20). Kings and politicians may be ignorant of his reign, but their ignorance makes his dominion no less real. Christ is the King in charge of all political elections and processes, and providence is a train of his political dispensations. The collapse of kingdoms and the commotion of revolutions all unfold according to a wisely determined plan that has as its final cause the kingdom of God.[45] This was not mere political theory for Newton, but the Christ-centered lens that he used to view all of human history. For example, Alexander the Great (356–323 BC), who conquered the entire known world and tirelessly labored to unite many people under one language (Greek), succeeded in a political move which Christ overgoverned as a means to spread the gospel to the nations. With Alexander's domination, God broke down language barriers and opened doors for the apostolic preaching of the gospel across the known Gentile world. Behind all that activity was a divine orchestration, and behind that orchestration was a kingdom, and behind that kingdom was the cosmic King born as a babe in

---

[42] *Letters* (Jones), 51.
[43] *W*, 4:295.
[44] *W*, 4:298.
[45] *W*, 4:22.

a dirty barn in a backwoods town called Bethlehem. That babe now governs every event in this world to further his eternal kingdom.

Friend

But of all the names Newton cherished for Christ, perhaps the most wide-ranging is *Friend*. For Newton, Christ is the all-sufficient Friend who protects us. He condescends to seek sinners who are poor and puny. No weakness in his friends withholds Christ's free and endless love, and no illustration shows this more clearly than in Christ's free willingness to ransom his life for his friends. Christ is a Friend who finds the sinner wandering a God-less desert, tripping toward eternal death. Christ steps in not only to save him, but also to give him eternal joy and comfort—true friendship in all its dimensions. The Christian lives "a strange mysterious life" that seems to swing daily from darkness into light, from peace into strife. Time and time again, our Friend breaks into this strange and mysterious riddle of life and empowers us for a sweet and stable life in the storm. And yet for all his help, we are enigmatic friends in return. We are forgetful and faithless and disloyal, but our neglect and distrust and disobedience does not diminish his love for us. He is steadfast. He's the Friend we wish we could be. He's the all-sufficient Friend we need. And if he were not, he would surely "spurn us from his sight."[46]

Christ is the perfect Friend. His sacrificial love is perfect. He left glory, took on flesh, submitted to shame, and delivered himself to death to save us from sin and misery and to open the kingdom to us, who were his enemies. "For he saw and pitied us, when we knew not how to pity ourselves."[47] He is transcendent in glory, but draws close to hopeless sinners in friendship (Matt. 11:19; Luke 7:34). We need a friend, and who better than a Friend who made heaven and earth, raised the dead, and hushed storms? He is always with us. "Jesus is always near, about our path by day, and our bed by night; nearer than the light by which we see, or the air we breathe; nearer than we are to ourselves; so that not a thought, a sigh, or a tear, escaped his notice."[48]

Christ majestically displays a daily, moment-by-moment friendship for his fickle friends, but his greatest act of friendship was performed on the cross. There he made the ultimate sacrifice for his friends—his own life,

---

[46] *W*, 3:340–41, 598–99.
[47] *Letters* (Taylor), 186.
[48] *Letters* (Taylor), 187.

a precious and pure life, a life that nobody took from him, a life that he laid down on the altar willingly (John 15:13). By naming Christ as his all-sufficient Friend, Newton spotlights a reality far deeper than Christ as our *buddy* or *chum*. Christ binds our friendship through the highest sacrifice ever conceived. Never before and never since has there been a friend who paid pure sinless blood for his friends.

> Which of all our friends to save us,
> Could or would have shed their blood![49]

None. This is friendship to the glorious extreme. Only Christ reconciles us to God and delivers peace with a holy God as the highest manifestation of his friendship. We either trust securely in this Friend or struggle to find our security in self-confidence and worldly safeties.[50]

With Christ as our Friend we find our source of daily joy in this tumultuous life.[51] *Friend* becomes for Newton an affection-loaded shorthand title to embrace the full scope of Christ's all-sufficiency, personally applied to us.[52]

"Ev'ry Precious Name in One"

Each of Newton's titles for Christ is a different face to the diamond of Christ's all-sufficiency, and he is a diamond of inexhaustible riches. To this list of Christ as our all-sufficient Shepherd, Husband, Prophet, Priest, King, and Friend, could be added many more. Christ is also our Lord, our Life, our Way, our End, our Head, our Root, our Meat, our Drink, our Portion, our Strength, our Hope, our Foundation, our Sun, our Shield, our Lawgiver, our Exemplar, our Forerunner, and our All, just to name a few other ways Newton described the excellencies of Christ. Christ is all of this, so we will expect and receive our all-sufficiency from his hands.[53] Yet only eternity will afford us time to discover and enjoy and worship Christ in the full dimensions of his all-sufficiency—"the unsearchable riches of Christ" (Eph. 3:8).

To use another Newtonian metaphor, Christ is like the sun in his endless supplies. Out of his all-sufficiency "he can cheer and enlighten thousands and millions at once, and give to each as bountifully as if there were

---

[49] *W*, 3:366.
[50] *W*, 3:380.
[51] *W*, 3:389.
[52] *W*, 3:340–41.
[53] *Letters* (Taylor), 224.

no more to partake of his favor. His best blessings are not diminished by being shared among many."[54] His greatness is not apportioned. A monarch may give a token gift to all of his subjects, but the gift must be divided.

> But Jesus has unsearchable, inexhaustible riches of grace to bestow. The innumerable assembly before the Throne have been all supplied from his fullness; and yet there is enough and to spare for us also, and for all that shall come after us. May he give us an eager appetite, a hunger and thirst that will not be put off with any thing short of the bread of life; and then we may confidently open our mouths wide, for he has promised to fill them.[55]

His all-sufficiency can make five loaves of bread and two fish stuff thousands of hungry stomachs. His grace cannot be exhausted (Matt. 14:13–21). His "unsearchable riches" are sufficient for millions of distressed sinners at the same time.[56] Christ is a sun, he is an endless feast, and he is an endless ocean in breadth, length, height, and depth of unsearchable love (Eph. 3:18–19). "This love of Christ to sinners is inexpressible, unsearchable, and passing knowledge; it is an ocean without either bottom or shore."[57] The treasury of life and salvation in Christ

> is inexhaustible, like a boundless, shoreless, bottomless ocean; like the sun, which having cheered the successive generations of mankind with his beams, still shines with undiminished luster, is still the fountain of light, and has always a sufficiency to fill innumerable millions of eyes in the same instant.[58]

Similarly, Christ, and him crucified, is the sun in the solar system of all knowledge and learning.

> As the eye cannot judge of sounds, nor the ear of prospects and colors, neither can our reason help us in our religious concerns, till it is first brought to the foot of the cross. The doctrine of Jesus Christ, and him crucified, is the Sun of the intellectual world. It can only be seen by its own light; but when the eyes of the mind are opened to behold it, it throws a light upon every other object and subject in which we are concerned.[59]

---

[54] *W*, 2:194.
[55] *W*, 2:194–95.
[56] *W*, 4:163.
[57] *W*, 6:502.
[58] *W*, 4:78.
[59] Letters (Palmer), 131.

Pick your metaphor, run its sufficiency to the farthest extent, then mix the metaphor with other metaphors, and you begin to understand the surpassing riches of Christ in Newton's mind.

It is not surprising, but it is striking, how consistently Newton focuses his writings and hymns ultimately on the *person* of Jesus Christ. All of Christ's work and all the combined doctrines of *justification* and *propitiation* and *adoption* are foremost communicated through the relational categories of Christ's *person*. At every point in his writings, Newton wants to point other Christians back to Christ, not merely to theological labels. And so Newton points often to the One who gives substance to the concepts and the promises—in order to point us again and again to a man, to the God-man, who accomplishes all these things for his eternal glory. A reader of Newton's works is struck by his frequent return to the person of Christ on whom hang all his hopes, not merely to correct outlines of orthodoxy. Newton was driven to expound the one Mediator between God and men, "the *man* Christ Jesus" (1 Tim. 2:5).

Newton will not allow us to abstract the Christian life from Christ. One day we will join Newton and plunge into the shoreless ocean of Christ's love to explore the far deeper reaches of Christ's all-sufficiency. But until that day, the Christian life is one of reading and singing and worshiping the full-sufficiency of Christ we see in Scripture. And to that end, in a Christmas hymn devoted to the joy of the incarnation, Newton's heart finds due expression.

> O my Savior, Shield, and Sun,
> Shepherd, Brother, Husband, Friend,
> Ev'ry precious name in one,
> I will love thee without end.[60]

It is a beautiful lyric of the all-embracing and all-sufficient Christ. And it's an optimistic lyric, though one we certainly cannot hope to fully realize in this lifetime.

Beatific Vision

To speak of the all-sufficiency of Christ is inevitably to see weaknesses in the present and to foresee hopes in the future. This was the counsel New-

---

[60] W, 3:502.

ton passed to his adopted daughter one day when the birthday cake she enjoyed was gone.

> Look at all that appears good and pleasant in this world; could you call it all your own, it would last but a little while, and when you go into another world, the remembrance of what you had in this, will be but like remembering you once had a cake, but it is gone, quite eaten up. But it is not so, my dear child, with respect to that feast which Jesus prepares for poor sinners. The pleasures which he gives are repeated from time to time, and are pleasing even when we reflect on them. And, in the other world, when earthly pleasures will be quite ended, they that love him shall have pleasure without interruption and without end, rivers of pleasure at his right hand for evermore.[61]

To know Christ perfectly—to be with Christ—is the zenith of eternal life, the consummation of our union to him. To behold his presence is the highest pleasure, joy's apex. To behold his glory is to be made holy, and to be made holy is to be made perfectly happy (John 17:24).

Apart from this ultimate hope, the created world would be a dungeon of despair for God's children. But faith animates our lives with an eschatological anticipation of the presence and glory of Christ. We will not find our full and permanent happiness here. Nor will we find Christian joy automatically, like a daily newspaper at the door. God intends for us to find joy kinetically, in action, as we work out our faith with fear and trembling, as we fight the good fight of faith, as we worship, fellowship, and engage in all the various dynamics of the Christian life together.[62] But even in this, our hope of eternal joy sobers our expectations for the joy we can expect to experience in this life.

To study the all-sufficiency of Christ in the writings of Newton is to be reminded that the pursuit of enduring joy requires that we set our face toward eternity. Through trials and pain and discomfort in this life, Christ is our Shepherd-Friend, leading us step-by-step along a pathway safely into his presence and toward our supreme eternal happiness, into the palace of his pleasures forever (Ps. 16:11). He is working out his ultimate good in the life of every believer (Rom. 8:18–30).

---

[61] W, 6:292–93. See *Theological and Expository Lectures by Robert Leighton, D.D., Archbishop of Glasgow* (London, 1828), 33–34, 106, 110, 116.
[62] See Rudolf Bultmann, *Theology of the New Testament* (New York: Charles Scribner's Sons, 1955), 2:83–84.

"It is sufficient for us at present to know that we shall see Jesus," Newton wrote.

> We shall see him as he is, and we shall be like him (1 John 3:2). The circumstances of the heavenly state, if I may so speak, are hidden from us; but this, which constitutes the essence of it, we can form some faint apprehension of, from our present experience. All that deserves the name of happiness here, consists of such conceptions of Jesus, and such measures of conformity to him, as are attainable while in a mortal and defiled nature. But we see him only as in a glass, darkly and in part, but, when that which is perfect arrives, that which is in part shall be done away. We shall be all eye, all ear, all activity, in the communications of his love, and in the celebration of his praise. Here we are almost upon a level with worms; there we shall rise to an equality with angels.[63]

The Motto

For Newton, the beatific vision of Christ not only shapes our hopes, but also shapes everything about the Christian life. But I am getting ahead of myself. Here we need only to see the centrality of Christ's all-sufficiency for every step of the Christian journey. Newton navigated the expansive oceans by compass just as he navigated the Christian life by Christ. In many similar ways, the Christian life is navigated by charts and maps, and, to use a term coined by contemporary theologian Kevin Vanhoozer, that chart is *Christography*. All the scenarios we face in this life are navigated by a Scripture map which always seeks to point the Christian soul to the all-sufficient Christ, alive and reigning in heaven. This is why Newton says that all the things deserving of the name happiness in this life are somehow connected with our comprehension of Christ.

So for now, the full and dazzling work of Christ precedes every step of our Christian lives and directs all our aims and pursuits. The Christian life is hidden within Christ's life (Col. 3:3–4). Or, to repeat the apostle Paul, "To live *is* Christ" (Phil. 1:21). Christ is the sum and substance of this all-encompassing thing we call life (John 11:25). This point is not reductionistic for Paul or for Newton; everything that John Newton said about the Christian life can be fitted into that short phrase, and it's clearly evident in his dying words.

---

[63] W, 6:371–72.

To imagine the Christian life as progress toward our own self-sufficiency is wholly wrong. All Christian maturity is advancement toward greater Christlikeness. And because Christ is a great Savior, Newton can own the fact that he is a great sinner. "I trust the great desire of my soul is that Christ may be all in all to me, that my whole dependence, love, and aim, may center in him alone."[64] Or, as he said earlier in his life, "'*None* but Jesus,' is my motto." Or, after penning this verse in a letter, "The cross of Jesus Christ, my Lord, / Is food and medicine, shield and sword," Newton writes, "Take that for your motto; wear it in your heart; keep it in your eye; have it often in your mouth, till you can find something better. The cross of Christ is the tree of life and the tree of knowledge combined."[65] The Christian life centers on Christ—the mighty, crucified, resurrected Christ.

> Look unto the Lord Jesus Christ; look unto him as he hung naked, wounded, bleeding, dead, and forsaken upon the cross. Look unto him again as he *now* reigns in glory, possessed of all power in heaven and in earth, with thousands of thousands of saints and angels worshipping before him, and ten thousand times ten thousand ministering unto him; and then compare your sins with his blood, your wants with his fullness, your unbelief with his faithfulness, your weakness with his strength, your inconstancy with his everlasting love.[66]

By fixing our eyes on Christ, our lives are filled with holy affection and delight, and we go forth in joyful obedience to him. In our daily lives, in our families, in our callings, in our ministries, and in our vocations, Christ is "our theme in the pulpit and in the parlor."[67] He is the core of the Christian life and ministry.

The person of Jesus Christ is the source of all grace (chap. 1). He is also the center, goal, and aim—the motto—of the Christian life (chap. 2). Christ both *empowers* and *aims* everything about the Christian life. These two core principles unlock Newton's works and help us understand the daily disciplines of prayer, Scripture reading, and pursuing communion with God.

[64] *Letters* (Jones), 57.
[65] *W*, 2:68. The lines of verse are likely a precursor to the final lines in Newton's hymn published ten years later under the title "Praise for the Continuance of the Gospel," which ends: "The precious Gospel sweetens all, / And yields us med'cine, food, and joy" (*W*, 3:514), and/or the hymn "The Word More Precious than Gold," which ends: "Jesus gives me in his word, / FOOD and MED'CINE, SHIELD and SWORD" (*W*, 3:529).
[66] *W*, 2:574–75.
[67] *Letters* (Bull 1847), 208.

CHAPTER 3

THE DAILY DISCIPLINE
OF JOY IN JESUS

Newton operates within a clear, two-pronged, universal axiom: (1) Every human is hardwired to thirst for abiding joy, and (2) these soul cravings can be satisfied only by the God who encoded those desires in us.[1] "He [God] has given us a capacity and thirst for happiness which, both experience and observation demonstrate, the world cannot satisfy. He has graciously invited us to seek his face and to place our happiness in his favor, in communion with him, and in conformity to him."[2] This triune God—Father, Son, and Holy Spirit—has enjoyed "supreme happiness" in mutual delight among the three persons from all eternity.[3] Now this expressive joy spills out in invitation to thirsty creatures who accept the beloved Son, Jesus

---

[1] W, 1:432, 634; 2:202, 219; 4:232, 577; 6:288, 343–44; *Letters* (Taylor), 235–36. See also *Theological and Expository Lectures by Robert Leighton, D.D., Archbishop of Glasgow* (London, 1828), 8–52, 103–30.

[2] Newton, *The Christian Character Exemplified* (London, 1793), xviii. He made this point elsewhere. "Man, considered as the creature of God, is the noblest and most important of his works in the visible creation, formed by him who originally made him for himself, with such a vastness of desire, such a capacity for happiness, as nothing less than an infinite good can satisfy; formed to exist in an eternal unchangeable state" (W, 5:132). "Until we are reconciled to God by the blood of Jesus, everything to which we look for satisfaction will surely disappoint us. God formed us originally for himself, and has therefore given the human mind such a vastness of desire, such a thirst for happiness as he alone can answer; and therefore, till we seek our rest in him, in vain we seek it elsewhere. Neither the hurries of business, nor the allurements of pleasure, nor the accomplishment of our wishes, can fill up the mighty void that is felt within" (*Letters* [Bull 1869], 201–2). "He made us to be happy; but as he made us for himself, and gave us a capacity, and a vastness of desire, which only he himself can satisfy, the very constitution and frame of our nature render happiness impossible to us, unless in a way of dependence upon him, and obedience to his laws" (W, 4:232). See also W, 1:300; 5:132.

[3] W, 6:213; John Newton, *365 Days with Newton*, ed. Marylynn Rouse (Leominster, UK: Day One, 2006), 15. See also Leighton, *Theological and Expository Lectures*, 13, 170.

Christ. "This capacity of being exquisitely happy or miserable, and that for-ever[,] renders the soul so valuable in the judgment of its Creator, that he gave the Son of his love to redeem it from sin and misery, by his obedience unto death, even the death of the cross."[4] In other words, man's inherent value is his potential capacity to delight in Christ, and Christ's death aimed to purchase for us an eternally abiding enjoyment of God's joy.

Regeneration marks a magnificent collision of aims. Regeneration de-livers a sinner from the love of sin and reaffixes his desires "supremely upon Jesus Christ."[5] Conversion realigns the affections to joy in God and recalibrates our lives to taste the glory of Christ. Newton pastored under the assumption that true security and hope and joy can only be rooted in our union to Christ. True faith in Christ unites the soul to Christ, and this unity brings a peace that passes understanding (Phil. 4:7) and a "joy that is inexpressible and filled with glory" (1 Pet. 1:8). Union with Christ teaches us that we are weak in ourselves, but strong in the Lord and in the power of his might (Eph. 6:10).[6] Union with Christ connects us to God, binding us to our supreme pleasures.[7]

Looking to Jesus

So what does *communion* with Christ look like in daily life? At the end of chapter 2 we looked at Newton's provocative maxim: "'*None* but Jesus,' is my motto. All wisdom, righteousness, holiness, and happiness, which does not spring from and center in him, my soul desires to renounce."[8] Now we look at the daily discipline of *how* this is pursued. For Newton, the *how* of the daily discipline emerges from the Christ-centering words of Hebrews 12:1–2.

> Therefore, since we are surrounded by so great a cloud of witnesses, let us also lay aside every weight, and sin which clings so closely, and let us run with endurance the race that is set before us, *looking to Jesus*, the founder and perfecter of our faith, who for the joy that was set before him endured the cross, despising the shame, and is seated at the right hand of the throne of God.

---

[4] W, 5:196.
[5] W, 1:203. In the words of Riccaltoun, the miracle of regeneration either brings new powers or resurrects dead powers, to enable the Christian "to perceive spiritual objects, to judge of their worth and excellency, and to find their pleasure, happiness, and joy, in God, through the Lord Jesus Christ" (*The Works of the Late Reverend Mr. Robert Riccaltoun*, 3 vols. [1771], 1:401).
[6] W, 1:612.
[7] See Leighton, *Theological and Expository Lectures*, 80.
[8] W, 6:42.

The imperative in the second verse—"looking to Jesus"—took special importance in Newton's mind. If the Christian life *is* Christ, then *looking to him* is the great duty of the Christian life. Looking to Jesus marks the beginning of the Christian life; looking to Jesus is the end goal of the Christian life; and looking to Jesus is the daily privilege of the Christian life, which is Newton's way of saying that we never outgrow the gospel.

The core of genuine faith reaches far deeper than a rational assent to the truth *about Christ*. On the negative side, the gospel cuts off our rebellious opinions to bring our "every thought into a sweet and willing subjection to Christ by faith" (2 Cor. 10:5).[9] On the positive side, genuine faith is the joyful embrace *of Christ*. Faith is aliveness to his beauty, writes Newton.

> Faith is the effect of a principle of new life implanted in the soul, that was before dead in trespasses and sins; and it qualifies not only for obeying the Savior's precepts, but chiefly and primarily for receiving and rejoicing in his fullness, admiring his love, his work, his person, his glory, his advocacy. It makes Christ precious, enthrones him in the heart, presents him as the most delightful object to our meditations; as our wisdom, righteousness, sanctification, and strength; our root, head, life, shepherd, and husband.[10]

This life of faith—looking to Christ and treasuring him—is the one great duty that simplifies the Christian life. In his hymn on Hebrews 12:2, Newton explains:

> But since the Savior I have known
> My rules are all reduc'd to one,
> To keep my Lord, by faith, in view;
> This strength supplies, and motives too.[11]

When we read Newton's words at the end of his life, we see how he succeeded at this calling to the very end of his journey. To say that the Christian life is Christ is at once to see the sufficiency of the Savior and to be ushered into a life of true discipline. "Looking unto Jesus," Newton wrote—"the duty, the privilege, the safety, the unspeakable happiness, of a believer, are all comprised in that one sentence."[12] Looking to Christ is

---

[9] *W*, 1:563.
[10] *Letters* (Scott), 205–6.
[11] *W*, 3:455.
[12] *W*, 6:4.

the preeminent Christian discipline, and Newton had good reason to hold
it so prominent.

Unveiled Eyes and Shimmering Bronze

Looking to Christ is a theme Newton bumped into all over Scripture. First,
he returned to the Old Testament story of the embittered Israelites who
were attacked by venomous snakes in the desert (Num. 21:4–9). The solution for Israel was found in Moses's bronze serpent impaled on a pole and
lifted up to shine in the desert sun. As the serpent was raised in the desert,
all who were dying from venom received physical healing. To gaze on the
impaled serpent brought renewed life to all who were dying. "Look and
live," was the call. Of course, the true importance of this story is fulfilled
in Christ. As Christ was lifted up on the cross, all who were dying from sin
received spiritual healing (John 3:14–15). To look upon Christ in faith is a
re-creation, an act of cleansing and sanctification.

Unlike the healing of grumblers in the desert, looking upon Christ is
not a one-time event. Newton believed that looking to Christ to remove the
venomous stings is not limited to the act of initial faith.[13] Returning to see
Christ on the cross is a reoccurring act for the Christian, a daily discipline
Newton learned from Paul: "May the Lord direct your hearts to the love
of God and to the steadfastness of Christ" (2 Thess. 3:5). In the cross, the
Christian finds daily forgiveness, spiritual power, godly motivation, daily
healing, and eternal hope. We find a cure only when we take our attention
off the bite wounds of our own sin maladies and stop comparing our bites
to the wounds of others. "It was not by counting their wounds, but by beholding the brazen serpent, the Lord's instituted means of cure, that the
Israelites were healed."[14] Pouring over sins and evils "will not cure them;
but he who was typified by the brazen serpent is ever present, lifted up to
our view in the camp; and one believing sight of him will do more to restore
peace to the conscience, and life to our graces, than all our own lamenta-
tions and resolutions."[15]

The Christian life will often remind us of the root of our own fruit-
lessness. We are powerless to save ourselves. And in our "total absolute
depravity" there is a poison so deep it has seeped down into the roots of

---

[13] See Newton's poem "The Spider and Toad" (W, 3:670–72).
[14] W, 1:696.
[15] W, 6:44; see also 3:374–75.

our being. Sin is a defeated poison, but not a wholly removed poison until the resurrection. And so whenever the bronze serpent is raised before our eyes, we find healing. First we find salvation, and then we find sanctification in the ongoing duty of looking outside of ourselves and upward to Christ—the same Christ.[16]

Finally, and most importantly, Newton was drawn to Paul's words about the glorious gospel that has broken into history in Christ: "And we all, with unveiled face, beholding the glory of the Lord, are being transformed into the same image from one degree of glory to another" (2 Cor. 3:18). Newton applied this point to Christian maturity. We behold "the light of the knowledge of the glory of God in the face of Jesus Christ" (2 Cor. 4:6), and this light shines full of glory in Scripture. As we behold Christ's beauty by the eye of faith, we are transformed from one degree of maturity to another. As we behold the glory of Jesus, we increasingly participate in his image, transformed into his resemblance and his character.[17] This transformation works incrementally as the Christian gazes deeper into the mystery of Christ's redeeming love; as the Christian sees deeper into the glory of Christ's person, offices, grace, and faithfulness; and as the Christian perceives more of the divine excellencies of God in Christ. In all these acts of faith, the Christian becomes more deeply engaged in this "great business" of beholding Christ's glory.[18]

When we open our Bibles and read divine words, we are illuminated by the power of the Holy Spirit and awakened once again to see and to delight in Christ's glory. In Christ we find spiritual nourishment for the soul: soul-sustaining happiness, pleasure, and joy; the very power and foundation for everything else in the Christian life—*life* in the fullest meaning of the term! In beholding Christ's glory, we are changed into his image and "then our hearts melt, our eyes flow, our stammering tongues are unloosed."[19] For many reasons we will discuss later, this transforming experience doesn't happen every time we open our Bibles—but it should be our aim. All throughout his writings, Newton is eager to remind his readers of this one essential core conviction about the Christian life: beholding the glory of Christ rouses joy, empowers obedience, and transforms the Christian into the image of Christ. "It is by looking to Jesus that the believer is enlightened

---

[16] *W*, 1:594.
[17] *W*, 2:193, 487.
[18] *W*, 1:211–12.
[19] *W*, 2:99.

and strengthened and grows in grace and sanctification." To understand anything else about the Christian life from Newton, this essential point must be grasped.[20]

Naked to the Nonfiction Imagination

But this raises a question. How exactly do *we* behold Christ? *Beholding* is more than *reading about*, so what does this discipline look like for us?

To see the glory of Christ requires a healthy imagination, and from childhood, Newton was blessed with one. In his letters, he often pushes his readers to visualize the life and work and glory of Christ with language appealing to the senses. In fact he reserves some of his most striking (and potentially offending) language to awaken Christians to the stark reality of Christ. Pushing Christ into a visual mold at times makes sense in light of what we see in relation to unveiled faces and shimmering bronze serpents. Newton presses us to *look to Jesus*, and to do that he engages our nonfiction imagination to make the point. "Look unto the Lord Jesus Christ; look unto him as he hung naked, wounded, bleeding, dead, and forsaken upon the cross," he pressed in one sermon.

> Look unto him again as he *now* reigns in glory, possessed of all power in heaven and in earth, with thousands of thousands of saints and angels worshipping before him, and ten thousand times ten thousand ministering unto him; and then compare your sins with his blood, your wants with his fullness, your unbelief with his faithfulness, your weakness with his strength, your inconstancy with his everlasting love. If the Lord opens the eyes of your understanding, you would be astonished at the comparison.[21]

When Newton focused on the person of Christ, he centered on the roles of Christ as Shepherd, Husband, Friend, Prophet, Priest, and King. But when Newton focused on his faith in Christ, he focused on three realities: Christ's death, resurrection, and ongoing reign. We look to Christ as the Savior who hung on the cross for our sins; we look to Christ who was raised victoriously on Easter; and we look to Christ in his eternal sovereign

---

[20] For a sampling of where this theme emerges in his writings, see *W*, 1:212, 522–23; 2:99, 146–47, 193, 487; 4:135–36, 446–47, 575; 5:257–58; 6:4–6, 73–74, 176–78; *Letters* (Taylor), 34, 44; *Letters* (Bull 1847), 124, 182; *Letters* (Bull 1869), 47–48, 123, 172. Newton would have found this theme throughout Riccaltoun's *Works*: "The whole business of a Christian is to behold the glory of God as it shines in the face of Jesus Christ; there is their life, there also lie all the materials of enjoyment" (2:451; see also 1:394–96; 2:282–85, 450–51).
[21] *W*, 2:574–75; see also 3:519–20.

reign now in heaven. Newton kept in focus these three distinct markers in the progression of Christ's life. Looking to Jesus was foundational.

Newton wields his vivid imagination like an offensive weapon in the battle against depression. In a letter to a troubled woman who was undergoing a lengthy trial and fell under seasons of dark depression as a result, he writes:

> They who would always rejoice, must derive their joy from a source which is invariably the same; in other words, from Jesus. Oh, that name! What a person, what an office, what a love, what a life, what a death, does it recall to our minds! Come, madam, let us leave *our* troubles to themselves for a while, and let us walk to Golgotha, and there take a view of *his*.

Then with a palate of stark and vibrant colors, Newton paints a picture of Gethsemane and Christ's tears of blood. Then he walks her to Golgotha to see the universe of suffering on Christ's shoulders. There he bids her to look into the bloodied face of the sagging and suffering Savior bearing the awful weight of sin. Then he leads her to the dusty tomb, where Christ is no longer. And a little later he points her eyes up and through the clouds, where the Lord sits, where there are no more trials, no more pains to hinder the Christian's ultimate and eternal happiness. With such pictures, Newton shows the woman the Christ who sovereignly orchestrates all our trials for his own glory and our ultimate happiness. On this virtual walk through the life of Christ, Newton encourages her to now reconsider her own pains and troubles in light of Christ's agony in redemption, and to weigh her pains in light of the coming tearless joys of eternity.

Is this pastoral insensitivity on Newton's part? No, not if he has succeeded through the imagination to reorient this woman toward the glory of Christ, who had grown invisible to her spiritual eyes.[22] This is what Newton called the *eye of the mind*. He would sometimes use this phrase in writing letters to friends, telling them they were often before the eye of his mind. It was a way to speak personally of those far off, and it's the same phrase he used of Christ, often for where Christ is right now in heaven. "The Lamb of God is an object proposed, not to our bodily sight, but to the eye of the mind, which indeed, in fallen man, is naturally blind; but the Gospel-message, enlivened by the powerful agency of the Holy Spirit,

---

[22] W, 6:377–81.

is appointed to open it."[23] We *see* the Lamb of God by the *eye of faith.* And we see our Savior in heaven interceding on our behalf. We are seated with him. "And even at present, by faith they ascend and are seated with him in the heavenly places (Eph. 2:6). They behold invisibles with the eye of their mind; they realize the glorious scene, from which they are separated by the veil of flesh and blood."[24]

Newton was a soul surgeon who opened hearts with the scalpel of vivid imagination-stirring images. This approach was shocking, but also healing.

> Behold the Beloved of God, perfectly spotless and holy, yet made an ex-ample of the severest vengeance; prostrate and agonizing in the garden; enduring the vilest insults from wicked men; torn with whips, and nails, and thorns; suspended, naked, wounded, and bleeding upon the cross, and there heavily complaining, that God had for a season forsaken him. Sin was the cause of all his anguish. He stood in the place of sinners, and therefore was not spared. Not any, or all, the evils which the world has known, afford such proof of the dreadful effects and detestable nature of sin, as the knowledge of Christ crucified.[25]

Newton used vivid depiction of Christ's work to prod the nonfiction imagi-nation.

> Come, sinners, view the Lamb of God,
> Wounded and dead, and bath'd in blood!
> Behold his side, and venture near,
> The well of endless life is here.[26]

Through vivid meditation on Christ's work, Newton modeled the daily dis-cipline of *looking to Christ.* "Faith can realize the presence of an unseen Savior."[27]

Such faith must withstand unbelief. "In ourselves we are all dark-ness, confusion, and misery; but in him there is a sufficiency of wisdom, grace, and peace suited to all our wants. May we ever behold his glory in the glass of the Gospel, 'till we are changed into the same image from

---

[23] W, 4:189.
[24] W, 4:327.
[25] W, 3:23–24.
[26] W, 3:519.
[27] *Letters* (Coffin), 115.

glory to glory by the Spirit'" (2 Cor. 3:18).[28] To behold the glory of Christ is ammunition against unbelief and power for sanctification. A life focused on Christ is a life of faith, and it's a life opposite to a life focused on self, self-sufficiency, and self-wisdom.[29] *Christ* and *self* are opposite aims. And when it comes to sin, in vain do we attempt to "beat down our corruptions" with resolutions. Rather, "a believing view of Jesus does the business."[30] If the business is holiness, there are proper means to pursue holiness, and Newton is not denying this. His point is that "a believing view of Jesus" has the power to mortify remaining sin within the Christian. This is the redemptive power of the nonfiction imagination. The opposite of selfishness is beholding Christ, and in the discipline of beholding Christ by the "eye of the mind," Newton wields a lethal weapon in the battle against sin. This weapon is available to any Christian who reads the Bible not merely as a book of motivation and inspiration, but as a manifestation of Jesus Christ and his glory.

The Christian Life at Its Hardest

This discipline of beholding the glory of Christ is also very difficult. From the letters of Newton we see that every step along the path of life is a battle for the Christian to keep two eyes on Christ. The Christian life *is Christ*—a truth that deeply reassures our souls, focuses our hearts, and simplifies our spiritual lives. But it's a calling that we perpetually fumble. The veil removed from our eyes in conversion gives way to clouds over our eyes in trials and sleepiness in our steps with the spiritual disciplines. The greatest challenges we face are Christ-clouding distractions. Even from within a busy life of family and work and responsibilities and complexities and ambiguities, the Christian must daily reorient his life to Christ. "Christ is all, and in all" (Col. 3:11), and our calling is to "rejoice in the Lord always" (Phil. 4:4). Whatever life throws our way, we must keep Christ in view—

> in afflictions, imperfections, temptations, and desertions; yet he [Paul] says, *always*; which can only be practiced by those who see and keep in mind that they are complete in Christ; that he is all in all to them; their Righteousness, Wisdom and Strength; their Sun and Shield; their Friend and Representative before the throne; their Shepherd and their Husband.

---

[28] *Letters* (Clunie), 185.
[29] *Letters* (Bull 1869), 264–65.
[30] *W*, 6:4–5.

And then Newton writes, "If I may speak my own experience, I find that to keep my eye simply upon Christ, as my *peace*, and my *life*, is by far the hardest part of my calling."[31]

In both the Christian life and the Christian ministry, we are tempted to assume and neglect the crucifixion of our Savior. One of Newton's pastor friends once preached an ordination sermon on the charge and calling of the minister, and sought to publish his remarks in a pamphlet. First he sent a draft to Newton for feedback. Newton wrote back with a warning that the pastor forgot (or assumed) the gospel in his remarks: "A minister may be diligent in his work, regular in his family, resident with his people and attentive to them, and in many respects exemplary in his outward conduct, and yet not preach *Jesus Christ, and him crucified*."[32] The precious truths of the gospel are too easily forgotten in the course of our busy lives, especially in the compound pressures of leadership. Newton's friend later made the proper edits and additions. Newton was aware of this neglectful tendency in others because he saw it in himself. "The Apostle, when speaking of the love and riches of Christ, uses remarkable expressions; he speaks of heights, and depths, and lengths, and breadths, and unsearchables, where I seem to find every thing plain, easy, and rational. He finds mysteries where I can perceive none."[33] "Pray for me," he wrote in a letter to another friend, "that my heart may be looking to Jesus for peace, wisdom, and strength. Without him all is waste and desert."[34]

Welcome to the lifelong battle for "a more simple dependence upon Jesus as my all in all" and to the lifelong struggle "to account every thing loss and dross that dares to stand in competition with him," and the lifelong ambition "to grow in grace, and the knowledge of our Lord and Savior; be more humble in our own eyes, more weaned from self, more fixed on him as our all in all, till at last we shall meet before his throne."[35] Keeping the eyes of our mind focused on the glory of Christ is the sweet battle of the ministry and the hardest part of the Christian life.

The Daily Battle for Joy

This battle to bring Christ into focus is a lifelong battle, but it's won in daily victories. Wrote Newton,

---

[31] *W*, 6:44–45.
[32] Letters (Palmer), 96.
[33] *W*, 1:597.
[34] *Letters* (Bull 1869), 154.
[35] *W*, 1:316.

The Daily Discipline of Joy in Jesus   77

> I wish you health, peace, and prosperity; but, above all, that your souls
> may prosper; that you may still prefer the light of God's countenance to
> your chief joy; that you may still delight yourselves in the Lord; be *daily*
> hungering and thirsting after him, and *daily* receiving from his fullness,
> even grace for grace; that you may rejoice in his all-sufficiency.[36]

The *all-in-all-ness* of Christ was to be tasted on a regular basis—every day
if possible. If we were to maintain our delightful communion with Christ,
the lures and temptations of the flesh and the world would prove paltry and
ineffective. But with indwelling sin remaining in our hearts, those petty
and futile joys still lure us. "Oh, if faith was in daily exercise, how little
would the world, and the things of time and sense, seem in my eyes! What
a dreadful thing would sin appear, that spilt my Savior's blood! And how
would my very heart rejoice at the sound of Jesus's name?"[37]

To tie this point with the previous two chapters, the daily fight for joy
is the fight to maintain faith in the all-sufficiency of Christ.[38] Which is why
daily joy in the Christian life is thwarted by personal sin. For two reasons,
it is impossible to live simultaneously in known sin and in the joy of the
Lord. First, sin is the soul's pursuit of a false pleasure that stands in as a
hollow replacement for the joy of Christ. Second, our sin chases out divine
joy, because holiness is the counterpart of happiness. Christlikeness is one
way we experience the joy of communion with Christ.

Yet indwelling sin lingers in our lives, clouding our joy in Christ in this
life. Sometimes we open the Bible and everything just seems flat and dull.
At this point we engage in a fight for joy, a fight for faith to cling to what is
true and what is supremely satisfying, says Newton.

> A delight in the Lord's all-sufficiency, to be satisfied in him as our present
> and eternal portion. This, in the sense in which I understand it, is not the
> effect of a present warm frame, but of a deeply rooted and abiding prin-
> ciple; the habitual exercise of which is to be estimated by the comparative
> indifference with which other things are regarded.[39]

The Christian's hope is based not on our unsettling *feelings of joy in Christ*,
but on *Christ himself.* "My best is defective and defiled, and needs pardon

---

[36] W, 6:47.
[37] W, 6:23.
[38] W, 6:378.
[39] W, 1:454–55.

before it can hope for acceptance; but, through mercy, my hope is built, not upon frames and feelings, but upon the atonement and mediation of Jesus."[40]

At a very deep level the Christian life is defined by a joy transfer, and it is this transfer that Newton describes autobiographically in his hymn "Looking at the Cross." There Newton looks back at the wicked sins in which he previously sought his delight. But he returns to the base of the cross, looks up, and engages his imagination to make eye contact with Christ.

> In evil long I took delight,
>   Unaw'd by shame or fear,
> Till a new object struck my sight,
>   And stopp'd my wild career.

> I saw one hanging on a tree,
>   In agonies and blood,
> Who fix'd his languid eyes on me,
>   As near his cross I stood.

Sinner Newton is stopped cold by "a new object." His *delight* in sin is confronted by the *sight* of Christ. Here at the base of the cross Newton is struck by his personal guilt in Christ's death.

> Sure, never till my latest breath
>   Can I forget that look;
> It seem'd to charge me with his death,
>   Though not a word he spoke.

> My conscience felt, and own'd the guilt,
>   And plung'd me in despair;
> I saw my sins his blood had spilt,
>   And help'd to nail him there.

> Alas! I knew not what I did;
>   But now my tears are vain;
> Where shall my trembling soul be hid?
>   For I the Lord have slain.

---

[40] *Letters* (Campbell), 110.

A second look he gave, which said,
  "I freely all forgive;
This blood is for thy ransom paid,
  I die, that thou mayst live."

The cross exposes the heinous evil of our sins. "Sin cannot be hated for itself, till we have seen the malignity of it in Christ's sufferings."[41] So after beginning the hymn with a sorrowful look back at the sinful joy that once captured his heart, Newton is now confronted with the Savior's sacrifice and closes the hymn with a contrast with true joy.

With pleasing grief and mournful joy
  My spirit now is fill'd,
That I should such a life destroy,
  Yet live by him I kill'd.[42]

The joy of the Christian is a costly joy, a blood-bought joy, and therefore a sobered joy, a "pleasing grief and mournful joy." Because this joy cost the Savior his blood, the Christian's joy is solid—albeit solemn—joy. This is true and living joy, a joy contrasted to the flippant and circumstantial amusements of the world. Joy in Christ is no shallow layer of icing over a prosperous life. Christ, our High Priest, "is supremely happy in himself, and is the fountain of happiness to all his redeemed"—a blood-bought fountain of happiness, purchased by his agonies, now offering us true joy even in our deepest pains and sorrows.[43] In Newton's mind, to behold the cross and to see Christ's death *for you*—and *because of you*—brings a transfer of indomitable joy. You have died to the delights of this world, and you are now alive to new heavenly joys in Christ. And when you find yourself lured toward the fleeting joys of this world, Newton points back to the victory of the Savior where joys are recalibrated, daily if necessary. Every *sight of Christ* we take is an attack on every *delight in sin* left in our hearts.

Clouds, Shrouds, and Trifles

So the "continual thirst for fresh communications from the Fountain of life"—Christ himself—is at the heart of Christian life.[44] "The hidden life of

---

[41] *Eclectic*, 278. See also *W*, 2:396; 3:440.
[42] *W*, 3:522–23.
[43] *W*, 6:213–14.
[44] *W*, 1:255–56.

a Christian, as it consists in communion with God by Jesus Christ," Newton says, is "a continual dependence on him for hourly supplies of wisdom, strength, and comfort."[45] The Christian life flows from hourly communion with Christ because "the more you know him, the better you will trust him; the more you trust him, the better you will love him; the more you love him, the better you will serve him."[46] But how easily we are distracted from him!

> Ah, what trifles are capable of shutting *him* out of our thoughts, of whom we say, he is the Beloved of our souls, who loved us, and gave himself for us, and whom we have deliberately chosen as our chief good and portion. What can make us amends for the loss we suffer here? Yet surely if we *could*, we *would* set him always before us; his love should be the delightful theme of our hearts. But though we aim at this good, evil is present with us; we find we are renewed but in part.[47]

And so we hunger and thirst again for the sufficiency of Christ. Christ is like the sun. One sun can easily provide for seven billion inhabitants on this planet, and the power of the sun abounds far beyond all this need![48] Now imagine the sustaining power of the sun, and Christ is like that, "complete and all-sufficient, the Sun of Righteousness, the Fountain of life and comfort; his beams, wherever they reach, bring healing, strength, peace, and joy to the soul."[49] As Newton liked to say, Christ is the soul's all-sufficient sun beheld by faith in the gospel.[50] And he is the sun of the soul, all-sufficient to give us fullness of spiritual joy now, for "if the whole creation around us were destroyed, and you or I were the only creatures in the universe—the Lord, the sun of the soul, could make us completely happy, and fill our capacities for happiness to the utmost, immediately from himself."[51] Both now and forever, Newton writes, Christ

> is the sun of the soul, and without him we should be like the earth if deprived of the light of the sun in the firmament. There is a spiritual sunshine of which I can speak but faintly from experience; but I would be thankful for daylight, by which I can see my way, and get a glimpse of my

---

[45] *W*, 1:33.
[46] *W*, 2:141.
[47] *W*, 1:442.
[48] *W*, 2:194.
[49] *W*, 6:289.
[50] *Letters* (Bull 1869), 350.
[51] *Letters* (Taylor), 82.

journey's end. Hereafter there will be a morning without clouds, a noon without night, a long, an everlasting day. Eternal sunshine![52]

In Christ we have both all the supplies of joy we could possibly ask for now and an eternity of pleasures forevermore awaiting us (Ps. 16:11; Rev. 21:23).

If we are convinced that communion with Christ is our chief good, why is living in the light of his presence so difficult? Why are we so Christ-negligent? Why is it that our minds are so scattered when it comes to Christ? Newton once admitted, "I approach the throne of grace encumbered with a thousand distractions of thought, each of which seems to engage more of my attention than the business I have in hand."[53] This is the battle of the Christian life and where Newton turns particularly practical. The Christian life is bound up with clear thinking, and the enemies are the clouds, the shrouds, and the trifles of life that take our eyes off Christ.

Distracted by Entertainment

Partly we are distracted by entertainment. Our fickle attention is far too easily distracted from Christ as our marauding affections jump from thrill to thrill in fictional entertainment that is wholly disconnected from us. Newton would warn us here against using entertainment and amusements as escapism. True religion is sufficient to provide joy. "That religion which does not engage the whole heart for the Lord can be little better than a name. The comforts of the gospel neither require nor admit such poor assistance as worldly amusements offer."[54] Binging on the cotton candy of worldly amusements cannot nourish a living soul. Christ's sufficiency bears directly on our lives, providing us a feast of eternal joy and significance. The tragedy is that

> we can read the history of Jesus Christ, his life and doctrines, his death and passion, with indifference, though we say, all he spoke, or did, or suffered, was for our sakes. What are our thoughts *of that eternity* to which we are posting, and to which, for aught we know, a few hours may introduce us? Is it not in the power of the meanest trifle that occurs, to hide this important point from our view?[55]

---

[52] *Letters* (Bull 1847), 261.
[53] W, 6:179–80.
[54] *Letters* (Bull 1869), 340.
[55] W, 2:264–65.

And yet our attention is easily distracted from the concrete reality of all Christ is and has accomplished on our behalf, and we turn to the entertaining fictional dramas of life that bear no effect on our soul's eternal good.

As we will see later, this is one of the blessings of trials. Trials remedy fictional escapism. Trials are the onrush of stinging realism crashing the idealized party we call "life." When these serious trials interrupt our lives, we "run simply and immediately to our all-sufficient Friend, feel our dependence, and cry in good earnest for help." But when all is well, when life seems peaceful and prosperous, and when the difficulties in life are small, then "we are too apt secretly to lean to our own wisdom and strength, as if in such slight matters we could make shift without him."[56] We lose out on communion with Christ when we gorge on entertainment.

Distracted by Worldliness

Likewise, we cannot serve God and money (Matt. 6:24), and yet we try, and the cost is our communion with Christ. Seeking ultimate joy in money makes financial profit trump spiritual profit. It would be a contradiction in the soul to cling to Christ as our highest good and cling to financial security as our highest good. We cannot keep our eyes focused on Jesus while our greed lusts for worldly security. We may go through the motions, but eventually the misplaced priority of worldliness will corrode the soul's joy.[57]

The world is a clamoring cauldron of idols all competing for the affections of men, a "tyranny of different and opposite passions," and all these "pretended pleasures" are "mingled with discontent, remorse, and foreboding fears of death and judgment."[58] Affections for Christ and desires for worldly comfort are mutually *expulsive*. A love for the world drives out affection for Christ. Admiration for Christ pushes out affections for worldly idols. Friendship with the world is enmity toward Christ, and love for Christ is enmity toward idols (James 4:4).

> The holiness of a sinner seems principally to consist in self-abasement, and in admiring views of Jesus as a complete Savior—these are the main principles from whence every gracious fruit is derived. In proportion as

---

[56] W, 1:622.
[57] W, 1:281.
[58] *Letters* (Taylor), 176.

we have these, we shall be humble, meek, patient, weaned from the world, and devoted to God.[59]

Newton is not forbidding Christians from properly enjoying the created gifts of this world (like food and sex), for confusing the value of such gifts is at the heart of Satan's attack on humanity (Gen. 3:1; 1 Tim. 4:1–5).[60] What Newton intends to show is that *knowing* all our temporal possessions are gifts enhances our *enjoyment* of each one. Every temporal gift and mercy we experience now is meant to be a tangible token of Christ's blessings upon us for eternity.[61] Every gift in this life not enjoyed to the glory of Christ is "like the crackling of thorns under a pot, a hasty, noisy, transient blaze, which will soon go out."[62] Therefore all the vain pursuit of joy that centers on the world—security in a spouse or riches, satisfaction in illicit sex, power grabs for personal authority—all these worldly aims cloud over admiring views of Christ's glory. For this reason Newton often points out the value of poverty as evidenced in the lives of Christ and Lazarus (Matt. 8:20; Luke 16:19–31).[63] False securities and worldly pleasures are flashes of vanity distracting us from the sunshine of Christ.

Distracted by Legalism

Religion itself can get in the way of Christ. When a sense of guilt and a lack of confidence in Christ push the Christian away from Christ, they tend to promote a wrong activity—an increasing confidence in self-righteousness. These insecurities before God quickly devastate communion with Christ. Legalism is a wicked lie that puts a mirror in front of our faces and makes us think we are looking at Christ when we are actually adoring the ghost

---

[59] *W*, 6:177.

[60] *365 Days with Newton*, 73; *W*, 1:455; 6:481–82.

[61] Newton: "We enjoy a thousand mercies in common with many who neither pray to him nor praise him; but to know that they come from *him* in answer to prayer, and as earnests of future and better blessings, gives them an additional relish of which worldlings can have no conception" (*Letters* [Campbell], 7). And in another letter: "Oh, my dear friends, are we not verily debtors for innumerable mercies and blessings, but especially for the Gospel, without which we could not have known the true value or right enjoyment of any thing else? But the knowledge of a Savior and a good hope of our acceptance in him, like the light of the sun, gilds every object. We are not only preserved and provided for in common with multitudes, but we know the hand that guards and feeds us, and can receive every instance of his kindness in our temporal concerns as a token and pledge of his love, and of the better things prepared for us within the veil, and all that we have, and all that we hope for, is not simply given to us. He shed his blood to redeem us from guilt and bondage; without this we could have had neither title nor capacity for happiness. How would it heighten our relish for all our comforts and prospects, if we could always think of the procuring price" (*Letters* [Taylor], 57–58).

[62] *Letters* (Coffin), 226.

[63] *W*, 2:411. One example of spiritual flourishing under a life of poverty is given in the story recounted by Newton of a woman who lived near Liverpool under the name "Dame Cross." See Letters (Palmer), 83–92.

of our own self-righteousness.[64] Eventually we see that our righteousness is filthy rags, and Satan pounces on our guilt and presses us toward condemnation to

> hold down the soul to the number, weight, and aggravation of its sins, so that it shall not be able to look up to Jesus, nor draw any comfort from his blood, promises, and grace. How many go burdened in this manner, seeking relief from duties, and perhaps spending their strength in things not commanded, though they hear, and perhaps acknowledge, the Gospel?[65]

When we feel the weight of remaining sin, looking to Christ is the only remedy, not looking in a mirror of self-righteousness, nor studying our snakebites. "There is a spice of legality in you," Newton once bluntly wrote a woman. "You want to have something that you might admire in yourself; but you will get more solid comfort by looking to Jesus and admiring him."[66] That was, and remains, the only answer to legalism, and it shows how easily our self-righteous hearts are clouded to Christ's glory.

Distracted by Self-Consumed Pride

We are distracted by our self-focus. All our boasting and pompous self-talk would be so utterly vain if we were to see Christ fully with our eyes of faith. Newton is perplexed at how often we find the time and the interest to talk so much about our puny greatness. The Christian life is a call to self-emptying. To one woman who struggled with doubts of her assurance and seemed to be overly focused on herself, Newton wrote, "let me endeavor to lead you out of yourself: let me invite you to look unto Jesus" (Heb. 12:1–2).[67] To his daughter he wrote, "This is God's way: you are not called to buy, but to beg; not to be strong in yourself, but in the grace that is in Christ Jesus. . . . Be humble, watchful, and diligent in the means, and endeavor to look through all, and fix your eye upon Jesus, and all shall be well."[68] And he testified of himself:

> I am nothing. He is all. This is foolishness to the world; but faith sees a glory in it. This way is best for our safety, and most for his honor. And

---

[64] W, 2:589.
[65] W, 1:527.
[66] Letters (Bull 1869), 389.
[67] W, 2:220–21.
[68] W, 2:141.

the more simply we can reduce all our efforts to this one point, "Looking unto Jesus," the more peace, fervor, and liveliness we shall find in our hearts, and the more success we shall feel in striving against sin in all its branches.[69]

The self-boasting life is a direct contradiction to the Christ-boasting life. Pride sucks away our spiritual joy and vitality and clouds over Christ. "O to live in and by and to and for and with Jesus by faith, this is life indeed. How different from that dry contentious self-applauding spirit, which makes so much noise and does so little good."[70] We are prone to exchange the glory of Christ for the lentil stew of self-consumed pride.

We cannot look *to* Christ without looking *beyond* ourselves. Assurance in the Christian life is measured not by our wins or our losses, even religious and moral wins and losses, but by Christ as we find our daily assurance in his all-sufficiency. "The best evidence of faith," Newton wrote, "is the shutting our eyes equally upon our defects and our graces, and looking directly to Jesus as clothed with authority and power to save to the very utmost" (Heb. 7:25).[71]

Distracted by Anxious Unbelief

Few things more quickly cloud over the Christian's joy in Christ than a lack of faith. Lack of faith chokes off all power in the Christian life, because faith is what makes it possible to look beyond ourselves for the remedy. Unbelief starts a downward cycle. The more anxiety we feel, the less we see Christ, and the less we see Christ, the more we feel our anxiety. "Unbelief, that injurious bar, interposes and starts a thousand anxious thoughts to hide him from us."[72] If Christ is the sun, anxiety is certainly one dark cloud overshadowing the soul. Indeed, Newton confessed, "an evil heart of unbelief fills my sky with many clouds."[73] This lack of trust in God "is the primary cause of all our inquietude."[74] Newton prayed hard against the unbelief in his heart: "For this I sigh and long, and cry to the Lord to rend the veil of unbelief, scatter the clouds of ignorance, and break down the walls which sin is daily building up to hide him from my eyes."[75] Yet in our pride we hold

---

[69] W, 6:140.
[70] *Letters* (Thornton), February 16, 1775.
[71] W, 6:178.
[72] W, 6:119.
[73] W, 6:78.
[74] W, 6:468.
[75] W, 2:202.

tightly to our cares and open ourselves to spiritual attack (1 Pet. 5:6–8). We pull anxiety close like a blanket, so close that we cover our faces and cloud our souls from the victory and sovereign reign of Christ in the heavens.

Even worse, unbelief makes us despondent. By faith we see our sin more clearly, and we see the sufficiency of Christ, which brings daily opportunities for joy in Christ. In turn, joy in Christ brings spiritual fortitude. "The joy of the Lord is the strength of his people: whereas unbelief makes our hands hang down, and our knees feeble, dispirits ourselves, and discourages others; and though it steals upon us under a semblance of humility, it is indeed the very essence of pride."[76] Pride exchanges joy in Christ for a cloud of spiritual despondency.

Unbelief also brings insecurity about our salvation, and insecurity in Christ carries compounded anxieties and doubts to snuff out joy in Christ. One pastor friend of Newton's was seeking to find his comfort in the work of grace in his own life, and this led to anxiety. Newton wrote:

> Indeed, my friend, you will not be steadily comfortable till you learn to derive your comfort from a simple apprehension of the person, work, and offices of Christ. He is made unto us of God, not only righteousness, but sanctification also. One direct appropriating act of faith in him will strengthen you more than all the earnest endeavors you speak of. Evidences, as you call them, are of use in their place; but the best evidence of faith is the shutting our eyes equally upon our defects and our graces, and looking directly to Jesus.[77]

You get the point. In these ways, and in many others, a sight of Christ is the cure. And yet we are so quickly and easily distracted.

> Wonderful are the effects when a crucified, glorious Savior is presented by the power of the Spirit, in the light of the Word, to the eye of Faith. This sight destroys the love of sin, heals the wounds of guilt, softens the hard heart, and fills the soul with peace, life, and joy; and makes obedience practicable, desirable, and pleasant. If we could see this more, we should look less at other things. But, alas! Unbelief places a veil before our sight, and worldly-mindedness draws our eyes another way. A desire to be something that we are not, or to possess something that we have not, or to do something that we cannot—some vain hope, or vain fear, or vain

---

[76] W, 2:175–76.
[77] Letters (Bull 1869), 173.

delight, comes in like a black cloud, and hides our Beloved from our eyes. This shows what poor creatures we are! Notwithstanding our hope that we are converted, we need a new conversion every day.[78]

In chapter 12, we will discover what's really behind the pride, legalism, anxiety, unbelief, and worldliness in our lives. The point to see here is how prone we are to find our identity in worldly comforts and in our vain self-sufficiency. This battle against pride makes communion with Christ the ongoing daily discipline of forming our personal identity by the worth of Christ. This is the daily reconversion. And this daily reconversion is Newton's way of signaling our desperate need for the transforming power of a living sight of Christ, by faith, in the gospel, every day.

Joy in the Lamb

In light of all the distractions we must overcome to keep two eyes on Christ, it should be obvious that the joy we pursue in Christ is not something to be presumed. Joy in Christ is an eschatological joy to be fully tasted and relished in eternity. We are not in heaven yet, but we intermittently join the saints and angels above and the saints on earth in this one, worshipful, joy-filled employment.[79] Right now the saints in heaven have two spiritual eyes fixed on Christ, and we will join them.

> Perhaps there is nothing but this thin partition of flesh and blood between us and those blessed spirits that are before the throne; if our eyes were open, we should see the mountains around us covered with chariots and horses of fire; if our ears were unstopped, we should hear the praises of our great Immanuel resounding in the air, as once the shepherds heard.[80]

But Newton is careful not to presume too much about our present experience of joy in this life, and neither does he make joy out to be a merely circumstantial hit-or-miss type of experience. Newton frequently reminded his friends that joy is a gift from God as much as it is sought after as a Christian discipline.

---

[78] *Letters* (Clunie), 59–60. Writes C. S. Lewis, "Continual re-conversion is, perhaps, the nearest most mortals come to stability" (*Image and Imagination: Essays and Reviews by C. S. Lewis* [Cambridge, UK: Cambridge University Press, 2013], 206).
[79] *W*, 6:18.
[80] *W*, 6:19.

I wish we may learn from all our changes, to be sober and watchful, not to rest in grace received, in experience or comforts, but still to be pressing forward, and never think ourselves either safe or happy, but when we are beholding the glory of Christ by the light of faith in the glass of the Gospel. To view him as God manifest in the flesh, as *all in all* in himself, and *all in all* for us; this is cheering, this is strengthening, this makes hard things easy, and bitter things sweet. This includes all I can wish for my dear friends, that you may grow in grace, and in the knowledge of Jesus. To know him, is the shortest description of true grace; to know him better, is the surest mark of growth in grace; to know him perfectly, is eternal life. This is the prize of our high calling; the sum and substance of all we can desire or hope for is, to see him as he is, and to be like him: and to this honor and happiness he will surely bring all that love his name.[81]

Christ is "all in all in himself, and all in all *for us*." The full spectrum of Christ's defeat of evil is intended to bring this full enjoyment of his presence eventually, and it is working toward our happiness now. Christ has come into the world to make an end of sin, to destroy death, and to destroy the one who has the power of death, to repair every disorder, and to remove every misery from this world. He will accomplish this so fully that "every thing contrary to holiness and happiness shall be swallowed up and buried beyond the possibility of a return, as a stone that is sunk in the depths of the sea."[82] And this joy is now breaking into our lives. It is a joy rooted in a magnificent act of God in our souls. New birth brings spiritual life, and from that life we thirst for God, delight in Jesus, renounce ourselves, and renounce the world so far as it contradicts the gospel.[83] It is the work of Christ—his *all-in-all-ness* for us—that works for our daily joy in Christ.

The Glorious Battle

"God is every where present; but only those who look to him in Christ can attain to love, trust, or serve him aright."[84] And this is a battle, a battle against self, legalism, worldliness, anxiety, and a host of other enemies. It is a glorious battle waged in hope as we move toward the greatest communion with Christ we can imagine—his perfect presence. One day our knowledge of Christ's glory by nonfiction imagination will be replaced

---

[81] W, 6:73–74.
[82] W, 4:480.
[83] W, 2:14–15.
[84] W, 6:294.

with a vision of Christ's glory by physical intimation. And in that day when we behold Christ face-to-face, we will experience full delight like we have never experienced on earth. "To see him as he is, and to be like him! This is worth dying for, and worth living for, till he shall say, 'Come up hither.'"[85] "In ourselves we are all darkness, confusion, and misery; but in him there is a sufficiency of wisdom, grace, and peace suited to all our wants. May we ever behold his glory in the glass of the Gospel, 'till we are changed into the same image from glory to glory by the Spirit.'"[86]

Beholding Christ is the key to the Christian life. We take in sermons and we open Scripture, and we slowly meditate on divine truth to enjoy the glory of our Savior Jesus Christ. By beholding Christ we are changed into the image of Christ and find our souls satisfied.

Newton was no stoic. Jesus endured the cross to win joy to share with us (John 15:11; Heb. 12:2). The Christian is driven by the anticipation of experiencing full joy with Jesus face-to-face. But for now, rejoicing in Christ is a daily pursuit. We aim to rejoice always: on the mountaintop and in the valley, as we conquer and while we fight, when the Lord is shining on us and when he seems to be hiding from us.[87] Therefore, nothing undercuts the Christian life like Christ-amnesia—thinking we can live safely for a moment without Christ, without his atoning blood, and without renewed communion with him.[88] Keeping Christ in view at all times is, by far, the hardest—and the most essential—part of our calling as Christians.

---

[85] *Letters* (Ryland), 336.
[86] *Letters* (Clunie), 185.
[87] W, 1:256–57.
[88] W, 6:139.

CHAPTER 4

GOSPEL SIMPLICITY

Everything in this world was beautiful and harmonious until sin spun all of creation into complication and disorder and misery.[1] This disorder touches close to home for all of us. Wrote Newton, "I labor under a complication of disorders, summed up in the word *sin*."[2] By definition, sin is the dis-ordering of what was once beautiful and harmonious. Individually, we were created to serve God, but sin confused everything, tangling our hearts with pride, false idols, false securities, and false saviors all knotted together into one disordered mess from which we cannot free ourselves. Only by grace are we given eyes to see the depth of our complex hearts and two-faced motives, and only by grace do we find a Great Physician committed to untangling our disordered hearts.

In this chapter we look at a few of Newton's fundamental categories to define the Christian life. What's critical for us to see at the outset is that for Newton, our sin fundamentally opposes a simple life of surrender to Christ. "A thousand such surrenders I have made, and a thousand times I have interpretatively retracted them."[3] And with each retracted surrender, the complicated knot of our sin tightens around us.

If for now we can simply assume sin is a knotted ball of complexity in the Christian life (we will look at just how tangled it really is in the next chapter), we can proceed here to ask, what is the authentic Christian life?

---

[1] W, 4:76.
[2] W, 1:257. See also W, 1:439; 2:259–75; 6:97–98, 203–4; John Newton, *365 Days with Newton*, ed. Marylynn Rouse (Leominster, UK: Day One, 2006), 264.
[3] W, 1:624.

There is nothing more frightening than a professing Christian who is eventually exposed as a fraud (Matt. 7:21–23; James 1:22–27). If the Christian life is inauthentic, then it's false, fake, and hypocritical. Few tragedies are more lamentable than the almost-Christian.

In this chapter we search for the meaning of the authentic Christian life, and we begin with Newton's category of *gospel simplicity*, an ultimate aim in the Christian life I hinted at in the introduction of this book. You may remember that Newton wrote: "If I may speak my own experience, I find that to keep my eye *simply upon Christ*, as my peace, and my life, is by far the hardest part of my calling."[4] But to define Christian authenticity we must understand how *authenticity* is tied up with *sincerity*.

Pauline Simplicity

For Newton, pastoring, preaching, and the Christian life are all framed by Paul's words about his own apostolic ministry in 2 Corinthians 1:12: "For our boast is this, the testimony of our conscience, that we behaved in the world with *simplicity* and *godly sincerity*, not by earthly wisdom but by the grace of God, and supremely so toward you." From this passage Newton witnessed the honesty and transparency of Paul's apostolic gospel ministry, and from this passage he developed a pattern for all his preaching and pastoral ministry to conform to simplicity and godly sincerity. He wrote, "The grand principle of gospel oratory [preaching] is simplicity."[5] The pulpit is not a place for oratorical cleverness. In the pulpit you will not find Newton talking about political debates, or quoting famous Greek poets, or dispensing flowery illustrations. The absence of adornment is intentional; it's rooted in Newton's conviction to remain biblically simple. And out of these categories for ministry emerges the rubric for the Christian life.

Simplicity (ἁπλότης) was a hallmark of Paul's ministry which Newton repurposed to define the authentic Christian life. This spiritual simplicity is a sense of wholeness and straightness—unmixed, pure, sincerity flowing from the heart and from a simple motive. Simplicity is single-hearted obedience, as opposed to halfhearted eye-service (Eph. 6:5; Col. 3:22). Indeed, all of creation and human history are aimed at one *simple* end: to glorify the Creator (Rom. 11:36; 1 Tim. 1:17; Jude 25; Rev. 4:9–11). The Christian life, therefore, is aimed at nothing short of the glory of the Creator, for if "the

---

[4] W, 6:45.
[5] W, 6:402.

Lord can design nothing short of his own glory, nor should we."[6] And this is why for Paul, any move away from the grand design to honor God echoes the seedy core of the very first sin: "I am afraid that as the serpent deceived Eve by his cunning, your thoughts will be led astray from a sincere and pure devotion to Christ" (2 Cor. 11:3). Sin is the move away from simple devotion to Christ. Sin is spiritual complexity.

Simplicity is what protects us from living for two masters. We cannot serve God and money. Such distraction is unhealthy and unsimple (Matt. 6:24). Living for two masters is failure in the Christian life. Living for two masters is entrapment in a tangled knot of sin. And so it was the unknotted simplicity of faith that became for Newton the hallmark of Christian life, and the great challenge we face in our struggles with sin. For John Newton, the Christian life boils down largely to this question: How do you maintain constant, undistracted, unmixed, single-hearted devotion to Christ?

Gospel Simplicity

The simplicity Paul aimed to produce and the simplicity Newton aimed to emulate both center on the gospel. This godly simplicity is strong, resilient, and substantive, and at the center of this strong simplicity is the gospel applied to our individual lives. "The true simplicity, which is the honor and strength of a believer," Newton writes,

> is the effect of a spiritual perception of the truths of the Gospel. It arises from, and bears a proportion to, the sense we have of our own unworthiness, the power and grace of Christ, and the greatness of our obligations to him. So far as our knowledge of these things is vital and experimental, it will make us simple-hearted.[7]

A life of gospel simplicity is a life focused on Christ and his all-sufficiency, a life in which we are aware of our sin and lostness, and confident of what Christ has done on our behalf. What we can call *gospel simplicity* is the essence of the Christian life, and no true character will be found where these simple convictions have not been grasped by the heart—a simple-hearted heart.

But how do we know when gospel simplicity has taken root in our lives?

---

[6] *W*, 1:456.
[7] *W*, 1:299–300.

According to Newton, gospel simplicity will show itself in two derivative forms: *simplicity of intention* and *simplicity of dependence.*

Simplicity of Intention

In Newton's own words, here is what he means by the first phrase:

> Simplicity of intention, implies that we have but one leading aim, to which it is our deliberate and unreserved desire that every thing else in which we are concerned may be subordinate and subservient—in a word, that we are devoted to the Lord, and have by grace been enabled to choose him, and to yield ourselves to him, so as to place our happiness in his favor, and to make his glory and will the ultimate scope of all our actions.[8]

It is a life of single-focused glory, and not our own glory. We place our happiness in his favor and find our joy in his glory. In other words, our happiness and God's glory have been inseparably bound together.[9]

God is the all-sufficient good, *our* all-sufficient good. We were created for him, and he is sufficient to fill us and satisfy every need he has created within us. We turn to him and find in his presence the full supply we need to thrive in spiritual comfort and joy.

We were created *by* God, we were created *for* God, and we find purpose for our lives when we resign ourselves *to* God's disposal. We offer ourselves for God's glory alone because God lives for his glory alone.[10] Newton once counted every mention in the Bible where God acts so that "they shall know that I am the LORD." He found the phrase seventy-three times.[11] This biblical discovery is essential to all other reality and knowledge in the universe. God intends with his every act to honor his own name—it is his highest

---

[8] *W*, 1:300.

[9] Leighton: "By a wonderful instance of wisdom and goodness, God has so connected his own glory with our happiness, that we cannot properly intend or desire the one, but the other must follow of course, and our felicity is at last resolved into his eternal glory" (*Theological and Expository Lectures by Robert Leighton, D.D., Archbishop of Glasgow* [London, 1828], 114).

[10] A point well made by theologian Jason DeRouchie: "The good news of God's end-times reign is nothing less than *the glory of God in the face of Jesus Christ*' (2 Cor. 4:6; cf. 1 Tim. 1:11). Jesus lived *for the glory of his Father* (John 7:18; 17:4), and his death and resurrection vindicated *God's righteousness* and exalted *God's glory* (John 12:27–28; 17:1; Rom. 3:25–26). God forgives sins and welcomes believers *for his glory* (Isa. 43:25; Ps. 25:11; Rom. 15:7), and he calls everyone to live *for his glory* always (Matt. 5:16; John 5:44; 1 Cor. 10:31; Phil. 1:11; 1 Peter 4:11), which includes a radical commitment to spreading a passion for God's supremacy throughout the world, both through sharing and suffering (Matt. 5:11–12; 28:18–20). Within this context, God promises to honor all who *seek to exalt him* and not themselves (1 Sam. 2:30; Luke 18:14; James 4:6; 1 Peter 5:5), even as they await the 'blessed hope, the appearing of the glory of our great God and savior Jesus Christ' (Titus 2:13)" (*What the Old Testament Authors Really Cared About: A Survey of Jesus' Bible* [Grand Rapids: Kregel, 2013], 40).

[11] *Letters* (Taylor), 132. By my count the phrase appears in Scripture ninety times, seventy-two of them in the book of Ezekiel alone.

end, his aim in every act.[12] He is the potter; we are clay, made in his image and created for his glory. And not only are we created for him; we have been redeemed from sin by him. Christ has paid the purchase price, and we are his by blood; therefore we can no longer live for multiple lords. We do not serve God and money, and we do not serve God and worldliness. Our bodies and souls have been created and redeemed for one ultimate end: to glorify God (1 Cor. 6:19–20).

This single end is key. "Conformity to the world is the bane of many professors in this day," Newton writes of those who think they have found a way to serve God and cash. They cannot. Double-mindedness only leads to spiritual instability, and those who love money can make no progress in the Christian life. No matter how often they attend church or study orthodox theology, they remain "destitute of the life, power, and comfort of religion, so long as they cleave to those things which are incompatible with it."[13] Gospel simplicity dies by split motives. Befriending the world and befriending God is impossible (James 4:1–10). You cannot have both a love of drunkenness and a desire for health. Split desires and split motives lead to sickness, decay, and death. Spiritual health is gained—and maintained—only by singular motives.

In purchasing our souls, Christ has become for us the perfect model of simple intention. He "willingly endured the cross, he gave his back to the smiters, he poured out his blood, he laid down his life. Here was an adorable simplicity of intention in him; and shall we not, O thou Lover of souls! be simply, heartily, and wholly thine?"[14] In this way, Christ's obedience to his Father was simple—and worthy of adoration. Christ was pained by the cost of redemption, but his heart was never torn between competing loves. His intentions were all dedicated to one end: his Father's pleasure.

This simplicity of aim covers every decision and situation faced in the Christian life. The heart blessed with simplicity of intention is a gospel-filled heart that can endure everything in this life. The gospel-simple heart knows that every trial or stroke of pain comes from God's hand, with his own glory at stake ultimately. The gospel-simple heart finds the love of God in Christ to be our highest temporal joy and finds freedom from the perpetual entanglements of sin and self. *Simplicity of intention* is self-denial before God—self-denial of our self-righteousness, self-denial of our self-wisdom,

---

[12] *W*, 4:122–24.
[13] *W*, 1:281.
[14] *W*, 1:300–301.

and self-denial of our self-will.[15] The gospel-simple heart takes its right-ful place under Christ's lordship, and there is protected from "low, sordid, and idolatrous pursuits." It entertains no rivals to Christ. It does not accept the bribes of the world. It lives for the glory of God. In enduring trials, or fighting sin, or living out our calling in the world, the gospel-simple heart is driven by one aim: "a single eye to [God's] glory, as the ultimate scope of all our undertakings."[16] Or, to use the Pauline language, "So, whether you eat or drink, or whatever you do, do all to the glory of God" (1 Cor. 10:31). Opportunities to fulfill this calling present themselves in the details of our lives—in our eating, drinking, talking, and serving. "Self likes to do great things; but grace teaches us to do little things with a great spirit—that is, for the Lord's sake. To fill up his appointed post with integrity, submission, and thankfulness, is all that an angel could do, if he was upon earth."[17]

This gloriously single aim drives the gospel-simple heart.

Simplicity of Dependence

If *simplicity of intention* is about our *aim* (living for God's glory alone), *simplicity of dependence* is about our *trust* (living in light of God's trustwor-thiness). Living for the glory of God alone is possible only by the moment-by-moment provision and support of God.

Remember, unbelief is the complexity that clouds our vision and mul-tiplies our difficulties in life. Faith is the key to simple dependence, and Abraham is our model. When he was told his aged and barren wife would conceive, Abraham believed. "No unbelief made him waver" (Rom. 4:20). When God called for Abraham to offer up his only son, he acted in faith (Gen. 22:1–19; Heb. 11:17–19). Abraham modeled simple dependence.

As Abraham discovered, the path of obedience requires a simplicity of trust in the wisdom and provision of God. As Newton writes:

> How comfortable is it to us, as well as ornamental to our profession, to be able to trust the Lord in the path of duty! To believe that he will supply our wants, direct our steps, plead our cause, and control our enemies! Thus he has promised, and it belongs to Gospel simplicity to take his word against all discouragements.[18]

---

[15] *Letters* (Jones), 28.
[16] *W*, 1:456.
[17] *Letters* (Campbell), 78.
[18] *W*, 1:302.

The lack of such dependence leads to a host of complications and problems. We are quick to look to the world to provide our comforts and our hopes, especially when life grows dark. We seek to serve false saviors that promise comfort and hope, instead of living on the promises of God. Spiritual insincerity emerges in our hearts. And when our perceptions of the world are governed by self-wisdom, we can quickly grow lukewarm in the attempt to find comfort and security in the world's riches, lusts, and powers. By failing to trust in God's wisdom and timing, we grow spiritually insincere, and some may eventually shipwreck their own souls by the complexity of self-wisdom and indecision. An inability to fully trust God creates a toxic "duplicity of conduct" that poisons the Christian life.

On the other hand, burdens in life are made lighter by simple dependence on God. "His grace is sufficient for us: and if he favors us with an humble and dependent spirit, a single eye, and a simple heart, he will make every difficulty give way, and mountains shall sink into plains before his power."[19] Even in faith, the circumstances of life will not be alleviated, the pain will still hurt, and life may be hard in many ways, but Newton is convinced all our trials are aggravated by unbelief. "Unbelief is continually starting objections, magnifying and multiplying difficulties."[20] When we fail to trust God, the difficulties of life loom larger, sting harder, and weigh heavier. The more we try to carry the load we were never called to bear, the more we trod on in unbelief; "we live so far below our privileges, and are so often heavy and sorrowful, when we have in him grounds of continual joy" (2 Cor. 6:10).[21]

Over every detail in this world, Christ reigns. His "sovereignty is but another name for the unlimited exercise of wisdom and goodness."[22] Nothing hinders his wisdom and goodness. Every drop of rain hits its appointed target, and every dust particle is carried by the wind to its appointed resting place.[23] If we could but grasp this in the depth of our being, our souls would be liberated to depend fully on God's governance over our lives and to learn to count trials "all joy" (James 1:2).[24] The joy of the Lord is our strength in the Christian life; unbelief is our Kryptonite.

---

[19] *W*, 1:160.
[20] *W*, 1:301.
[21] *W*, 2:578.
[22] *W*, 1:446. On the sovereignty of Christ, see *W*, 2:421.
[23] *Letters* (Campbell), 182.
[24] Leighton: "Can any thing give greater consolation or more substantial joy, than to be firmly persuaded, not only that there is an infinitely good and wise Being, but also that this Being preserves and continually governs the universe which [he] himself has framed, and holds the reins of all things in his powerful

Serious Simplicity

Gospel simplicity is a deadly serious concern for Newton. At stake is a life that glorifies God in its eternal aim and enjoys God in its daily routine. What can be more serious than that?

The gospel-simple life does not suggest that life will never get complicated. Even the most godly lives will be tied up by complexity in their inboxes and their marriages and their children and their relationships, but the complications in everyday life are distinguished from a simplicity in the spiritual life. Sin remains, and complexities remain, but Christians can maintain gospel simplicity by frequent returns to the gospel. As we rehearse the gospel in our own lives, we recall the gravity of our sin and the price of our redemption. From that awareness, we make it our daily aim to live for God's glory alone (not seek our own glory), to depend on God's strength and wisdom (not rest in false securities), and to thrive on the joy offered to us by God (not feed on the pleasures of the world). The simple life is an abundant life, a pleasant life, and often a delightful life, but it is a life that requires nothing short of an ongoing war this side of eternity. We fight for gospel simplicity.

Yet there is also a hidden side to the simple life. Gospel simplicity shapes our lives in the private places where others cannot pry, in the quiet moments when we wrestle with God, and in the decisive moments when we struggle with conflict. Gospel simplicity is often shrouded in privacy, but its consequences cannot be hidden. Not for long.

Gospel Sincerity

Gospel simplicity produces something beautiful. While displayed in both *simplicity of intention* and *simplicity of dependence*, it results in *gospel sincerity* (εἰλικρίνεια, 1 Cor. 5:8; 2 Cor. 1:12; 2:17). Those who aim to please God live sincere lives before others. In the healthy Christian life, there are no double standards, no dual aims. The private life and the public life are equally oriented to the glory of God. This is manifested as true Christian authenticity in the world.

> For they who love the Lord above all, who prefer the light of his countenance to thousands of gold and silver, who are enabled to trust him with all their concerns, and would rather be at his disposal than at their own,

---

hand, that he is our father, that we and all our interests are his constant concern?" (*Theological and Expository Lectures*, 33–34).

will have but little temptation to insincerity. The principles and motives upon which their conduct is formed, are the same in public as in private. Their behavior will be all of a piece, because they have but one *design*. They will speak the truth in love, observe a strict punctuality in their dealings, and do unto others as they would others should do unto them; because these things are essential to their great aim of glorifying and enjoying their Lord.[25]

The sincere Christian sees nothing to gain through cunning hypocrisy, crafty evasion, or insincere motives with others. The sincere Christian preacher will not peddle God's Word to get rich (2 Cor. 2:17). Likewise, the Christian businessman in the workplace aims to be godly in his own calling. He is honest, self-disclosing, purposeful, kind, and loving. In a word, he is *sincere*. He lives in no fear of being "found out" because he walks by the light of God's wise Word, he aims at God's glory alone, and he walks by God's power in Christ. By this power he walks in liberty and sincerity before the world and others.

As Newton makes very clear, gospel sincerity is not the product of religious conformity to external standards of justice and holiness. True Christian character in the world is deeply rooted in the simple motives and simple dependence of daily faith. True Christian godliness is rooted fundamentally in the conviction that we have found our ultimate joy, and our sole confidence, in Christ and in no other. Gospel sincerity in the world is achieved in no other way.

And so we return to the question at the beginning of the chapter: what are the roots under true Christian authenticity? Newton supplies the answer, via the apostle Paul: simplicity. The authentic Christian life is impossible if the aims and motives of the heart are double-dealing. The truly authentic Christian life—the life of faith—is exemplified by gospel simplicity: waiting on God *alone*, receiving all from him, rendering all to him, resting in him, and acting solely for his glory.[26]

Godly Sincerity (and Its Weirdness)

Daily we are drawn back to the gospel to be shaped by the life and work of our Savior, Jesus Christ. To live *is* Christ, and to live *simply in Christ* is the

---

[25] W, 303–4.
[26] W, 6:55.

aim of the Christian life. This is why we fight against the entanglements of sins that complexify our hearts.

The Christian life does not call us to be cynical toward the world. We need humility to acknowledge the ways the world will tempt us to slowly abandon gospel simplicity.[27] Attempting to walk *fashionably* in the eyes of the world and walk *simply* in the presence of God are two roads that part into mutually exclusive paths. The gospel of Christ inspires sacrificial love and kindness toward others, attributes that we would think appeal to the world. But Christlikeness doesn't appeal to the world, certainly not for long. Even if we display Christlike kindness, we still face the reality that peace with all men is simply impossible (Rom. 12:18). The Christian who walks in godly simplicity and sincerity will testify to the world of God's grace, but he or she will also rub the world's fur in the wrong direction.

> A consistent Christian, whose integrity, humility, and philanthropy, mark his character and adorn his profession, will in time command respect; but his attachment to unfashionable truths, and his separation from the maxims and pursuits of the many, will render him in their eyes singular and precise, weak and enthusiastic.[28]

In other words, godly simplicity may come across to the world as dated, stale, and foolish simplemindedness. Or it may incite jeers and dislike, and even perhaps slander and persecution.[29] In the act of exalting God alone, we will "stain the pride of all human glory."[30] We can expect opposition, but this should not throw us Christians off, as Newton states it (rather bluntly), "When the conscience is clear and the heart simple, neither the applauses nor the anathemas of worms are worth twopence per bushel."[31]

In the gospel-simple life we do not live to please men; we live to please the Lord alone. As Puritan Thomas Boston (1676–1732) said it, "Men-pleasers, and those who please Christ, divide the whole world."[32] Sometimes that division becomes very clear, and in those times gospel simplicity causes our tension with the world. There are two ways to live, and the Christian who seeks to live a life pleasing to God finds himself uncomfortably out of place in this world at times. Like a pilgrim.

---

[27] *W*, 6:272–73.
[28] *W*, 4:510.
[29] *W*, 4:509–10.
[30] *W*, 1:372.
[31] *Letters* (Bull 1847), 150.
[32] Thomas Boston, *The Whole Works of Thomas Boston* (Aberdeen, 1849), 4:243.

Simplicity as Treasuring

But gospel simplicity and its result (godly sincerity) do not merely simplify our lives; they also amplify our deepest desires. Gospel simplicity is about adoring rightly, treasuring singularly, and embracing wholly. Nineteenth-century Danish writer Søren Kierkegaard titled a book *Purity of Heart Is to Will One Thing*. That's getting close to gospel simplicity. Or to say this in a slightly more robust way, purity of heart is to *treasure one thing*.[33] Newton comes very close to this when he prays, "May we be enabled from hence-forth to serve him with a single eye and a simple heart, to be faithful to every intimation of his will, and to make him our All in all!"[34] A single-eyed obedience correlates to having found Christ to be our all in all (Eph. 1:23).

To obey sincerely is a supernatural phenomenon growing out of daily communion and adoration of Christ in his all-sufficiency. Newton best explains this in this beautiful excerpt we studied earlier.

> I wish we may learn from all our changes, to be sober and watchful, not to rest in grace received, in experience or comforts, but still to be pressing forward, and never think ourselves either safe or happy, but when we are beholding the glory of Christ by the light of faith in the glass of the Gospel. To view him as God manifest in the flesh, as *all in all* in himself, and *all in all* for us; this is cheering, this is strengthening, this makes hard things easy, and bitter things sweet. This includes all I can wish for my dear friends, that you may grow in grace, and in the knowledge of Jesus. To know him, is the shortest description of true grace; to know him better, is the surest mark of growth in grace; to know him perfectly, is eternal life. This is the prize of our high calling; the sum and substance of all we can desire or hope for is, to see him as he is, and to be like him: and to this honor and happiness he will surely bring all that love his name.[35]

We adore Christ for his immeasurable love.[36] As we do, the glory of God shining in the face of Jesus Christ simplifies the Christian life by focusing our attention on the treasure. Here, in the adoration of Christ, all acts of obedience (hard things) and all trials (sour things) take on new sweetness under the illuminating glow of Christ's transfigured glory.

This gospel simplicity is inseparable from spiritual pleasure. Proper

---

[33] John Piper, *What Jesus Demands from the World* (Wheaton, IL: Crossway, 2006), 206.
[34] *W*, 2:210.
[35] *W*, 6:73–74.
[36] *W*, 2:180–81.

gospel simplicity binds together our joy, our obedience, and God's glory. Gospel simplicity means that we so

> yield ourselves to him, as to place our happiness in his favor, and to make his glory and will the ultimate scope of all our actions. He well deserves this from us. He is the all-sufficient good. He alone is able to satisfy the vast capacity he has given us; for he formed us for himself: and they who have tasted he is gracious, know that 'his loving-kindness is better than life'; and that his presence and fullness can supply the want or make up the loss of all creature-comforts.[37]

God's all-sufficiency in Christ is the only basis for single-minded obedience. All else is "a poor pretense, a lifeless shadow of religion."[38]

In other words, a heart truly aimed at glorifying God alone expects its heart-sustaining joy from God alone. The Christian life is not only about simplicity of dependence and intention, but also about a simplicity of affection. We give up all vain attempts to self-medicate our souls with the broken-cistern pleasures of the world. The simple Christian looks to God alone to supply him with spiritual joys, understanding that there will be times when those joys may be withheld by God for a divinely appointed reason. Yet, because he aims to live for God's glory alone, he looks to God alone for his soul's pleasure (Ps. 86:4).

In Newton's mind, single-minded obedience and wholehearted embrace of Christ's all-sufficiency are inseparable. Mopey, sour Christians live in a state that works against sincere obedience. But joyful, treasuring Christians rest upon Christ's all-sufficient power against sinful selfishness, as Newton explained in a letter to Lord Dartmouth.

> A single eye to his glory, as the ultimate scope of all our undertakings.—The Lord can design nothing short of his own glory, nor should we. The constraining love of Christ has a direct and marvelous tendency, in proportion to the measure of faith, to mortify the corrupt principle *Self*, which for a season is the grand spring of our conduct, and by which we are too much biased after we know the Lord. But as grace prevails, self is renounced. We feel that we are not our own, that we are bought with a price; and that it is our duty, our honor, and our happiness, to be the servants of God and of the Lord Jesus Christ. To devote soul and body, every talent, power, and

[37] W, 1:300.
[38] *365 Days with Newton*, 203.

faculty, to the service of his cause and will; to let our light shine (in our several situations) to the praise of his grace; to place our highest joy in the contemplation of his adorable perfections; to rejoice even in tribulations and distresses, in reproaches and infirmities, if thereby the power of Christ may rest upon us, and be magnified in us; to be content, yea glad, to be nothing, that he may be all in all; to obey *him*, in opposition to the threats or solicitations of men; to trust *him*, though all outward appearances seem against us; to rejoice in *him*, though we should (as will sooner or later be the case) have nothing else to rejoice in; to live above the world, and to have our conversation in heaven; to be like the angels, finding our own pleasure in performing his:—This, my lord, is the prize, the mark of our high calling, to which we are encouraged with a holy ambition continually to aspire. It is true, we shall still fall short; we shall find that, when we would do good, evil will be present with us. But the attempt is glorious, and shall not be wholly in vain. He that gives us thus *to will*, will enable us to perform with growing success, and teach us to profit even by our mistakes and imperfections.[39]

All this obedience is connected to our adoration of the glorious perfections of Christ. Our communion with Christ is the "the greatest happiness we are capable of," and this happiness opens the way of obedience for us. In the delight of communion with Christ, the will of God opens for us, and obedience is called forth.[40] We are not called to be recluses in the world; rather, we are each given a daily role to play in the drama. And daily obedience requires daily treasuring of Christ. For the Christian life to work properly, Christ must first be our "all in all." In Christ, the Christian life is aimed and empowered.

> When indeed we are willing to be nothing, that he may be all in all, *in* us and *for* us, then I think we reach the very *acme* [pinnacle] of our profession. Then, while we feel that we have no sufficiency of ourselves, we shall be enabled to do all things that occur in the line of duty, through him strengthening us [2 Cor. 12:9–10].[41]

Successful Simplicity

This is no grand theory. Newton's dear friend William Wilberforce, the abolitionist, wrestled as a young man with doubts about pursuing a life in politics. He also wrestled with doubts about the health of his own soul.

---

[39] *W*, 1:456–57.
[40] *Letters* (Bull 1869), 190–91.
[41] *Letters* (Coffin), 171–72.

Wilberforce recalled his first meeting with Newton: "When I came away I found my mind in a calm, tranquil state more humbled and looking more devoutly up to God." It is a simple testimony, and it speaks of Newton's skill in applying his counsel to the most complex of lives and callings. Gospel simplicity is not removal from the world—it is finding our identity tied up in Christ who is our "all in all." Nor does it call us to choose between the sacred and the secular; it simply calls us to live for the glory of God alone. Newton clearly made this point to the young Wilberforce, who would later choose to play a significant political role in abolishing the British slave trade.[42]

Success in the Christian life is about simplicity of intention and simplicity of dependence leading to genuine obedience. True Christian faithfulness to God "is not to be measured by our sensible feelings, by what we can say or write, but rather by the simplicity of our dependence, and the uniform tenor of our obedience to his will."[43] This uniform tenor is the genuine mark and measure of Christian maturity. Which means, we must always check our sinful hearts and our motives. In every decision of life, we can ask two questions:

1. Sustained by the all-sufficiency of Christ, am I motivated by God's glory alone?
2. Eternally secured by the blood of Christ, am I dependent upon God's wisdom, timing, and his power alone?

All other behavior modification in the Christian is ultimately hollow when these questions are answered no. Only the gospel of the all-sufficient Christ is powerful enough to make the yes a reality in our lives, to grab our affections, and to awaken all our ambitions to magnify God. Sin is an entangling power in our lives that pulls our hearts away from Christ and gospel simplicity, and pushes us toward the world, splitting our aims and multiplying spiritual complexity. At the core of every human life are joy-seeking motives. Sin muddles our intentions, motives, and our securities. And at the core of the healthy Christian life our intentions, motives, and securities are shaped by Christ's all-sufficiency. This is gospel simplicity.

There's one final point Newton would stress here. Such gospel simplicity is an active *grace* in the heart, and it is precious, more precious than

[42] Aitken, 299–307.
[43] *Letters* (Bull 1869), 364.

eminent spiritual *gifts*.[44] Newton supposes that if he could search out the world to award a man, woman, or child with a trophy for being the most godly Christian on the planet, the award would not go to an eminent Christian, or even to a public Christian—not to a pastor, seminary professor, or author. The greatest Christian in the world, Newton supposes, is most likely a man of faith who just barely survives in this world thanks to a homeless shelter and the meager employment he finds on the lowest rungs of the social ladder. Or perhaps, Newton speculates, the greatest Christian is a bedridden old woman in a mud cottage who has learned through years of trials to adore Christ and trust him and his timing in everything. Low thoughts of self and high and admiring thoughts of Christ are the sure marks of the godliest Christian, even if such a Christian is likely unnoticed by the world and overlooked by most Christians. The best models of gospel simplicity are the poorest and the weakest Christians who have been emptied of all self-sufficiency, and who have learned to fully submit their lives to the lordship of Christ, his will, his wisdom, and his timing.[45]

For John Newton, the path of Christian maturity is nothing less than *gospel simplicity* leading to *godly sincerity*. Christ is the source of the power to transform our hearts, and he is the model of what this life of simple aim and simple dependence looks like in its full sincerity.

> Was it as easy to do as to say, I should be happy, for the Lord has shown me how true peace is to be possessed, even by a simple reliance on his all-sufficiency and love, living upon his free grace, and sure mediation, and receiving strength continually from him suited to the occasions of every hour.[46]

Yes, gospel simplicity and sincerity are easy to write and read about, but hard to live out.

In the pursuit of the freedom to be found in gospel simplicity, we must untangle our knot-tying foe of the Christian life—indwelling sin.

---

[44] Grace is more valuable than gifts, in other words, because the genuine work of God in the heart to humble us and to make Christ more beautiful to us is a grace more valuable than our gifts and practical usefulness in the eyes of others. This is one of Newton's themes through his letters, particularly to leaders. See *Letters* (Bull 1869), 169; *W*, 1:163–66; 5:77–78; 6:115, 127–28, 171.

[45] For all these points, see *W*, 6:171–72; *Letters* (Bull 1869), 169, 364; *Letters* (Campbell), 36–37.

[46] *Letters* (Clunie), 17.

CHAPTER 5

INDWELLING SIN

John Newton was locked behind prison doors in the fall of 1775. It wasn't exactly a prison, but more of a correctional institution for thieves. And he wasn't sent there by force, but entered the facility voluntarily as a fifty-year-old pastor.

The correctional facility in London was known as Westminster Bridewell. The inmates in the facility were subjected to hard labor and, in the spirit of behavior reform, to physical lashings for disobedience. Those floggings were meted out publicly in full view of the good citizens of London, further enlarging the social distance between the law-abiding citizens on the outside and the law-breaking miscreants on the inside. Newton entered Bridewell with his Bible and with a very personal story of God's saving grace. Soon after, he recounted the trip to a friend.

> You would have liked to have been with me last Wednesday. I preached at Westminster Bridewell. It is a prison and house of correction. The bulk of my congregation were housebreakers [burglars], highwaymen [a highway robber on horseback], pickpockets, and poor unhappy women, such as infest the streets of this city, sunk in sin, and lost to shame [prostitutes]. I had a hundred or more of these before me. I preached from 1 Tim. 1:15 ["The saying is trustworthy and deserving of full acceptance, that Christ Jesus came into the world to save sinners, of whom I am the foremost"]; and began with telling them my own story: this gained their attention more than I expected. I spoke to them near an hour and a half. I shed many tears myself, and saw some of them shed tears likewise. Ah! Had

you seen their present condition, and could you hear the history of some of them, it would make you sing, "O to grace how great a debtor!" By nature they were no worse than the most sober and modest people; and there was doubtless a time when many of them little thought what they should live to do and suffer. I might have been, like them, in chains, and one of them have come to preach to me, had the Lord so pleased.[1]

Walking into the prison forced Newton to think on his own past, though that recollecting was a daily habit for him already. Given his preconversion life, it was not difficult for him to imagine a reversal of roles—himself wearing the chains, bearing public floggings, and needing a preacher to proclaim to him the good news of the gospel. The miscreants Newton addressed in the correctional facility were sinners, and they knew it, and the citizens of London knew it. Likely the biggest surprise for the prisoners was the pastor's candid story.

This prison visit is illuminating on three levels. First, Newton believed that the grace of God could reach anyone, no matter how dark or prevailing the sin, and he was living proof of it. Second, Newton found in 1 Timothy 1:15 a natural transition from his own life of sin to Paul's claim on the title of "chief sinner." Newton could make such a smooth transition because he genuinely believed that he was the worst sinner he knew—even in a room where he was circled by one hundred thieves and prostitutes. Third, sin is sin. No matter how squeaky clean the Christian appears in society compared with a burglar, a prostitute, a pickpocket, or any other social miscreant, in both resides a powerfully wicked bent called indwelling sin.[2] Newton's preaching, whether in a vile prison or from a varnished pulpit, always addressed those who were "criminals condemned already."[3]

Newton sensed his own sin deeply and profoundly. In his letters, he is quick to apply to himself the contemptible designation *chief of sinners*.[4] "In my days of folly and vanity, I was a chief sinner indeed—a vile blasphemer, and profligate to an extreme."[5] And just like the apostle Paul, Newton was self-aware that his redemption as chief sinner was a means of hope for every other sinner (1 Tim. 1:15–16). "It has pleased him to set me forth

---

[1] W, 2:150.
[2] W, 1:697.
[3] W, 1:586.
[4] For a sampling, see W, 1:517; 2:180, 246–47; 5:570; 6:58; *Letters* (Ryland), 397; *Letters* (Jones), 107; *Letters* (Campbell), 28.
[5] *Letters* (Coffin), 151.

as a pattern of his long-suffering and patience to other chief sinners, that none may despair when they see me."[6] And because God opened the eyes of this chief of sinners to the depth of indwelling sin in his own heart and to the greatness of the Savior, Newton walked into the Westminster Bridewell prison not as a self-righteous authority, but as a broken and humbled brother to fellow sinners. This was perhaps the key to his pastoral gentleness to all other sinners, writes John Piper. "Glad-hearted, grateful lowliness and brokenness as a saved 'wretch' was probably the most prominent root of Newton's habitual tenderness with people."[7]

Our own biographies do not require the dark degeneracy of a John Newton in order to make a similar self-evaluation. In a sermon Newton explained,

> It is probable that all who are convinced and enlightened by the Holy Spirit, having a clearer knowledge of the nature, number, and aggravation of their own sins, than they can possibly have of those of any other person, account themselves among the chief of sinners, though many of them may have been preserved from gross enormities.[8]

Whether or not our lives have been tainted by scandalous sins, and whether or not we literally claim for ourselves the title *chief of sinners*, Newton operates with a fundamental assumption: the Christian life can be successfully lived out by one who has looked into the pit of sin in his own heart and found evil down deep in the core of his being.

Sensing Sin

But awareness is not permission. Newton never vindicated his sin. He was never comfortable with his indwelling sin. If John Newton was a pastoral cardiologist with a stethoscope upon his flock, he could diagnose the maladies of their hearts because he was first a careful student of his own heart. What he discovered inside was a myriad of evils and rebellions against his Creator. "My heart is like a highway," he wrote, "like a city without walls or gates: nothing so false, so frivolous, so absurd, so impossible, or so horrid, but it can obtain access, and that at any time, or in any place;

---

[6] *Letters* (Taylor), 178. See also *Letters* (Bull 1869), 259.
[7] John Piper, *The Roots of Endurance: Invincible Perseverance in the Lives of John Newton, Charles Simeon, and William Wilberforce* (Wheaton, IL: Crossway, 2002), 73.
[8] W, 5:173.

neither the study, the pulpit, nor even the Lord's table, exempt me from their intrusion."[9] In another place he says:

> My heart is like a country but half subdued, where all things are in an unsettled state, and mutinies and insurrections are daily happening. I hope I hate the rebels that disturb the King's peace. I am glad when I can point them out, lay hold of them, and bring them to him for justice. But they have many lurking-holes, and sometimes they come disguised like friends, so that I do not know them, till their works discover them.[10]

In another place Newton personifies his rebellion.

> I want to deliver up that rebel Self to him [God] in chains; but the rogue, like [the mythical Greek god] Proteus, puts on so many forms, that he slips through my fingers: but I think I know what I would do if I could fairly catch him. My soul is like a besieged city: a legion of enemies without the gates, and a nest of restless traitors within, that hold a correspondence with them without; so that I am deceived and counteracted continually. It is a mercy that I have not been surprised and overwhelmed long ago: without help from on high it would soon be over with me.[11]

Remaining sin is an enemy of the soul, a selfish morass of complications disrupting our spiritual peace and making life into a perpetual warfare, as we discovered in the last chapter.

But it's not enough just to read in the Bible about our remaining sin. It's not enough to hear from a preacher that our sin remains even after redemption. "We are so totally depraved," Newton wrote, "is a truth which no one ever truly learned by being only told it."[12] We must discover our sin—we must *feel* our own sin and it must *shake* us—and this *feeling* of our sin is a sure mark of the work of grace. In Christ there is all-sufficient hope and forgiveness for a murderer who has killed one thousand people, but there's no hope for any sinner who has not come face-to-face with the indwelling disease of sin.[13] We must *feel* our malady before we rightly prize our Physician, and appeal to him as our all-sufficient solution.[14] The pain is a necessary, grace-given pain. "The gospel affords no hope but to

---

[9] W, 1:444–45.
[10] Letters (Clunie), 78.
[11] W, 2:122.
[12] W, 1:451. See also W, 6:251; Letters (Coffin), 220.
[13] Letters (Taylor), 239–40.
[14] See W, 1:583; 2:444; 4:173, 351; Letters (Taylor), 240; Letters (Coffin), 119, 229.

those whose hearts are contrite, and broken by a conviction of sin; for, while we feel not our malady, we cannot duly prize, or rightly apply to the only Physician."[15] This sting is felt when God's grace breaks into your life, like a sharp knife, cutting deep into motives and intentions (Heb. 4:12).[16] Without this sting, we would never be compelled to confess our sins. We would be left in the condition of the legalist, who can only make excuses for his sin, but who cannot repent because he remains numb to his depravities.[17] There are times when God willingly withholds his presence from us in order that we can *feel* the weight of our indwelling sin for ourselves.[18] To *feel* sin for what it is, an offense against a holy God, is a bone-chilling sensation explained by no human cause, but only the "good work" of the Spirit.

When the Spirit bears witness to indwelling sin, we discover that evil is no occasional thing, but an abiding presence, an unwanted guest in our hearts complicating every step in the Christian life.

> Every day draws forth some new corruption which before was little ob-
> served, or at least discovers it in a stronger light than before. Thus by
> degrees they are weaned from leaning to any supposed wisdom, power, or
> goodness in themselves; they feel the truth of our Lord's words, "without
> me ye can do nothing" (John 15:5).[19]

In one sense we want to progress daily in holiness, and yet each day we discover new levels of sinfulness in our hearts, and in our spiritual inabilities.

As we will see later, grace gave Newton the freedom and confidence he needed to face his own personal sins directly. He did not whitewash the darkness of his own sin, because the deeper and darker his sin, the more glorious became his Savior. Newton was open and honest about his weaknesses, and this honesty marked his entire forty-year ministry. Nothing in his service was not in some way "debased, polluted, and spoiled by my depraved nature." "I am a riddle to myself," he wrote, "a heap of inconsistence."[20] This was never an excuse to shrug off obedience or justify scandalous sin, but it was a disclosure of grace intended to break and humble him. Every Christian must *feel* something of the same.

---

[15] *Letters* (Taylor), 240.
[16] *Letters* (Bull 1869), 264.
[17] John Newton, *365 Days with Newton*, ed. Marylynn Rouse (Leominster, UK: Day One, 2006), 134.
[18] *W*, 1:259.
[19] *W*, 1:452.
[20] *W*, 6:97–98.

The Effects of Indwelling Sin

But let's stop, back up, and dig a little deeper into the effects of indwelling sin in the Christian life. Indwelling sin is not something we can discover merely by being told about it, but rather a discovery we must make on our own. So where do we begin to look in our own lives? This question engaged Newton for many self-reflective hours.

A key text for him on indwelling sin in the Christian life was Galatians 5:17: "For the desires of the flesh are against the Spirit, and the desires of the Spirit are against the flesh, for these are opposed to each other, to keep you from doing the things you want to do." We want to do things—noble things, holy things—because as Christians we are motivated to act. And if we could act in perpetual faith, our lives would shine in holiness, love, and obedience. Apart from sin, a Christian "would tread in the very footsteps of his Savior, fill up every moment in his service, and employ every breath in his praise. This he would do; but, alas! he cannot."[21] No we cannot. As C. S. Lewis wrote, "No man knows how bad he is till he has tried very hard to be good."[22]

Newton uses a fitting metaphor to make the point. Imagine a Christian sitting down with a blank page and pen. He begins to write out his perfectly scripted life, explaining how he would love others, how he would structure his prayer life, or how he would sanctify his wife by the Word. But indwelling sin and Satan crouch at his elbow, disrupting every pen stroke and messing up every word and sentence as our Christian friend tries to write the script. At every point in the Christian life Satan jabs our elbow, and our pen skids across the page as our perfect plan is reduced to scribbles. This is a metaphor of the Christian life with indwelling sin. Yet the biggest problem is that sin is not at our elbow—our sin is in us![23]

Newton used a lot of metaphors for indwelling sin. When a carnival brought a tame lion to his town, he went to see it and was told not to touch it. For however tame, the lion still had violent fits. Newton saw in the lion a metaphor for his own heart.[24] Or indwelling is like a squatter who has taken permanent residence in the house of the Christian life. He may be relegated to smaller and smaller rooms—even into a closet—

---

[21] W, 1:689.
[22] C. S. Lewis, *Mere Christianity* (1952; repr., San Francisco: HarperCollins, 2001), 142.
[23] W, 1:698.
[24] W, 2:236. The experience inspired his hymn "The Tamed Lion" (W, 3:559–60).

but he will not leave. The house (flesh) must be demolished and rebuilt (death and resurrection).[25]

The presence of indwelling sin at its root makes it impossible for us to live out the full extent of holiness we know to be right and true. Our intentions are good, but we flounder and flop. This is the perplexing mystery of the Christian life, and this conundrum vividly emerges in one poignant letter from Newton to a friend.

> It may sound like a contradiction to say, we cannot do what we can do: but there are many enigmas in a believer's experience, at least in mine; and I never expect to meet the man that knows his own heart, that will say he is always faithful, diligent, and obedient, to the full extent of his ability: I rather expect he would confess, with me, that he feels a need of more ability, and fresh supplies of grace, to enable him to make a better improvement of what he has already received. If some, as you suppose, in their dullest frames can read the Bible, go to the Throne of Grace, and mourn (as they ought) over what is amiss, I must say for myself, I can, and I cannot. Without doubt I *can* take the Bible in my hand, and force myself to read it; I *can* kneel down, and I can see I *ought* to mourn: but to understand and attend to what I read, to engage my *heart* in prayer, or to be duly humbled under the sense of so dark and dissipated a state of mind; these things, at some seasons, I can no more do than I can raise the dead; and yet I cannot plead positive inability: I am satisfied that what prevents me is my sin, but it is the sin of my nature, the sin that dwelleth in me. And I expect it will be thus with me at times, in a greater or less degree, till this body of sin shall be wholly destroyed.[26]

Here in this paragraph is the key to understanding indwelling sin. Sin is what makes the things we know we ought to do so difficult and lifeless. We

---

[25] Newton: "I have a troublesome inmate, a lodger, who assumes as if the house were his own, and is a perpetual encumbrance, and spoils all. He has long been noted for his evil ways; but though generally known, is not easily avoided. He lodged with one Saul of Tarsus long before I was born, and made him groan and cry out lustily. Time was when I thought I would shut the door, to keep him out of my house, but my precaution came too late; he was already within; and to turn him out by head and shoulders is beyond my power; nay, I cannot interdict him from any one single apartment. If I think of retiring into the closest corner, he is there before me. We often meet and jostle and snarl at each other; but sometimes (would you believe it?) I lose all my suspicion, and am disposed to treat him as an intimate friend. This inconsistency of mine I believe greatly encourages him, for I verily believe he would be ashamed and afraid to be seen by me, if I always kept him at a proper distance. However, we both lay such a strong claim to the same dwelling, that I believe the only way of settling the dispute will be (which the Landlord himself has spoken of) to pull down the house over our heads. There seems something disagreeable in this mode of proceeding; but from what I have read in an old book, I form a hope that when things come to this crisis, I shall escape, and my enemy will be crushed in the ruins" (*Letters* [Bull 1869], 307–8).
[26] W, 1:394–95. On the enigmas of the Christian, see also W, 1:251–52; 6:275–76.

know we *want* to read the Bible, or at least we know we *ought* to desire to read it. We know we *want* to pray, or at least we know we *ought* to desire to pray. And yet we don't. Even with our Bibles open and our hands folded, there is no guarantee we are doing what we *want* to or *ought* to be doing. The spiritual disciplines are rather simple, yet we find them dreadfully hard because of this enigma. Our *knowledge* of what is right and our good intentions cannot overcome our sinful *desires* opposed to the Spirit.

Behind our lacking disciplines, behind our spiritual lethargy, behind our ebbing heart numbness, the deepest problem we have is a God-problem. Indwelling sin is nowhere more evident in our lives than when we turn from God, the fountain of living waters, and hew out for ourselves broken cisterns that can hold no water and can provide no spiritual joy (Jer. 2:13). Turning *away* from God and turning *to* creatures for our joy is one perpetual reminder that sin continues to indwell our hearts. "We seem more attached to a few drops of his grace in our fellow-creatures, than to the fullness of grace that is in himself. I think nothing gives me a more striking sense of my depravity than my perverseness and folly in this respect: yet he bears with me, and does me good continually."[27] There it is. The most striking sense of depravity, where we feel it strongest, is in the dehydrated affections that are starved for God. Indwelling sin is never more evident than when we are content to forego communion with Christ (the fountain of special grace) in favor of enjoying the comforts of this world (the drops of common grace).

The Advantages of Indwelling Sin

And yet at a profound level, covered by the sovereignty of God's goodness and held secure in the sufficiency of Christ, Newton could see "benefits" to indwelling sin. Clearly, indwelling sin remains in the Christian life for one important reason: it promotes the ultimate good of the Christian (Rom. 8:28). Newton harbored something of an appreciation for the effects of indwelling sin on the Christian life, and was the subject of one particular letter.

In the letter, Newton begins with the comforting truth that while sin remains in our hearts, it no longer rules us, and more importantly, sin cannot separate us from the love of Christ. "Though sin wars," he wrote,

---

[27] W, 2:155–56.

it shall not reign; and though it breaks our peace, it cannot separate from his love. Nor is it inconsistent with his holiness and perfection, to manifest his favor to such poor defiled creatures, or to admit them to communion with himself; for they are not considered as in themselves, but as one with Jesus, to whom they have fled for refuge, and by whom they live a life of faith.[28]

A Christian may self-identify as the chief of sinners, but indwelling sin is not the chief identity of the Christian. The Christian finds his identity in union to the Chief Shepherd.

Apart from Christ, indwelling sin only angers God; for those in Christ, indwelling sin draws out his compassion. Apart from Christ, the sinful soul will be completely judged; in Christ, the sinful flesh will be completely destroyed. For now, we are his children, supported in the battle against indwelling sin and led toward certain victory. Like a leper's house that must be completely destroyed and rebuilt, so too our vile bodies are incurably contaminated and will one day be completely recreated in the likeness of Christ in the presence of Christ. This ultimate victory in Christ, realized in our own resurrection, brings hope amid the Christian's battle against indwelling sin and magnifies the power of God's influence in our lives.

For Newton, a profound mystery exists in the work of sovereign grace. God could completely remove all the roots of indwelling sin from our hearts in a moment, and yet he chooses not to. Sin remains in the Christian *because* Christ is overruling it, not because sin is stronger than grace.[29] But if the cross of Christ has broken the power of sin, if Christ is stronger than the remaining evil in my heart, how do we explain remaining sin in the Christian life? Newton offers six answers.

First, *indwelling sin remains to make us wonder how such a weak sinner's faith has been sustained.* Indwelling sin should cause us to marvel when we awake each morning with a remaining spark of hope and faith in Jesus. A sinner living with sustained faith and assurance of eternity in the presence of God is the sure mark of grace. This faith-sustaining grace proves the power, wisdom, faithfulness, and love of God toward us. How can it not? Faith survives in the most unlikely of places: *within us!*

The gracious purposes to which the Lord makes the sense and feeling of our depravity subservient, are manifold. Hereby his own power, wisdom,

---

[28] *W*, 1:448–49.
[29] *W*, 1:205–6, 443, 448, 664–66.

faithfulness, and love, are more signally displayed. His power, in maintaining his own work in the midst of so much opposition, is like a spark burning in the water.[30]

The oceanic torrent of evil—the world, the flesh, and the Devil all conspired—cannot extinguish the smallest spark of faith when that spark has been ignited and sustained by God. Indwelling sin provides us with marvelous proof of God's sustaining grace.

Second, *indwelling sin magnifies the extent of redemption.* By experiencing the battle between the Holy Spirit and the flesh in our hearts, we taste the incredible accomplishment of what Christ defeated at the cross. Indwelling sin affords us the firsthand experience of sin's potency, thereby magnifying the work of Christ's power in its defeat. Only a powerful Savior could defeat evil this stubborn and strong.[31]

Third, *indwelling sin humbles us in our awareness of its presence.* If God must save us and preserve us to the end, the final work is all due to him. He gets the glory. If a sailor escapes with his life in a storm on the open sea, he will be grateful but soon forget his deliverance, Newton writes (no doubt looking back to the storm that nearly took his life). But even more permanently thankful will be the sailor who escapes storm after storm, swell after swell, near-death experience after near-death experience, and then after such an odyssey finally finds his way to safe harbor. The Christian is the second sailor, and the waves and the billows are the swells of indwelling sin that rock our lives and conscript us to daily battle. The Christian is safe on the journey home, but not arrogantly safe—properly humbled, we can say. Moreover,

> whoever is truly humbled will not be easily angry, will not be positive and rash, will be compassionate and tender to the infirmities of his fellow-sinners, knowing, that, if there be a difference, it is grace that has made it, and that he has the seeds of every evil in his own heart; and, under all trials and afflictions, he will look to the hand of the Lord, and lay his mouth in the dust, acknowledging that he suffers much less than his iniquities have deserved. These are some of the advantages and good fruits which the Lord enables us to obtain from that bitter root, indwelling sin.[32]

Indwelling sin makes us humble friends.

[30] W, 1:449–50.
[31] Letters (Jones), 31.
[32] W, 1:452–53.

Ezekiel 16:62–63, says Newton, proves that our sense of sinfulness should endure even after our full and sufficient personal atonement: "I will establish my covenant with you, and you shall know that I am the LORD, that you may remember and be confounded, and never open your mouth again because of your shame, *when I atone for you for all that you have done,* declares the Lord GOD." The reminder of our preatonement sin confounds us by grace, and we stop comparing ourselves to others. Or to use Paul's words, "Do nothing from selfish ambition or conceit, but in humility count others more significant than yourselves" (Phil. 2:3). Paul and Newton preach the same point. In Newton's mind, a deep awareness of our own sin-filled insignificance comes from a humble awareness of both our preatonement sins and our ongoing indwelling sin.

This real and tangible perception of our own indwelling sin explains the varying degrees of Christian maturity in the world. "It is chiefly by this frame of mind," Newton writes about feeling the weight of sin, "that one Christian is differenced from another; for, though it is an inward feeling, it has very observable outward effects."[33] In other words, the degrees of awareness in relation to indwelling sin explain the varying degrees of Christian maturity. "The tip-top Christians do not say, 'behold I am perfect,' but, 'behold I am vile.'"[34] In the mature Christian *more aware* of his sin (in private) there will be found an authenticity to his humility (in public) that cannot be faked by those who are *less aware* of indwelling evil. A deep sense of indwelling sin is essential to humble living.

Fourth, *indwelling sin magnifies Christ's sovereignty.*

> The righteous are said to be *scarcely saved* (1 Pet. 4:18), not with respect to the certainty of the event, for the purpose of God in their favor cannot be disappointed, but in respect of their own apprehensions, and the great difficulties they are brought through. But when, after a long experience of their own deceitful hearts, after repeated proofs of their weakness, willfulness, ingratitude, and insensibility, they find that none of these things can separate them from the love of God in Christ, Jesus becomes more and more precious to their souls.[35]

And so, if the righteous are "scarcely saved," their salvation is owing to Christ's magnificent power, not to the sufficiency of the Christian. "In a

---

[33] W, 1:452.
[34] *Letters* (Coffin), 162–63.
[35] W, 1:450–51.

word, some of the clearest proofs they have had of his excellence, have been occasioned by the mortifying proofs they have had of their own vileness. They would not have known so much of him, if they had not known so much of themselves."[36]

> Hereby Christ is made more precious to us when our insurmountable evils encompass us about like bees—when we see them more in number than the hairs of our head; then, and then only, we are properly apprized both of the exceeding value and the absolute necessity of that better righteousness than our own, whereon our hope is founded.[37]

This is a perpetual theme in Newton's writings. The more aware we are of indwelling sin and its vile nature, the more precious and beautiful Christ grows. "The repeated experience we have of the deceitfulness of our own hearts, is a means which the Lord employs to make us willing debtors to his free grace, and teach us to live more entirely upon Jesus. He is our peace, our strength, our righteousness, our all in all."[38] If our awareness of indwelling sin humbles us and makes our sovereign Christ more precious to us, we are safe.[39]

Fifth, *indwelling sin humbles all our attempts at charity*. Newton was convinced Romans 7 was a realistic and normative picture of the struggles in the Christian life. When we seek to do good, evil lies close at hand to thwart our attempts (Rom. 7:21). No act of love or obedience is free from the sludge of self and sin. And therefore Christ is honored by our broken and contrite hearts (Ps. 51:17).

Finally, *indwelling sin sets our hopes off this world*. God would never allow sin to remain inside his children if he did not purpose to ultimately defeat its presence.[40] Which is to say, our indwelling sin causes us to cherish the forthcoming day when it will be removed forever. The sense of our indwelling sin now entices our anticipation for the day we see Jesus, the day when every evil and every imperfection and every hindrance to full joy in Christ—every desire we have for sin—will be exterminated from our hearts. With the eradication of indwelling sin will come a full possession of eternal happiness to perfectly reflect the

[36] W, 1:451.
[37] *Letters* (Jones), 32.
[38] W, 6:51–52.
[39] W, 6:138.
[40] W, 1:205–6.

riches of God's love for us and the sufficient work of Jesus. We will live in a curse-less creation, all will be made new, and all things will once again be freed from sin.[41] But for now, indwelling sin is what sets our hope on this future day, prevents us from storing up treasures on earth, readies us for death, and keeps us in eager anticipation of our "glorious liberty" to come.[42]

This cannot be stressed enough: these so-called "benefits" of indwelling sin are never an excuse for sinning. Sin is our mortal enemy, sin killed our Savior, and mortifying indwelling sin is the daily work of the Spirit in our lives now. God ever "abhors pride and self-importance," and he has committed in mercy to "pound them as in a mortar, to beat it out of them, or to prevent its growth."[43] And yet even within the battle to purge his children from all evil, evil plays a role. For now we in our flesh harbor sin—an enemy, a viper of lingering enmity against God that eludes our mortifying efforts by the cunning of a snake, and the shifting shape of a mythological sea creature.

When Paul said that all things work together for our good, he meant it, all the way down to the core of our indwelling sin (Rom. 8:28).

> The evils of which we mutually complain, are the effects of a fallen nature; and though we feel them, if the Lord gives us grace to be humbled for them, if they make us more vile in our own eyes, and make Jesus more precious to our hearts, they shall not hurt us, but rather, we may rank them among the all things that shall work for our good.[44]

Indeed, the Lord who could make us as holy as angels in a moment "is rather pleased to accomplish our deliverance gradually, and we may be sure it is for wise and gracious ends, and because he knows how, and designs to overrule this remaining evil to the advancement of his glory."[45] This is a profound reality in the Christian life: "We serve a gracious Master, who knows how to over-rule even our mistakes to his glory and our own advantage."[46] We remain watchful over ourselves, but confident in him.

---

[41] *W*, 1:334.
[42] *W*, 1:443–44.
[43] *Letters* (Bull 1869), 377.
[44] *W*, 6:138.
[45] *Letters* (Jones), 30–31.
[46] *W*, 2:74. See also *Letters* (Bull 1869), 92.

Complaints and Assurances

Throughout his ministry, Newton received stacks of letters from depressed friends who were deeply aware of indwelling sin, dissatisfied with a lack of holiness, and battling fits of depression compounded by unbelief and hard thoughts about God. "We cannot shake off our natural unbelief," Newton wrote to one such woman who was overwhelmed with her sin.

> What you complain of in yourself, comprises the best marks of grace I can offer. A sense of unworthiness and weakness, joined with a hope in the Savior, constitutes the character of a Christian in this world. But you want the witness of the Spirit. What do you mean by this? Is it a whisper or a voice from heaven, to encourage you to believe that you may venture to hope that the promises of God are true, that he means what he says, and is able to make his word good? Your eyes are opened, you are weary of sin, you love the way of salvation yourself, and love to point it out to others, you are devoted to God, to his cause and people. It was not so with you once. Either you have somewhere stolen these blessings, or you have received them from the Holy Spirit."[47]

By magnifying the initiating grace of God in the Christian life, and by rooting every hope of the Christian life in Jesus Christ, Newton helped his friends look honestly and realistically at their remaining evil and besetting sins *without* feeding their personal condemnation. I will say more about perseverance in a later chapter, but here it is important to note the pastoral skill of Newton. His confidence in the all-sufficient Savior is the key that frees him to dive deep into the evils of his own heart and not lose his mind.

By engaging in such Christ-centered pastoral care, Newton could truly encourage a Christian who felt the deep weight of sinfulness and the emptiness of self-righteousness, without minimizing the reality of the sin or ignoring Christ himself. Only a high view of Christ's all-sufficiency makes this possible. To feel the weight of sin is a sure mark of God acting upon the soul, because apart from the Holy Spirit we are numb to the gangrene sin in our lifeless hearts. As reborn creatures, we are given new eyes to truly perceive the dreadful darkness of sin that remains. By discovering our personal sin, we feel the weight of sin and experience the sorrow of sin. To feel this pinch of indwelling sin is not disqualification from God;

---

[47] *Letters* (Bull 1869), 388.

rather it's a gift from God, an evidence of his work, and an essential piece of maturity in the Christian life.

Depraved but Not Discouraged

Indwelling sin becomes for Newton the daily provoking reminder for us all to believe that Jesus Christ alone is our "wisdom from God, righteousness and sanctification and redemption," and in becoming all these things for us, he is our only boast (1 Cor. 1:30–31).

> Humbled I ought to be, to find I am so totally depraved; but not discouraged, since Jesus is appointed to me of God, wisdom, righteousness, sanctification, and redemption; and since I find that, in the midst of all this darkness and deadness, he keeps alive the principle of grace which he has implanted in my heart.[48]

Christian growth is never measured by a Christian's satisfaction in himself. On this point Newton often returns to the testimony of the apostle Paul.

> The evils which you complain of are inseparable from our fallen nature—you never will be free from them in this world. Paul felt them no less than you, perhaps more, because he was more advanced in grace. They ought to humble us, but nothing need break our peace, which has not the consent of the will. Why should you confess to the Lord that you are a poor helpless unworthy sinner if you did not feel yourself to be one![49]

Our humbling experience of sin is a mark of maturity. To be humbled by sin is to be marked by grace. Christian holiness is not the eradication of the sin nature, at least not on this side of eternity.

According to God's wise plan, and for his own glorification, indwelling sin will not be eradicated from the Christian's life until the resurrection. For now, we remain at war with the sinful nature, like the apostle Paul (Rom. 7:7–25; Gal. 5:17). If we measure progress by the absence of indwelling sin, we will be endlessly frustrated and depressed. The reality is that indwelling sin

> will be universally and always felt during our present state. It insinuates into, and mixes with all our thoughts, and all our actions. It is inseparable

---

[48] *W*, 1:259.
[49] *Letters* (Coffin), 56.

from us, as the shadow from our bodies when the sun shines upon us. The holiness of a sinner does not consist in a deliverance *from it*, but in being sensible *of it*, striving *against it*, and being humbled *under it*, and taking occasion from thence to admire our Savior, and rejoice in him as our complete righteousness and sanctification.[50]

"But if you will look for a holiness that shall leave no room for the workings of corruption and temptation; you look for what God has nowhere promised, and for what is utterly inconsistent with our present state."[51]

In another place Newton wrote to a pastor who could not believe God would use such a sinner as himself. Such self-doubt was a trespass against the all-sufficiency of Christ, Newton responded. "You say, you find it hard to believe it compatible with the divine purity to embrace or employ such a monster as yourself. You express not only a low opinion of yourself, which is right, but too low an opinion of the person, work, and promises of the Redeemer; which is certainly wrong."[52] Yes, there are monsters in the heart of a man, as there are monsters under the surface of the ocean, but there is a line we must never cross, and the line is crossed when indwelling sin clouds the Savior from our eyes. Newton dealt with this time after time with his friends, and it's an enduring lesson for anyone who takes personal sin seriously.

> Blessed be God, amidst so many causes of mourning in myself, it is still my duty and my privilege to rejoice in the Lord; in him I have righteousness and strength, pardon and peace. I have sinned—I sin continually—but Christ has died, and forever lives, as my Redeemer, Priest, Advocate, and King. And though my transgressions and my enemies, are very many and very prevalent, the Lord in whom I trust is more and mightier than all that is against me.[53]

We should take sin seriously and readily admit of the monster we find

---

[50] *Letters* (Coffin), 171.

[51] *W*, 6:177.

[52] *W*, 6:185. On this Newton letter, Timothy Keller said, "Don't you see there's an awful lot of moral reformation which does not have Jesus at the heart? It's willpower, but it's a kind of willpower that actually keeps Jesus away and puts you more deeply locked into the grip of the flesh. Self-control is not something you can do for yourself. Running the Boston Marathon in order to overcome your low self-esteem so you can get control over your substance abuse is self-control for yourself. In the end, you're giving yourself a new master: your pride. You got rid of one little bondage to move into a far worse bondage, a more spiritual one, and a more subtle one. Self-control is not something you do for yourself. Indeed, self-control only comes when we want something more than the self" (sermon, "Self-Control, Part 2" [April 15, 1990]). In a sermon in the next year, Keller quoted this line from Newton and said, "If God cannot work with you, that means your sins have more glory, more weight, than the work of the Redeemer" (sermon, "The Marks of the Spirit" [July 7, 1991]).

[53] *Letters* (Jones), 21–22.

roaming the yet half-conquered land of our hearts. But sin should never consume our focus at the expense of our confidence in the power and sufficiency of Christ. There is little danger in thinking lowly of ourselves. The ever-present danger faced by the Christian is thinking too lowly of Christ. Christ is our identity, not indwelling sin.

The Infallible Physician

With beautifully edifying pastoral care, Newton pointed his still-sinful flock to the all-sufficient Christ. He showed that our standing before God cannot rest on our own sinlessness, but must rest upon Christ's sinlessness. In this confidence, Newton is free to speak frankly about the ugliness of indwelling sin and its effects and consequences. His brilliantly balanced pastoral technique brings health and hope to the Christian life. *To not feel* the sting of sin is a form of sickness, a deadness, a leprosy of the soul.[54] But *to feel* the sting of sin is a mark of health, a sign of life, and a necessary experience if we are to appreciate the sin-conquering work of Christ. "In ourselves we are all darkness, confusion, and misery; but in him there is a sufficiency of wisdom, grace, and peace suited to all our wants. May we ever behold his glory in the glass of the Gospel, 'till we are changed into the same image from glory to glory by the Spirit.'"[55] Under this sense of our sin, Christ is our hope.

Christ is made our hope as we *feel* our sins. In Newton's mind, our eternal security and unconditional acceptance before God in Christ (in justification) do not prohibit God from experiencing genuine grief by our sins. God *is* grieved over the sin of his children, and he chooses sometimes to respond to our sins by hiding his face from us. God is not grieved that indwelling sin remains in us, as a father does not lament the weak muscles of his infant. But God is grieved (like any father) when the child he loves *willfully* disobeys him. In response to our *willful sins*, God is pained, and he will often choose, for a time, to send into our lives dark clouds that hide his face and "suspend his influence" in our communion with him (Psalm 51; Eph. 4:30). Our justification remains untouched. But the lack of our experienced communion with him and the drought of our joys and affections are intended to expose our weaknesses.

In these experiences we *feel* our sin again, and by them we *feel* our need

---

[54] *Letters* (Campbell), 24.
[55] *Letters* (Clunie), 185; *Letters* (Bull 1869), 388.

for the delivering power of Christ again. These experiences are meant to humble and benefit us, ultimately building our assurance in Christ rather than destroying us, and we should never lose heart in the darkness. "For sin the Lord will often hide his face and permit dark clouds to hang over us. Yet we must not give way. We cannot recover ourselves but by believing." But God is genuinely grieved by our willful sins, a profoundly important reality in the Christian life well captured by Puritan Thomas Watson: "The sins of God's own children go nearer to his heart."[56]

And so we never shrug our shoulders at sin. "Dread whatever might grieve the Spirit of God." The job of the sin-sick Christian is to repent and turn from sin and press into Christ for continued healing. In him we find our *Infallible Physician* (a favorite name Newton applied to Christ), for our *sin-sick souls* (a common title he applied to himself).

> There is but one Physician
> Can cure a sin-sick soul![57]

And so we come.

> Physician of my sin-sick soul,
> To thee I bring my case;
> My raging malady control,
> And heal me by thy grace.[58]

"It is my part to commit myself to him as the Physician of sin-sick souls, not to prescribe to him how he shall treat me. To begin, carry on, and perfect the cure, is his part."[59] Newton was the chief of sinners; Christ is the only Infallible Physician for sin-sick souls. In his cross and resurrection, Christ has taken our sin-sick hearts under his care, and he will not finish until the cure is complete (Phil. 1:6).

Christ's all-sufficient care gives the Christian perfect freedom and honesty to face his or her sins, to confess them genuinely, and to rejoice in hope.[60] The progressive cure for our maladies is looking to Christ's glory as

[56] *W*, 2:598; 3:625; 6:322, 467; *365 Days with Newton*, 69, 221, 326; Thomas Watson, *The Ten Commandments* (Edinburgh: Banner of Truth, 1967), 134.

[57] *W*, 3:375.

[58] *W*, 3:397.

[59] *W*, 1:681.

[60] *Letters* (Taylor), 206. Newton: "Satan knows, that if he can keep us from confession, our wounds will rankle (Ps. 32:3–5)" (*W*, 2:49).

we endure the proper medications of necessary pain and trials, the bitter circumstances that make us whiny patients.[61] Yet Christ is always on call, his patience is infinite, and he bears with our complaints as he works out our spiritual health.[62] Only in him do sinners find healing.

> The more sick I am, the more need I have to apply to such a great, compassionate, infallible physician. I cannot heal myself, and why should I wish I could, when he has undertaken my case. Depend upon it, our hearts are all alike. To know that they are deceitful and desperately wicked, and to look to Jesus for mercy, help, and salvation, are, I think, the greatest attainments we can rise to in this imperfect state.[63]

And so these two convictions stand as marvelous evidences of grace: an awareness of our heart's depravity and an awareness of our Physician's infallibility. "The sum of my complaints amounts but to this—that I am a sick sinner, diseased in every part; but then, if he who is the Infallible Physician has undertaken my case, I shall not die but live, and declare the works of the Lord."[64]

When it comes to the deeply entrenched sin in our hearts, we can complain of sin maladies all day long—"Our *all* is little, our *best* is defiled."[65] But as Newton grew more and more aware of his own sin and the evil that debased his best service, he was careful not to take his eyes off Christ. "I could go on complaining," Newton wrote a friend, "but I check myself. I am vile indeed, but Jesus is full of grace and truth. He leads and guides, he feeds and guards, he restores and heals. He is an all-sufficient Savior."[66] Under the care of such an all-sufficient Christ, the chief of sinners does not despair, but presses on toward holiness.

---

[61] Newton: "The Lord is an infallible physician; you shall not suffer more than he sees needful, nor I trust suffer in vain. Were health at all times and in all respects best for those who fear him, they would not feel a moment's illness. But the promise of strength according to the day, and that all things shall work together for good, may make us easy. He prescribes all our afflictions, in number, weight, and measure, and season, exactly according to what our case requires" (*Letters* [Coffin], 15).

[62] *W*, 1:257–58.

[63] *Letters* (Coffin), 37.

[64] *Letters* (Campbell), 32.

[65] *Letters* (Taylor), 50.

[66] *Letters* (Clunie), 84.

CHAPTER 6

CHRIST-CENTERED HOLINESS

While at sea, and before his conversion, John Newton began reading a spiritual classic, *The Imitation of Christ* by Thomas à Kempis (c. 1380–1471).[1] When or where he got a copy is not clear, but the book was with him on the fateful journey where he nearly died at sea on the battered *Greyhound*. How far into the book he read is equally unclear, but at some point Newton made the decision to shut the book and to put off religious thoughts. The next day his ship nearly sank in the Atlantic Ocean.

Whatever role the book had on Newton's spiritual awakening and eventual conversion is hard to discern, but it is easy to see the importance of Christ's example for the Christian life in Newton's writings. Christ is our *victor*, Christ is our *life*, and Christ is also our *example*—this is the Christian life in 3-D, three dimensions held together by the person, life, and work of Christ. In the Christ of the Gospels, the Christ to whom the Christian is united, we find every provision for every situation in the Christian's life: "a balm for every grief, an amends for every loss, a motive for every duty, a restraint from every evil, a pattern for every thing which he is called to do or suffer, and a principle sufficient to constitute the actions of every day, even in common life, acts of religion."[2] For Newton, the Christian life, in

---

[1] Aitken, 72–73.
[2] W, 1:669.

all its motives and patterns and comforts, is wholly Christocentric. Christ is always the Christian's *victory, life,* and *example.*

In Step with Christ

As our moral example, the life of Jesus patterns for us every virtuous behavior. Especially in the very depths of suffering and in the experience of pain and disappointment in this life, we look to him and follow his lead (1 Pet. 2:21). The sudden appearance of Christ in history inaugurates new covenant godliness training, as Paul explains in Titus 2:11–14:

> For the grace of God has appeared [that is, Christ has appeared (see 3:4)], bringing salvation for all people, training us to renounce ungodliness and worldly passions, and to live self-controlled, upright, and godly lives in the present age, waiting for our blessed hope, the appearing of the glory of our great God and Savior Jesus Christ, who gave himself for us to redeem us from all lawlessness and to purify for himself a people for his own possession who are zealous for good works.

Newton treasures this passage as "an epitome of the whole faith, practice, and hope of a Christian."[3]

In the second appearance of Christ (yet to come) we find daily motivation to keep our focus on Jesus now. God's plan of salvation doesn't end with our freedom from hell, but presses us on, training us as disciples who think and act and speak like Christ. Putting these together, we see that Christ's coming and Christ's return are bookends around a gathering of redeemed sinners who flourish in Christ-centered holiness. In one hymn, Newton wrote,

> Since the Savior I have known
> My rules are all reduc'd to one,

---

[3] *Letters* (Coffin), 215. Newton: "To have a real conviction of our sin and unworthiness; to know that Jesus is the all-sufficient Savior, and that there is no other; to set him before us as our Shepherd, Advocate, and Master; to place our hope upon him alone; to live to him who lived and died for us; to wait in his appointed means for the consolations of his Spirit; to walk in his steps, and copy his character; and to be daily longing for the period of our warfare, that we may see him as he is. All may be reduced to these heads: or the whole is better expressed in the apostle's summaries, Titus, 2:11–14, and 3:3–8. But, though the lessons are brief, it is a great thing to attain any good measure of proficiency in them; yea, the more we advance, the more we shall be sensible how far we fall short of their full import" (*W*, 6:211). "Though there is a height, a breadth, a length, and a depth, in this mystery of redeeming love, exceeding the comprehension of all finite minds; yet the great and leading principles which are necessary for the support and comfort of our souls, may be summed up in a very few words. Such a summary we are favored with in Titus 2:11–14; where the whole of salvation, all that is needful to be known, experienced, practiced, and hoped for, is comprised within the compass of four verses" (*W*, 1:680).

To keep my Lord, by faith, in view;
This strength supplies, and motives too.[4]

In Newton's mind the Christian life of obedience can be simplified to one rule: follow Christ. It's a rule Newton develops around two driving realities.

First, *Christ is our pattern because he's the perfect image of God in human form*. In biblical language, the perfect picture of God's intention for humanity in Psalm 8 is left unfulfilled until the appearance of Jesus Christ (1 Cor. 15:27; Eph. 1:20–23; Heb. 2:6–8). The incarnation becomes key for Newton.[5] Christ could have entered our world as a morally perfect angel, but by taking on flesh he shares our nature and offers what no angel could: a perfect model of *human* godliness. And although sinfully twisted and fallen, every human retains something of the *imago Dei*, with Jesus alone as the *perfect* image of God (Col. 1:15).[6] By taking on our human nature, Jesus becomes our concrete, touchable, enfleshed expression of God's highest purposes for human morality. Thus, as seventeenth-century mathematician Blaise Pascal expressed it, "Not only do we know God by Jesus Christ alone, but we know ourselves only by Jesus Christ."[7] Christ reveals God's truest and highest purposes for humanity. He is the second Adam, the first faithful expression of godliness, the first truly *human* human. Christ now serves as the pattern for this new humanity called the church (2 Cor. 3:18). In Christ we find true humanity reflected and modeled, in him we find our moral identity, and in him we discover God's moral intentions for humanity. In other words, in Christ we find our ideal selves and catch a glimpse of our future perfected selves.

Second, *Christ is our pattern because he's our forerunner* (Heb. 4:14; 6:20; 8:1; 9:24). Our sins excluded us from God's kingdom, but Christ has purchased and taken possession of glory in our name.

> Hence he is styled their [believers'] forerunner, because, by virtue of their relation to him, and their interest in him, they shall surely follow him. This is the encouragement of believers. He is the head of his body the church: and though the church, while in this world, is in a suffering perilous state; yet as the body of a man is not in danger of drowning while

---

[4] *W*, 3:455.
[5] *W*, 4:58.
[6] John Newton, *365 Days with Newton*, ed. Marylynn Rouse (Leominster, UK: Day One, 2006), 26.
[7] Blaise Pascal, *Thoughts, Letters, and Minor Works*, trans. Charles W. Eliot, The Harvard Classics (New York: P. F. Collier & Son, 1910), 177.

his head is out of the water, so our forerunner and head being in heaven
on their behalf, he will assuredly draw all his living members to himself.[8]

Christ is our safety, and he is our magnet, drawing us to himself, pulling
us along a path marked out with his own feet, into a heaven opened to us
by his crushed body.

Following the Forerunner

As we follow our forerunner, our eyes and our directions are firmly fixed on
the end. If we become too intent upon the ground for the next footprint to
follow, and not focused upward to where Christ is (Col. 3:1), then we stumble and sputter and stall in discouragement on the path. There is a *pathway*
to be followed in the Christian life because there is an *end* to the Christian.
By this emphasis, Newton protects the Christian from interpreting Christ's
life as nothing more than a situation-to-situation moral model to be copied. The footsteps of Christ mark out a pathway *leading into his presence.*

We walk on the straight and narrow pathway our Lord marked with his
feet, even when it leads through the most difficult pain and suffering. His
joy is our strength. Paradoxically, the only way to *look like Christ* is to *walk
behind Christ*, and to *walk behind Christ* is to *suffer with Christ.* "Undoubtedly,
so far as we are partakers in the doctrine of his sufferings, and have real
fellowship with him in his death, we shall resemble him."[9] For Newton,
the only way to reflect Christ is to suffer like Christ (Phil. 3:10; Col. 1:24;
1 Pet. 4:19).

In a real sense, we follow Christ by pursuing Christ. To model our lives
after Christ presupposes a personal relationship with him. In this relationship we imitate Christ, our all-sufficient Savior, at every step of the Christian life. His life is the glorious example of true gospel-simple obedience
and sincere holiness. And when this obedience seems too hard, Jesus says
to us: "Take *me* for your example: I require nothing of you but what I have
performed before you, and on your account; in the path I mark out for you,
you may perceive my own footsteps all the way."[10] Jesus is unlike the Pharisees, who command an obedience they cannot model. Jesus is the perfect
image of God, modeling obedience for us in a variety of circumstances so

---

[8] W, 4:299. See also *Letters* (Bull 1847), 108.
[9] W, 4:279; see also 3:608–10.
[10] W, 2:485.

we may learn from him. If you find it hard to live under the pushback of your Christian life, look to Christ and imitate his constancy (Heb. 12:3). Compare the opposition he lived with and your own opposition. Admire his meekness and his love for his enemies. Learn from Jesus, who did not live to please himself (Rom. 15:3), who did not take the safe and easy angle on anything, but was driven by the glory of God and full obedience to his will (gospel simplicity). Look to Jesus, who in the midst of his darkest hour asked, "Shall I not drink the cup that the Father has given me?" (John 18:11). No jot of obedience called for in the Christian life has escaped the obedience of Christ.

Glory Exemplified

Now, if we return to Newton's core theological priority in the Christian life, we see quickly why Jesus is far more than our model of godliness. All of Christ's words, thoughts, and actions are given to us to behold the glory of God shining in him *before* they are given to us as our personal example to emulate. The life of Christ is divine glory, and as we behold the glory of his life, we ourselves are changed (2 Cor. 3:18). Christ's glory is the operating power in our Christian holiness. "It is thus by looking to Jesus, that the believer is enlightened and strengthened, and grows in grace and sanctification."[11] "To behold the glory and the love of Jesus is the only effectual way to participate of his image."[12] In other words, gospel holiness is possible only to those who behold the glory of Christ in disciplined and expectant Bible reading. This protects sanctification from any misunderstanding about whether our maturity is a passive or active process. Newton is clear: we *become* by *beholding*. "By beholding we are gradually formed into the resemblance of him whom we see, admire, and love."[13]

Here's the point for Newton: "If Christ died, rose from the dead, and entered into glory, only to assure us 'that the practice of virtue is the duty and dignity of man, and at all events his safest and wisest course'; I may venture to say, that he died and rose in vain."[14] It was not in vain, however, because in his atonement Christ achieved far beyond a respectable model of religious duty and virtue. Every act, every word, and every moral example we

---

[11] *W*, 2:485–87.
[12] *W*, 2:193.
[13] *W*, 2:487.
[14] *W*, 6:429.

see in Christ is a substitutionary revelation of glory, and every revelation of his glory, when beheld by the Christian, transforms us incrementally.

Beauty-Driven Duty

In other words, it's the beauty *in Christ* that fuels true obedience *in us*. Newton expresses this truth in one hymn:

> Our pleasure and our duty,
>   Though opposite before,
> Since we have seen his beauty,
>   Are join'd to part no more:
> It is our highest pleasure,
>   No less than duty's call,
> To love him beyond measure,
>   And serve him with our all.[15]

Quoting this hymn in a sermon, Timothy Keller followed it with a question: "What is it that has taken the whipsaw out of John Newton's life from between *pleasure* and *duty* and has brought them together?" Answer: "A beauty. In other words, the gospel doesn't primarily give you a duty; it gives you a beauty,"[16] a beauty, without which, "your duty will be impossible."[17] In other words, long-term Christian obedience will fail if not fueled by the glorious beauty of Christ in the gospel. Apart from this revelation of glory, the Christian life has no combustion. The tension leaves a tortured life, pitting *right duty* over and against *selfish pleasures*, one pulling *left* and one pulling *right*. The beauty of Christ brings the two into harmony, rightly aligning into one pursuit our joy in him and our obedience to him.

A Love to Imitate

Here's how this beauty-to-duty harmony works out in one particular area. It's the beauty of Christ that softens us to Christlike duty, like caring for

---

[15] *W*, 3:572.

[16] Timothy Keller, sermon, "Prayer" (March 2, 2003).

[17] Timothy Keller, sermon, "The Patience of Jesus" (May 17, 1998). In an earlier sermon, Keller quoted Newton's hymn and said, "Our pleasure and our duty used to be opposite. In other words, when I thought God was just this kind of tyrant and I had to obey him and maybe I'd get to heaven if I obeyed him, I knew I could either have fun (that's pleasure) or I could go ahead and obey him. I've had many people say, 'I'd like to become a Christian someday, but I'd like to have some fun first.' Our pleasure and our duty were opposite before, but when you have seen his beauty, they're joined to part no more" (sermon, "The Parable of the Farmer" [August 21, 1994]).

others. "None can truly love it but those who have tasted it," writes Newton. "When your hearts feel the comforts of God's pardoning love, you will delight to imitate him. When you can truly rejoice that he has freely forgiven you that immense debt, which is expressed by ten thousand talents, you will have no desire to take your fellow-servant by the throat for a few pence" (Matt. 18:21–35). A daily renewed sense of Christ's beauty softens our heart and erodes angry and resentful thoughts against those who have offended us. When the love of Christ rules our hearts, we can put on "compassionate hearts, kindness, humility, meekness, and patience" (Col. 3:12–14). "If you find this practice difficult," Newton writes, "it is owing partly to the remaining depravity of your nature, and partly because you have had but a faint sense of his mercy. Pray for a more powerful manifestation of it, and you will do better; mercy will be your delight." Or to say this in another way, it's impossible to *love like Christ* until we are first *loved by Christ* (1 John 4:19).[18] Newton understood the imitation of Christ's love to be an outward display of an inner receiving of Christ's love. Christ's love must first be received before Christ's example of love can be pursued. As we will see later, it's impossible to follow Christ if we fail to display Christlikeness (chap. 11).

By trusting in Christ, we behold his blood-spilled love. We love Christ, and in loving him we seek to become what we love. By beholding what is true, good, and beautiful in Christ, we cannot but hate what is false, twisted, and ugly in contradiction to him. As our love and appreciation for Christ reorient our affections, we begin to take on characteristics of the Savior. In Christ we are *counted righteous* before God (justification); but in Christ we are also *made righteous* (sanctification). The "love of righteousness is implanted in [believers'] hearts; they believe what the Lord says, they heartily strive to obey his commands, to avoid what he forbids; they place their happiness in his favor, and in doing his will."[19]

The entire Christian life finds its orbit around the sun of Christ: his perfect person, his perfect works, and his perfect substitutionary death for us. The Christian is drawn toward Christ and his attractive beauty, and a sure mark of health is an appetite for more of Christ. The Christian is attracted to books about Christ and sermons about Christ and songs about Christ. Duty and pleasure merge. Simultaneously, the world's foolish vanities become like child's toys in the light of Christ. All of this works to produce a

[18] W, 2:548–49.
[19] W, 6:318.

Christian who thinks like Christ (1 Cor. 2:16; Phil. 2:5). In Christ we find our true selves and we unearth the evils that remain in our selfish lives: our impatience, our pride, our envy, our anger, our lust, and our malice. Those sins grieve us because they grieve our Savior. In those remaining areas of sin we run *to* the Savior, not *away* from him. He exposes our sins, but then he covers them.[20]

Loving Eternal Souls

And yet when it comes to people, we are prone to playing favorites. To make the point, Newton contrasted the lot of a newborn prince and a pauper. At the birth of a prince, the palace erupts in a celebration, attracting wealthy gifts to match the prestige and honor of the occasion. Meanwhile, in the dumpy city, an impoverished mother gives birth to a little boy, an event marked with no pomp, very little celebration, and no public notoriety. Yet the births of the prince and the pauper are equally priceless for a simple and profound reason: both children are immortal souls. "When a child is born, a new existence begins which will never end." Therefore, "the present life of the children before you is precarious, but their souls are, by God's constitution and appointment, immortal."[21]

Rich or poor, perfect or fallen, humans remain the capstone of God's creation. At our most culturally refined levels, we can make art and music and poetry. And yet for all the beauty that reveals our privileges in God's creation, the unredeemed soul is stone-cold dead. Newton writes:

What the poet ascribes to Beelzebub is true of man; he still retains some marks of his pristine greatness; he is majestic though in ruins; he is alive as to the concerns of this world, and his attempts and success give indications of his native dignity: the sciences and the fine arts exhibit proofs of his genius and ability: he undertakes to measure the earth, to weigh the air, and almost to number and marshal the stars. What discoveries have been made in geometry, natural history, and chemistry! What powers are displayed in architecture, sculpture, painting, poetry, and music! But, with respect to the concerns of his immortal soul, and the great realities of the unseen world, man, by nature, is dead as a stone. The dead body of Lazarus was not more incapable of performing the functions of common life than we, by nature, are of performing one spiritual act, or even of

[20] W, 6:317–18.
[21] W, 6:512–13.

feeling one spiritual desire; till he, who, by his commanding word, raised
Lazarus from the grave, is pleased, by the power of his Holy Spirit, to raise
us from the death of sin unto a new life of righteousness.[22]

Profoundly majestic, spiritually dead, eternally existing: this was Newton's
understanding of each prince or pauper born into the world, and it significantly influenced how Newton considered his role as a pastor. At times he
struggled to find the right words to express his earnest love for the immortal souls in his church.[23] The eternal soul is a terrible thing to waste, and
Newton was aware of the stakes. He maintained a "just regard to the worth
and danger of immortal souls."[24]

Because the soul is immortal, every soul is priceless.

God, who formed the soul originally for himself, has given it such a vast
capacity, that nothing short of himself can satisfy its desires; and it is
likewise, by its constitution, immortal. This capacity of being exquisitely
happy or miserable, and that for ever, *renders the soul so valuable in the
judgment of its Creator*, that he gave the Son of his love to redeem it from
sin and misery, by his obedience unto death, even the death of the cross.[25]

For Newton, the mere capacity to delight in God for eternity is what gives
the soul its priceless valuation, a value that would demand the beloved
Son's blood.

This soul value frames the pastor's calling. For a pastor,

the end at which he aims, in subordination to the will and glory of God,
is the salvation of souls; and the recovery of one immortal soul to the
favor and image of God, is, and will at length be found, a greater and more
important event, than the deliverance of a whole kingdom from slavery
or temporal ruin.[26]

These are strong words, given Newton's role in abolishing the British slave
trade (alongside William Wilberforce). The high value of freedom from iron
chains is trumped by a freedom from eternal chains.

Privilege, wealth, education, learning, and culture are all powerless to

---

[22] W, 6:507.
[23] W, 6:563.
[24] W, 3:248.
[25] W, 5:196; see also 4:549.
[26] W, 4:161.

convert the immortal soul. The only hope for the prince or the pauper, or for that matter the boy born to a slave, is the gospel of Jesus Christ. "Colleges can never make up the want of the knowledge of Christ."[27] Only in the gloriously revealed Christ do we find the object to satisfy our vast thirst for unending pleasures. In him is our eternal wealth: "For you know the grace of our Lord Jesus Christ, that though he was rich, yet for your sake he became poor, so that you by his poverty might become rich" (2 Cor. 8:9). In Christ's model we find the incredible value and dignity of the human soul, even the poorest human soul.[28]

This "worth and danger" of immortal souls for Newton was perhaps best articulated nearly two centuries later by Anglican C. S. Lewis:

> It is a serious thing to live in a society of possible gods and goddesses, to remember that the dullest and most uninteresting person you can talk to may one day be a creature which, if you saw it now, you would be strongly tempted to worship, or else a horror and a corruption such as you now meet, if at all, only in a nightmare.

Every day we influence others in one of two directions: (1) toward faith in Christ and eternal glory, or (2) toward rejection of Christ and eternal judgment. "It is in the light of these overwhelming possibilities, it is with the awe and the circumspection proper to them, that we should conduct all our dealings with one another, all friendships, all loves, all play, all politics," writes Lewis. "There are no *ordinary* people. You have never talked to a mere mortal. Nations, cultures, arts, civilizations—these are mortal, and their life is to ours as the life of a gnat. But it is immortals whom we joke with, work with, marry, snub, and exploit—immortal horrors or everlasting splendors."[29]

Newton would have agreed, and would have admitted to playing both roles—first in leading others into sin and immortal horrors, and then investing his life in serving souls toward Christ and everlasting splendors. Newton will argue along this line when he addresses controversy (chap. 13). Like Lewis, John Newton was dead serious in the handling of priceless, immortal souls. This did not make Newton indifferent to the physical needs of the poor, any more than it made him indifferent to the physical and

---

[27] *Letters* (Campbell), 158.
[28] *W*, 6:512–13.
[29] C. S. Lewis, *The Weight of Glory: And Other Addresses* (1949; repr., San Francisco: HarperCollins, 2001), 45–46.

emotional suffering of African slaves by the evil British slave trade. In light of eternity, the simple acts of giving food to the hungry, drink to the thirsty, shelter to the stranger, clothes to the naked, care to the sick, and company to the imprisoned are all potential ways to honor Christ (Matt. 25:31–46).

Such acts of physical kindness are patterns taken from Christ's love for humans, body and soul. He healed the paralytic, telling him to sin no more (John 5:1–16). How much more is our love called for when it comes to our brothers and sisters in Christ who "are washed by the same blood, supplied by the same grace, opposed by the same enemies, and have the same heaven in view."[30]

A Universe of Blessings

Our resistance against sin, this holiness, causes us to look back to Christ— the beautiful image of God—to discover God's will for how we reflect God's glory in practical situations. Our failures and sins empty us of self-confidence without driving us to disillusionment. Newton can accomplish all this because his thinking is so rooted in 1 Corinthians 1:28–31, a favorite text of his and a paradigm for gospel holiness.

> God chose what is low and despised in the world, even things that are not, to bring to nothing things that are, so that no human being might boast in the presence of God. And because of him you are in Christ Jesus, who became to us *wisdom from God, righteousness* and *sanctification* and *redemption*, so that, as it is written, "Let the one who boasts, boast in the Lord."

Newton finds the only hope for following Christ's moral model in the *wisdom, righteousness, sanctification,* and *redemption* of Christ. In these four little words are a universe of blessings for the Christian all brought together, in Christ, in one passage (1 Cor. 1:30).

In recent years theologians have debated how these four elements hold together and apply to the Christian. Is each of these four categories *forensic* and *imputed*? Or are they *experiential* and *imparted*? Or a mixture of each? Without detailing the current debate, there's good reason to believe that these four categories mix different applications without diluting the specifics, a position Newton seems to hold. In Christ our spiritual deadness is overcome, our guilt and condemnation before God are removed, our

---

[30] *W*, 1:353.

captivity to sin is broken, our sanctification is made possible (and is em-powered!), and all our hopes for freedom from this fallen world are made certain and secured. All these realities converge in 1 Corinthians 1:30.[31] In the all-inclusive language of Newton,

> Jesus is mine: in him I have wisdom, righteousness, sanctification, and redemption, an interest in all the promises and in all the perfections of God: he will guide me by his counsel, support me by his power, comfort me with his presence, while I am here; and afterwards, when flesh and heart fail, he will receive me to his glory.[32]

Newton is comfortable finding in 1 Corinthians 1:30 both the Christian's new forensic standing before God (justification) and the Christian's empowered spiritual life (sanctification). Christ's righteousness is *imputed* to the Christian, and Christ's power is *imparted* to the Christian.[33] First Corinthians 1:30 throws the door open to all the various blessings and graces of Christ's perfect work for our daily Christian life.

"Though [the believer is] weak in himself," said Newton,

> he is strong in the grace that is in Christ Jesus the Lord, upon whom he relies, as his wisdom, righteousness, sanctification; and expects from him, in due time, a complete redemption from every evil. His faith is not merely speculative, like the cold assent we give to a mathematical truth, nor is it the blind impulse of a warm imagination; but it is the effect of an apprehension of the wisdom, power, and love displayed in the redemp-tion of sinners by Jesus Christ. It is a constraining principle, that works by love, purifies the heart, and overcomes the world, it gives the foretaste and evidence of things invisible to mortal eyes, and, transforming the soul into the resemblance of what it beholds, fills the heart with benevo-lence, gentleness, and patience, and directs every action to the sublimest ends, the glory of God, and the good of mankind.[34]

---

[31] John Piper comments on this passage: "In our union with Christ he becomes wisdom for us in overcom-ing the blinding and deadening *ignorance* that keeps us from seeing the glory of the cross (1 Cor. 1:24). Then he becomes righteousness for us in overcoming our *guilt and condemnation* (Rom. 8:1). Then he becomes sanctification for us in overcoming our *corruption and pollution* (1 Cor. 1:2; Eph. 2:10). Finally, he becomes redemption for us in overcoming, in the resurrection, all *the miseries, pain, futility, and death* of this age (Rom. 8:23). There is no reason to force this text to mean that Christ becomes all these things for us in exactly the same way, namely, by imputation. He may become each of these things for us as each reality requires" (John Piper, *Counted Righteous in Christ: Should We Abandon the Imputation of Christ's Righteousness?* [Wheaton, IL: Crossway, 2002], 86–87).
[32] W, 1:488.
[33] W, 6:239–40.
[34] W, 3:295–96.

Thus, following the perfect pattern of Christ and living out of the all-sufficient vicariousness of Christ are not at odds.

> The life of a Christian is a life of faith in the Son of God. He, undoubtedly, is the greatest Christian who most exemplifies in his own practice what is recorded in the Gospel of the temper, converse, and actions of the holy, the harmless, and undefiled Jesus, and depends the most absolutely upon him, for wisdom, righteousness, sanctification, and redemption.[35]

The successful Christian life can follow the *pattern of Christ* only by the *power of Christ*.

A Riddle and a Race

This all-sufficiency in Christ works the other way around. God's aim in saving us is not to boost our self-esteem or self-evaluation, but to expose our self-sufficiency as a sham. Newton trembled at his own sins and marveled at how he had been loved so much and how he loved so little in return. We are invested with all the mercies of heaven, and what is our daily response? Forgetfulness and spiritual laziness. "Every new day is filled up with new things—new mercies on the Lord's part, new ingratitude on mine."[36] Instead of living in joyful obedience to Christ, we mourn and stumble because of the den of vipers that is our remaining sin. The good we want to do, we fail to do. The evil we don't want to do, we do (Rom. 7:15–20).

Newton finds in Romans 7 a reflection of his Christian experience, something like a mirror "in which," he says, "I often see my face, and a wretched figure I make."[37] "My sins of omission are innumerable," he confesses. Newton laments the darkness in his understanding, the perverseness in his will, the disorders in his affections, and the folly and madness in his imagination. He desires to rejoice in God, but the aim is frustrated daily. In short, he writes, "I am a riddle to myself; a heap of inconsistence."[38] This heap of inconsistency and instability found his hope outside himself in the Christ whose love and holiness are perfect. Why? Very simply, Newton returns to 1 Corinthians 1:30. In our union with him, Christ is our *wisdom from God, righteousness and sanctification and redemption.* "On this rock I build."[39]

---

[35] *Letters* (Jones), 33.
[36] *W*, 6:20.
[37] *Letters* (Ryland), 63.
[38] *W*, 6:98.
[39] *W*, 6:97–98.

The beauty of Christ works in both ways: (1) it empties us of our futile self-sufficiency, and (2) it fills us with the empowering sufficiency of Christ.

> The Gospel, rightly understood and cordially embraced, will inspire the slothful with energy, and the fearful with courage. It will make the miser generous, melt the churl [rude] into kindness, tame the raging tiger in the breast, and, in a word, expand the narrow selfish heart, and fill it with a spirit of love to God, cheerful unreserved obedience to his will, and benevolence to mankind.[40]

Over and over again, Newton labors to show why the successful Christian life hinges on the sufficiency of Christ. The Christian life centers on one rule—one man. Christ is our example and our pattern. He is the measure and the means of all our holiness (Eph. 4:13). We follow in the footsteps of the Savior by the power of him who has completed the race and who now empowers us for the race. Christ is the example we follow, the forerunner we emulate, and the finish line we anticipate.

But all of this remains a little abstract. What does gospel holiness look like as it grows? And what are the daily incremental stages that mark its growth? To these important points of application we turn next. Christ is the Christian life in 3-D.

---

[40] W, 5:199.

CHAPTER 7

THE GROWTH CHART OF
THE CHRISTIAN LIFE

Before he uprooted his pastorate and replanted it in the heart of London's financial district—that is, before he lived near the constant "rumbling of wheels" on busy cobblestone roads, before he elbowed his way through crowded streets from morning to night, and before he inhaled the smoke and soot and smog of the big city—John Newton enjoyed daily walks in the clean air and quiet landscapes of Olney, a village sixty miles north of London. In the country landscape he wandered through fields, by brooks, and along hedgerows, listening to the singing birds and bleating lambs, and enjoyed climbing a small hilltop to stand under the shadow of one old, large, spreading oak tree.[1] When Newton gave up his pastorate in Olney after sixteen years, he lamented parting with these rural luxuries,[2] but he would take the large oak tree and put it in his pocket of metaphors to help picture growth in the Christian life.

The pace of growth and maturity in the Christian life is not like a mushroom; it's like an oak tree. A mushroom sprouts overnight and vanishes just as fast. An oak tree begins from an acorn by sending a deep

---

[1] W, 6:365.
[2] In a letter (February 15, 1777), Newton hinted: "I have expressed my desire of living and dying at Olney. I own [admit] the death of many of my people, the desertion of others, the general deadness and wickedness of the town (the bulk of whom seem sermon proof), and the visible increase of sin and contempt of light amongst us from year to year, have made me of late apprehensive that my work here might be nearly done. But I never said so to anybody out of Olney" (*Letters* [Ryland], 108–9). Newton's first service at St. Mary Woolnoth in London took place on December 19, 1779. For more on his transition out of Olney, see Aitken, 263–70.

taproot straight down into the earth before it begins working its way into the sky. The oak grows slowly, with deep roots to endure droughts, absorb rain, and withstand harsh seasonal changes, and while the tree looks more alive in the summer than in the winter, it's always alive. "The full-grown oak that overtops the wood, spreads its branches wide, and has struck its roots to a proportional depth and extent into the soil, springs from a little acorn," wrote Newton to his friend, eminent writer and philanthropist Hannah More. "Its daily growth, had it been daily watched from its appearance above ground, would have been imperceptible, yet it was always upon the increase. It has known a variety of seasons. It has sustained many a storm, but in time it attained to maturity, and now is likely to stand for ages."[3]

The Stages of Grace Growth

Just as the branches of an old oak on a hill served as a metaphor of Christian growth in Newton's letters to others, the seasons of planted corn in a field illustrated the phases of spiritual growth in a trio of letters under the titles "On Grace in the Blade," "On Grace in the Ear," and "On Grace in the Full Corn."[4] Taken together they form a sixty-five-hundred-word tract on progressive sanctification in the Christian life and are the closest thing we have to Newton's comprehensive vision of growth and development in the stages of the Christian life. The letters focus on the maturity of a *child* who becomes a *teen* and then a *father*. Whether by accident or intent, the movement parallels the stages of spiritual maturity in 1 John 2:12–14.

Like the apostle John's words, Newton's trio of letters features male characters and strikes an autobiographical tone at times. But the letters are not straight autobiography; they set forth three archetypes for distinct stages in Christian maturity. In these three letters Newton brings together many years of pastoral reflections from the close study of his own soul and those around him. The letters describe specific stages, but not in prescriptive, cookie-cutter categories. Newton, the blaspheming sailor and slave-trader-turned-pastor, was fully aware of the unpredicted turns of sovereign grace in an individual's life. His life was anything but normative. But God also works in similar ways to develop Christians in general; and so Newton writes from the outset,

---

[3] *Letters* (Bull 1869), 350–51.
[4] The letters are published in *W*, 1:197–217.

I shall not therefore give you a copy of my own experience, or of that of any individual; but shall endeavor, as clearly as I can, to state what the Scripture teaches us concerning the nature and essentials of a work of grace, so far as it will bear a general application to all those who are the subjects of gracious operations.[5]

With that qualification, Newton gets to work in explaining common stages of Christian maturity.

"On Grace in the Blade" (or, Grace in the Christian Child)

The story begins at conversion. All conversions start with the drawing grace of an all-sufficient Father (John 6:44). We are dead in trespasses and sins, strangers to God, hostile to him and his grace. All of us, "whether wise or ignorant, whether sober or profane, are equally incapable of receiving or approving Divine truths."[6] Every Christian testimony begins with a necessary transformation from spiritual death to new birth by the glorious work of God.

The first experience of the boy is an awakening to spiritual light, however weak. This new light on his soul is the sure mark of God's initiative, and one that promises more light will come in the future—like awakening from a long, dark sleep into the faint dawn. A new light shines, yet a person's awareness of his dark sinfulness will often develop later as he better understands the holiness, majesty, goodness, and truth of the God against whom he has sinned. This understanding will come in due time.

This first stage of grace—grace in the blade—is like a green shoot poking up from the soil. Something has happened. New life has begun. It doesn't matter if your conversion occurs at age eight or eighty, and it doesn't matter if you're naturally smart or dull, a leader or a follower, wealthy or poor; every Christian begins as a spiritual baby. And as spiritual infants we all do foolish things, like attempting to appease God and rest our security in religious and spiritual duties such as Scripture reading and prayer. This self-righteous misunderstanding of salvation must be shown to be empty, and, as we will see, it's a lesson years of personal experience will teach.

Because of the weakness of his faith, our infant Christian will struggle with spiritual insecurity. In reflecting on Newton's point, Timothy Keller explains the two systems of salvation: self-salvation and Christ-salvation.

---

[5] W, 1:197.
[6] W, 1:197.

Baby Christians are people who, though they intellectually believe Christ is their Savior, actually and psychologically and functionally in their day-to-day lives act as if something else is their savior. Radically, they are still insecure. They still really don't believe Jesus loves them. They still don't really believe they're forgiven. In a sense, they still are really trying to earn that forgiveness, and as long as you're in that state, you're still a baby. You'll never get out of babyhood.

In fact, Keller says, "Most Christians stay babies all their lives, and only very few even get out of that."[7]

The only hope of escaping this infancy is to find more stable security in Christ. All Christians have been loved and forgiven in Christ—this truth must rattle our minds and hearts and significantly alter our own self-identity. But security takes time and experience. The toddler will find that his security grows, writes Newton, as

his heart is affected and drawn to Jesus by views of his glory, and of his love to poor sinners; [he] ventures upon his name and promises as his only encouragement to come to a Throne of Grace; waits diligently in the use of all means appointed for the communion and growth of grace; loves the Lord's people, accounts them the excellent of the earth, and delights in their conversation [or fellowship]. He is longing, waiting, and praying, for a share in those blessings which he believes they enjoy, and can be satisfied with nothing less. He is convinced of the power of Jesus to save him; but, through remaining ignorance and legality, the remembrance of sin committed, and the sense of present corruption, he often questions his willingness; and, not knowing the aboundings of grace, and the security of the promises, he fears lest the compassionate Savior should spurn him from his feet.[8]

These are the first wobbly, insecure, baby steps of the Christian. He has so many uncertainties and weaknesses and distractions. Temptations assault, doubts arise, indwelling sin stings. He trusts in false securities, false idols, and false self-righteousness, none of which can support him. He wonders if he is truly qualified to be a child of God, and gets buffeted from various directions. Sometimes he is motivated by selfishness; sometimes he is motivated by God's glory (he thinks). He loves himself, yet sometimes loves others. He is surprised

---

[7] Timothy Keller, sermon, "Principles of Christian Growth: Part 1" (November 28, 1993).
[8] W, 1:200.

by the commotion and unpredictable changes in his heart. "Then he is at his wits' end; thinks his hopes were presumptuous, and his comforts delusions. He wants to feel something that may give him a warrant to trust in the free promises of Christ."[9] Even worse, the infant Christian looks *inside* himself for security and finds nothing to stand on. Insecurities increase, rattle his affections, and stifle his daily desires. What the baby Christian cannot perceive at this point is why and how these trials, these emptyings, these falling downs, are building his precious strength and fortitude.

The Christian life is a training of the intellect and the affections. And those must rise together. Warm affection with spiritual ignorance is an emotional superstition. True spiritual knowledge that fails to warm the affections is hypocritical knowledge. At this early stage there's often more religious affection than spiritual knowledge. The infant Christian attempts to live off his fluctuating affections and as a result finds his tank empty. Later, he will learn to live off truth in the all-sufficiency of the unchanging Christ, and he will see how spiritual knowledge informs and stokes his affections. "The old Christian has more solid, judicious, connected views of the Lord Jesus Christ, and the glories of his person and redeeming love: hence his hope is more established, his dependence more simple, and his peace and strength more abiding and uniform than in the case of a young convert."[10]

And yet the young Christian's life is sweetened with beautiful new growth. His faith is weak and ill-informed, but his heart is genuinely warm. He falls often, but he's learning to walk by holding his Father's hand. And his knowledge is quickly growing. Most important of all,

> the Lord has visited his heart, delivered him from the love of sin, and fixed his desires supremely upon Jesus Christ. The spirit of bondage is gradually departing from him, and the hour of liberty, which he longs for, is approaching, when, by a farther discovery of the glorious Gospel, it shall be given him to know his acceptance, and to rest upon the Lord's finished salvation.[11]

As he moves out of insecurity into Christ-centered security, and as his affections increasingly focus upon Christ, the spiritual infant begins to transition into an adolescent.

---

[9] *W*, 1:201.
[10] *W*, 1:202–3.
[11] *W*, 1:203.

"On Grace in the Ear" (or, Grace in the Christian Adolescent)

As our little wobbly infant grows in the knowledge of Christ, marks of adulthood begin to show, and none are more important than a growing confidence in the saving power of Christ. The soul rests in Jesus "by a spiritual apprehension of his complete suitableness and sufficiency, as the wisdom, righteousness, sanctification, and redemption of all who trust in him, and is enabled by an appropriating faith to say, 'He is mine, and I am his.'"[12] So long as this confidence remains a confidence *outside* oneself and is unobstructed by emotional fluctuations and finds its root in the permanent and abiding sufficiency of Christ, it grows deep and begins to produce personal assurance. The adolescent Christian begins to echo the apostle Paul: "Who is to condemn? Christ Jesus is the one who died—more than that, who was raised—who is at the right hand of God, who indeed is interceding for us" (Rom. 8:34). The adolescent's faith is stronger and more robust than the child's. And the teen will need it, for what's to come is a season of prolonged conflict in his life.

God intends that his children be delivered not only from the power of sin, but also from the presence of sin. The long toil of sanctification is especially engaged in this adolescent stage. God hates sin, he loves his people, and he will not leave sin to dwell in them forever. Through his imperatives, God commands the adolescent Christian to strive against sin and pursue sanctification, to keep his heart fixated on the work ahead, and to keep his eyes open to the target. His conviction of God's acceptance of him and his security in Christ are no guarantee that he will experience a steady love, joy, peace, gratitude, and praise in his own heart. And as these experiences fluctuate, the world, the Devil, and his own flesh will scheme to "draw forth corruptions." And while the adolescent Christian has read of the spiritual battles in Scripture, he has not yet experienced the battlefield.

The Christian who has tasted the goodness of divine grace and has rejoiced in his Christ-secured salvation is now exposed to new storms of spiritual confrontation he likely never experienced in his early years. But the time is right. He's an adolescent, and it's time for him to begin acting on his own faith-informed initiative against his enemies. At this stage some Christians will be caught in gross public sins for which they will be exposed and humbled. But for most Christians, the sins that emerge in their

---

[12] W, 1:204.

hearts are largely private, known only to themselves, the Lord, and perhaps a few close friends. In either case, the root of public and private sin is the same. There's no room for self-righteousness, but much need for personal humility and Christ-motivated mortification.

As the adolescent Christian faces his enemies, he will be exposed to seasons of isolation when God will withdraw his perceived presence. This isolation will help the adolescent feel the vileness of his remaining sin, will expose his weaknesses, and will undermine any roots of spiritual pride, self-sufficiency, or other Christ-substitutions. In these first clashes against sin, self-confidence will erode, and in its place confidence in Christ will grow. These seasons of spiritual temptations have a design in the sovereign plan of God. This young man is learning to live like an adult. He is learning not to grieve the Holy Spirit with sin (Eph. 4:30). He is learning (by experience) the pledge of covenant theology—the unshakable bond of God's love covering over all the changes and weakness exposed in his life. Painfully, but necessarily, the young Christian learns this lesson especially when he cannot *feel* the presence of God.

This stage of spiritual development, just like in physiological development, is a stage of independent decision making. We dress ourselves, we feed ourselves, we take responsibilities, and we no longer seek immediate rewards for every act. Spiritual maturity is made evident by obedience. The Word of God dwells in our young man, and he acts and wars and makes spiritual decisions based on what he knows from that Word—a sure sign of maturity. The spiritual toddler lived off his moods and ill-informed intuition; the spiritual adolescent lives more off spiritual knowledge, especially when his feelings and affections wane. The only way out of spiritual immaturity is to walk by faith when the affections are dry and the presence of God appears to have been withdrawn.

At this stage in life, our young Christian becomes exposed to the weaknesses of his own life. This makes him more loving and kind to others. He does not confuse sin and godliness, but he becomes a mature Christian who has learned from personal experience how to offer forgiveness and how to show pity and tenderness and forbearance to others. He is meek, not self-righteous, toward others who are caught in sin, and seeks their restoration (Rom. 15:1; Gal. 6:1–2). Such an adolescent, with such care for the souls of others, now moves into full spiritual manhood.

"On Grace in the Full Corn" (or, Grace in the Christian Father)

Newton labels the progression of the inner life of the Christian at these various stages from *desire*, to *conflict*, and now to what he calls *contemplation*. This third stage of Christian maturity is reached through long experiences of God's faithfulness throughout life. Gospel maturity never means self-sufficiency—quite the opposite. The spiritual man, the father, always lives in "absolute dependence" on God. His ever-present mindfulness of his weakness *is his strength*. "In a sense he is much stronger, because he has a more feeling and constant sense of his own weakness," Newton writes.

> His heart has deceived him so often, that he is now in a good measure weaned from trusting to it; and therefore he does not meet with so many disappointments. And having found again and again the vanity of all other helps, he is now taught to go to the Lord *at once* for "grace to help in every time of need" (Heb. 4:16). Thus he is strong, not in himself, but in the grace that is in Christ Jesus.[13]

Spiritual maturity is expressed by a suspicion of the heart's tendencies and a quick turn to the sufficiency of Jesus Christ in every time of need. This childlike trust in the face of all need is the measure of mature faith. There's no secret to maturity in the Christian life; it's reached through a Christian's consistent application of the means of grace in years and years of need.

Newton summarizes how the spiritual adult (stage C) excels the infant and the adolescent stages (A and B).

> C's happiness and superiority to B lies chiefly in this, that, by the Lord's blessing on the use of means—such as prayer, reading and hearing of the word, and by a sanctified improvement of what he has seen of the Lord, and of his own heart, in the course of his experience—he has attained clearer, deeper, and more comprehensive views of the mystery of redeeming love; of the glorious excellency of the Lord Jesus, in his person, offices, grace, and faithfulness; of the harmony and glory of all the Divine perfections manifested in and by him to the church; of the stability, beauty, fullness, and certainty of the Holy Scriptures; and of the heights, depths, lengths, and breadths of the love of God in Christ. Thus, though his sensible feelings may not be so warm as when he was in the state of A, his judgment is more solid, his mind more fixed, his thoughts more habitu-

---

[13] *W*, 1:211.

ally exercised upon the things within the veil. His great business is to behold the glory of God in Christ; and by beholding, he is changed into the same image, and brings forth in an eminent and uniform manner the fruits of righteousness, which are by Jesus Christ to the glory and praise of God. His contemplations are not barren speculations, but have a real influence, and enable him to exemplify the Christian character to more advantage, and with more consistence, than can in the present state of things be expected either from A or B.[14]

The mature Christian life is marked by a daily return to the Lamb of God and diligent Bible reading, not merely as a daily discipline, but as a means to lead to heart-satisfying delight in the all-sufficient Savior. The mature Christian prays not out of a sense of mere duty, but because the all-sufficiency of Christ draws him to ask and plead in confidence. He listens intently to sermons because he awaits a glimpse of the precious Savior. The more he sees of Christ, the more he seeks by the means of grace (Scripture reading, prayer, and fellowship with the gathered church). His spiritual life is structured by discipline.

By contrast, the new believer's zeal is hot and wonderful, but also immature, ill-informed, and short-lived. The new believer's confidence in his affections arises from "the lively impressions of joy within," rather than from "a distinct and clear apprehension of the work of God in Christ." The new believer is overconfident in himself and has yet to discover the true depths of his sin. It will take time "to learn that we are nothing, have nothing, can do nothing but sin," in order that "we are gradually prepared to live more out of [from outside] ourselves, and to derive all our sufficiency of every kind from Jesus, the fountain of grace." The father has learned this hard lesson. He bases his hope not on his unstable feelings but on his unchanging Christ. This reorients all his expectations.

Years after conversion, if we find ourselves growing in knowledge of the gospel, maturing in our spiritual thinking, humbled by our indwelling sin, increasingly tenderhearted toward others, and desiring God's truth, ordinances, and people, "we may warrantably conclude, that his good work of grace in us is, upon the whole, on an increase." But we might not *feel* it. To be sure, there are "seasons of refreshment, ineffable glances of light and power upon the soul, which, as they are derived from clearer displays of

---

[14] *W*, 1:211–12.

Divine grace, if not so tumultuous as the first joys, are more penetrating, transforming, and animating." But, Newton adds,

> if the question is, How are these bright moments to be prolonged, renewed, or retrieved? we are directed to faith and diligence. A careful use of the appointed means of grace, a watchful endeavor to avoid the occasions and appearances of evil, and especially assiduity in secret prayer, will bring us as much of them as the Lord sees good for us. He knows best why we are not to be trusted with them continually. Here we are to walk by faith, to be exercised and tried; by and by we shall be crowned, and the desires he has given shall be abundantly satisfied.

So while our life, in the long run, rightly lived, will give evidence of increasing light and heat, the wearisome pathway will see frequent diminishing of both: sometimes because of our sin, and sometimes merely because God wants us to trust him when we cannot *feel* anything for him. An increasingly muscular faith demands our occasional exercise without the support of comfortable affections. Newton approaches frank disbelief that such a state—*growth in grace* coinciding with *decline in fervor*—is even possible, and yet he finds proof and evidence of this paradox in his own life. This is the experience of the advancing faith of the Christian father.[15]

Day by day, the Christian father beholds the glory of God shining in the face of Jesus Christ and is thereby continually transformed into the same image from one degree of glory to another (2 Cor. 3:18; 4:6). His life is marked by a tangible knowledge of God (1 John 2:14). The transforming power of Christ's beauty continues to work its influence in the cycle of daily discipline. Here we begin to reach what was for Newton the very pinnacle stage of maturity in the Christian life—and it's a stage marked by ordinary faithfulness and consistency in pushing through the weariness of life and the shackles of worldliness, and getting daily glimpses of Christ's glory.[16]

---

[15] W, 1:427–30.

[16] This point is well summarized by Keller: "A father or mother in the faith is someone who has learned through spending the time, through relentless passion, a deep yearning that is consistent. You finally start to penetrate. You have regular communion with him. You know the One who is from the beginning. Put it this way: You're babies until you understand the difference between grace and works. You're adolescents until you understand everything is necessary that he sends and nothing can be necessary that he withholds. You stop blubbering about the hardness of life. You learn how to live according to the bare Word of God. Lastly, you become a father or mother in the faith when you start to learn the disciplines of prayer and communing with him, so you regularly are seeing his glory. . . . Spiritually, people very often want spectacular things. They want great preaching. They want a great church. They want miracles. They want to see dramatic things happening in their lives. They don't like the routines. They don't like praying and reading their Bible every day. They don't just like learning the truth. Don't you see the spiritual babyness in you? You're unstable. You're undiscriminating. You're easily fooled. You tend to

The father in Christ looks back over the abounding grace shown him through the years, and this memory works deep to give his entire life a flavor of humility. If you walk closely with God for forty years, Newton admits, "you will at the end of that time have a much lower opinion of yourself than you have now."[17] The toddler and the adolescent know they should be humbled, but the father truly reaches levels of humility in his life. Newton asked one old man who had reached the end of his Christian life on earth, "What, my dear sir, is the proper attainment of an advanced and veteran believer, which distinguishes him from a young convert?" Newton summarizes the man's answer:

> From what he has seen and felt in the course of his experience, he has acquired a quicker and more abiding sense of his own nothingness, and the desperate deceitfulness and wickedness of his heart, than he could possibly be possessed of at his first setting out; and therefore has made a nearer approach to the character of a broken and contrite spirit, which the Lord speaks of as his peculiar delight. (Ps. 51:16–17)[18]

This father has learned humility firsthand. Yet his humility has been hard-won through many trials. He knows how to manage his anger and bitterness, he has learned to distrust his own impulses, and he humbly trusts the wisdom of his sovereign God. He grows tender toward his fellow believers who are younger and less mature, and he grows more courageous toward others who are living in self-destructive sins. The toddler may seek to correct others, but is often motivated by prideful ignorance of his own personal faults. But a father corrects others from a due sense of his own failures and God's faithfulness shown to him. "In reproving, our danger is to say what should not be said, and to leave unsaid what should have been spoken." The father understands this balance. When it's needed, the father reproves others "in *secret*, in *season*, and in *love*."[19] His attitudes and

---

be exhibitionistic. You tend to like the spectacular, and you don't like the grind. These are marks of the average Christian. These are the characteristics of the average church congregation. All I'm urging you to do is to humble yourself and encouraging you to say, 'Yes, this is true of me, but I'm going to outgrow it'" (sermon, "Principles of Christian Growth: Part 1").

[17] *Letters* (Bull 1869), 389. See also *Letters* (Coffin), 95. Spurgeon: "When John Newton wrote a book about grace in the blade, and grace in the ear, and grace in the full corn in the ear, a very talkative body said to him, 'I have been reading your valuable book, Mr. Newton; it is a splendid work; and when I came to that part, 'The full corn in the ear,' I thought how wonderfully you had described me.' 'Oh!' replied Mr. Newton, 'but you could not have read the book rightly, for it is one of the marks of the full corn in the ear that it hangs its head very low.' So it is; and when a man, in a careless, boastful spirit, says of his work, 'It is finished,' I am inclined to ask, 'Brother, was it ever begun?'" (*The Metropolitan Tabernacle Pulpit Sermons*, vol. 40 [London, 1894], 34).

[18] *Letters* (Jones), 111–12.

[19] *Eclectic*, 106.

relationships grow by a wisdom that shuns jealousy and selfish ambition and embraces godly purity, peacemaking, gentleness, and reasonableness. The wisdom of the mature Christian results in a life flowing with mercy, good fruits, impartiality, and sincerity (James 3:13–18).

Spiritually, the idols of the world have grown hollow to the mature believer. All Christians "are prone to an undue attachment to worldly things," and it is the spiritually mature, who are aware of the allurements in their hearts toward broken cisterns, to whom are given victory over the worldliness. The father in Christ has grown familiar with the insufficiency of worldly comforts and securities, and simultaneously familiar with the all-sufficient grace of the sovereign goodness of God. He is increasingly aware that communion with Christ offers pleasures superior to the false comforts of the world. He is being weaned from worldliness. There's a rock-solid stability emerging in his life, and when evil comes upon others and the hearts of others shake in fear, he can stand with confidence in the God who is working all things for his good according to the counsel of his will (Rom. 8:28; Eph. 1:11). The Christian father cares for others and steadies Christian toddlers in moments like this.

And, finally, he is genuine. The unmistakable evidence of gospel simplicity marks his life. This man has reached a level of maturity because he truly treasures the glory of God as his chief aim. He lives in victory over self-centeredness. Convinced that his own personal good and God's glory are bound up together, he takes pleasure in living solely for God's glory. He is resolved to honor Christ in his God-centered life or in his God-appointed death. In either case he lays his life down at the disposal of the Lord (Phil. 1:18–26). If the power of Christ will be best manifested in his life by trials, then he welcomes the trials (2 Cor. 11:16–12:10). The man may be educated or illiterate, extroverted or introverted, cheerful or depressed, a pastor or a layman, healthy or sick, but whatever the circumstances of his life, he is "ripening for everlasting glory."[20] His race hastens toward a finish line, and as it does, he is compelled by the splendor of God's magnitude.

> That God in Christ is glorious over all, and blessed for ever, is the very joy of his soul; and his heart can frame no higher wish, than that the sovereign, wise, holy will of God may be accomplished in him, and all his creatures. Upon this grand principle his prayers, schemes, and actions, are formed.[21]

---

[20] W, 1:217.
[21] W, 1:216.

When the man can say this, he is very nearly fitted for heaven.

Maturity (by Category)

When Newton's stages of maturity are put together, they form a robust picture of Christian growth. In order to see the stages, it may be helpful to briefly review the categories individually:

- Maturity moves away from a self-centered life and toward a gospel-simple, God-centered orientation aimed at God's glory.
- Maturity moves away from a circumstantially centered roller coaster of emotions and toward a disciplined life rooted in daily spiritual habits.
- Maturity moves away from a legalistic, works-oriented relationship with God and toward a stable, gospel-centered security in Christ.
- Maturity moves away from a self-centered evaluation of the assurance of salvation and toward a firm confidence in Christ as the ground of assurance.
- Maturity moves away from exalted thoughts of self and toward lower and more humbled opinions of self and greater awareness of the remaining sin within.
- Maturity moves away from the impulse to correct others in harsh arrogance and toward a humbled and loving correction of others motivated by a deep sense of the worth of souls.
- Maturity moves away from a fearful apprehension about life's circumstances and toward a confidence in God's sovereign orchestration over every detail in life.
- Maturity moves away from worldly securities and toward an increasing willingness to leave this world in the Lord's timing.

In time I will address some of these spiritual marks of progress in more detail, but we must now turn to an essential component that emerges in Newton's understanding of Christian maturity.

New Affections Eject Old Habits

Emerging in this series of letters on Christian maturity is the primacy of Christ's glory in the Christian's ongoing growth. For Newton, the irreducible and irreplaceable core power for Christian growth is the daily discipline of treasuring God's glory shining in the face of Jesus Christ. Newton

clearly saw the centrality of this point in Paul (2 Cor. 3:18; 4:6) and structured his own pastoral ministry around it.

Within this theme is a point hinted at earlier, one we need to address
directly. In the Christian life, new affections for Christ clash with habitual
sin patterns. To put it more strongly, new affections for God eject old habits of sin. Or to say it in the negative, failure to find satisfaction in Christ
leaves in the soul a vacuum filled by self, idols, and false securities. Thomas
Cha' ners (1780–1847) would later call this phenomenon *the expulsive
powe ̆ of a new affection*. It was a biblical concept Newton no doubt came
across in the writings of Robert Riccaltoun (1691–1769), Ralph Erskine
(1685–1752), and others.[22]

Essential to our sanctification is a clash of competing affections. Wrote
Newton, "A believing view of the land that is far off, where the King reigns

---

[22] Riccaltoun: "Men as well as children may be pleased with trifles. With these life begins: and however
one object may drive out another, it is but an exchange of trifles, unless one could fix upon what is
perfectly good; i.e. such as is fitted to give perfect pleasure: and thence it has been the business of the
wisest men to find out what they called *the chief good*, such as could make one happy in the want, and
even in the loss, of every thing else; i.e. such as perfectly suits the human constitution, so as to raise
and maintain perfect pleasure" (*The Works of the Late Reverend Mr. Robert Riccaltoun*, 3 vols. [1771],
1:167); "Wherever the love of God is so shed abroad in the heart as to become the ruling principle,
there the world loses its hold; the light of his glory, as it shines in the face of Jesus Christ, casts shame
and disgrace on all worldly glory" (2:123–24); "So long as the love of the world rules in the heart, the
ways of God must be insupportable; and nothing can turn out the love of the world, but the love of God
shed abroad in the heart. This is the proper business of faith; the victory which overcomes the world
(1 Jn. 5:4)" (2:187–88).

    Erskine: "Thoughts of Christ are assimilating thoughts, sanctifying and transforming thoughts:
'But we all with open face, beholding as in a glass the glory of the Lord, are changed into the same
image, from glory to glory, even as by the Spirit of the Lord' (2 Cor. 3:18). They that see Christ, cannot
but love him, and desire to be like him, for there is a smitting [infectious] favor in his face. They that are
in heaven are like him, because they see him as he is: the beautiful vision brings in full conformity to
him. Now, a spiritual thought, and a believing thought, is a mental sight, a fiducial vision of him, and
the more of this, the more conformity to him in holiness. The thought that endears Christ, embitters
sin. A man cannot think duly of the loveliness of Christ, without thinking of the loathsomeness of
sin. O! When the Sun of righteousness ariseth, there is a heat that accompanies the light, and warms
the heart. And, indeed, high thoughts of Christ do warm the heart, and make it burn within him. And
heart-warming thoughts tend to burn up corruption, for, as Christ comes into the heart, sin must go
out, according to the measure and degree of his coming. As a talent of gold, or some weighty metal,
falling into a vessel of water, dashes out all that is in the vessel to make room for itself, so Christ coming into the heart, dashes out sin to make room for himself. And, indeed, they that have honorable
thoughts of Christ in their hearts, cannot have favorable thoughts of sin, because, whenever Christ
comes into the thoughts, if he do not wash out the life, yet he dashes out the love of sin. . . . So far as
Christ comes in, sin goes out. It is possible, indeed, that a believer that hath Christ in him may think
that he hath more sin than ever, and that sin is on the growing hand, instead of the decaying. But he is
mistaken. It is in this case as it is with a cup of water. Put silver and gold in a cup, and the water swells
up, and the more you put in, the more will the water swell and run over, that you would think there is
still more water than before, the more gold is put in. Christ is the tried gold, and the more the vessel
of the believer's heart is filled with it, the more may sin appear to rise and swell, and run over all its
banks. This frightens and terrifies the poor soul, because now he sees that which it may be, was hid
in the vessel of his heart before, and out of his sight. But it is not that there is more sin, more water
than before, but more gold cast in, only every dash perhaps makes the water flee about, that he thinks
he was never so full of sin and corruption as now, yet still it holds good, Christ's coming in makes sin
flee out, and the more it seems to rise and swell, the more does the soul's indignation rise and swell
against it. All right thoughts of Christ are sanctifying thoughts" (*The Sermon and Other Practical Works
of the Reverend and Learned Ralph Erskine* [London, 1821], 4:78–79).

in his beauty, will wean our affections from the present evil world."[23] Similarly, in a hymn, he wrote:

> Jesus, source of excellence!
> All thy glorious love reveal!
> Kingdoms shall not bribe me hence,
> While this happiness I feel.[24]

These tastes of happy adoration in Christ now, and the anticipation of a more glorious uninterrupted adoration of Christ in the beatific vision, are adorations at the very heart of Christian obedience. Holiness grows out of an inner change within the affections, the fruit of the Spirit's awakening a dead sinner to the beauty of God's holiness in Christ (Pss. 29:2; 96:9). Holiness must first be rooted in *new tastes* and *new desires* if it is to lead to *right actions*. The world looks on baffled. The natural man loves "the perishing pleasures of sin, the mammon of unrighteousness, and the praise of men," yet in stark contrast, the new man "loves Jesus."[25] And so Newton can say with confidence, "In vain we oppose [set up] reasonings, and arguments, and resolutions, to beat down our corruptions, and to silence our fears; but a believing view of Jesus does the business."[26] Opposing sin and temptation with mere resolutions to holiness proves to be powerless; only a sight of Christ crucified is powerful enough to wean us from the world (Gal. 6:14).[27]

It is spiritual suicide to claim Christ as your fountain of joy but then feed your soul on sin, idols, and worldliness. The sinful pleasures of this world usurp true affection for Christ, and vice versa.[28] The love of Christ must control us (2 Cor. 5:14), and "the constraining love of Christ is alone able to purify the heart from selfish and sinful principles, and to overcome the world with all its allurements and threatenings."[29] This controlling power of Christ is the *new affection*, part of what Newton calls a *new principle*, a gift in conversion to enable the believer to withstand the world's

---

[23] *Letters* (Clunie), 191. On the power of our anticipation of the *future* beatific vision of Christ ("that boundless ocean of happiness") to wean us from worldly lusts and securities *today*, see one of Newton's cherished books, *Theological and Expository Lectures by Robert Leighton, D.D., Archbishop of Glasgow* (London, 1828), 33–34.

[24] *W*, 3:638.

[25] *W*, 2:493.

[26] *W*, 6:4.

[27] Newton: "The knowledge of Christ crucified (like Ithuriel's spear) removes the false appearances by which we have been too long cheated, and shows us the men and the things, the spirit, customs, and maxims of the world, in their just light" (*W*, 2:12).

[28] *W*, 3:404.

[29] *W*, 6:391. Newton: "Experience and observation proves, that no doctrine, but Jesus Christ and him crucified, will turn the stream of the heart, or withstand the stream of the world" (Letters [Barlass], 583).

temptations and to mortify remaining sin.[30] By this new affection, beholding Christ's glory in Scripture becomes dynamite to loosen sin from us, and
a superior pleasure to shield us from worldly enticements. "Let us look to
Jesus in his offices, power, compassion, grace, and example; when he and
his glories are presented to the eye of faith in the light of the Word and
Spirit, then obedience is easy, and temptations lose their force."[31] Temptations lose potency, and obedience finds its power in the glory of Christ
beheld in Scripture.

> So, if obedience be the thing in question, looking unto Jesus is the ob-
> ject that melts the soul into love and gratitude, and those who greatly
> love, and are greatly obliged, find obedience easy. When Jesus is upon
> our thoughts, either in his humbled or his exalted state, either as bleed-
> ing on the cross, or as worshipped in our nature by all the host of heaven,
> then we can ask the apostle's question with a becoming disdain, "Shall
> we continue in sin that grace may abound?" God forbid.[32]

Confidence in God's love is a powerhouse for strengthening obedience
and advancing sanctification. Whenever hard thoughts of God plague the
Christian (God is *against me*), obedience must grow feeble and temptations
grow alluring. But where the conviction of God's favor is certain (God is *for
me*), faith and holiness are properly joined, sin is subdued, and temptations are silenced.[33] Which is why for Newton the beholding of Christ's
all-sufficient glory as a daily discipline is essential. The mature Christian
does not live on the roller coaster of experience, but draws upon this secret
to holiness. He has learned that "his great business is to behold the glory
of God in Christ; and by beholding, he is changed into the same image, and
brings forth in an eminent and uniform manner the fruits of righteousness, which are by Jesus Christ to the glory and praise of God" (Phil. 1:11).[34]

John Flavel (1628–1691), one of Newton's favorite Puritan authors,[35]
wrote, "The more frequent and spiritual your converse and communion
with Christ is, the more of the beauty and loveliness of Christ will be
stamped upon your spirits, changing you into the same image, from glory

[30] W, 1:370; 3:556.
[31] Letters (Jones), 73.
[32] W, 6:6.
[33] Letters (Jones), 42–43.
[34] W, 1:212.
[35] Newton recommended that William Wilberforce read anything and everything written by Flavel
(Aitken, 306).

to glory."[36] This works because the beauty and loveliness of Christ outshine the sparkle of sin. It's worth looking again at one quote from Newton we studied earlier to see how this dynamic process functions in the Christian life:

> Wonderful are the effects when a crucified, glorious Savior is presented by the power of the Spirit, in the light of the Word, to the eye of Faith. This sight destroys the love of sin, heals the wounds of guilt, softens the hard heart, and fills the soul with peace, life, and joy; and makes obedience practicable, desirable, and pleasant. If we could see this more, we should look less at other things. But, alas! Unbelief places a veil before our sight, and worldly-mindedness draws our eyes another way. A desire to be something that we are not, or to possess something that we have not, or to do something that we cannot—some vain hope, or vain fear, or vain delight, comes in like a black cloud, and hides our Beloved from our eyes. This shows what poor creatures we are! Notwithstanding our hope that we are converted, we need a new conversion every day.[37]

The glory of Christ annihilates sin's glamour. Beholding Christ's glory is *affective* and *effective* at killing sin, and it is a practical way we experience the vital sap of spiritual life flowing to us from our vital union with Christ himself, depending on our faith.[38] If we are to mature, we mature *in Christ* (Col. 1:28), and this happens as we make biblical discoveries of his glory—a sin-expelling diet for the soul.

The takeaways here are relevant for every Christian advancing in maturity, but especially for any Christian leader, writer, parent, or spouse who is called to lead others toward holiness. The chief task of distinctive *Christian* leadership is laboring to get clear and affecting views of the splendor of Christ before others as often as possible, a plea that shaped Newton's friendships and ministry.

> May you have such increasing knowledge of his person, character, and offices, that beholding his glory in the Gospel glass, you may be changed into his image, drink into his Spirit, and be more conformable to him. The highest desire I can form for myself, or my friends, is, that he may live in us, we may live to him, and for him, and shine as lights in a dark world.

---

[36] John Flavel, *The Whole Works of the Reverend John Flavel* (London, 1820), 2:224.
[37] *Letters* (Clunie), 59–60. See also *W*, 3:455.
[38] *W*, 4:85.

To view him by faith, as living, dying, rising, reigning, interceding, and governing for us, will furnish us with such views, prospects, motives, and encouragements, as will enable us to endure any cross, to overcome all opposition, to withstand temptation, and to run in the way of his commandments with an enlarged heart.[39]

In other words, the expulsive power of Christ's glory is the secret to Christian maturity. It's the glory moving Christians from *blade* to *ear* to *full corn*—from *infant* to *adolescent* to *father.*

An Oak for the Ages

And now we return to that hill in Olney. The Christian life grows, not hastily like a mushroom or like the speed-sprouting plant over Jonah's head, but rather like Newton's oak, a tree buffeted by winds and hailstorms and winters and scorching summers, but firm and resolute from branch to root. Such growth requires patience because Christ "works powerfully, but for the most part gently and gradually."[40] "We are hasty, and would be satisfied at once, but his word is: 'Tarry thou the Lord's leisure'" (Pss. 27:14; 37:34).[41]

In our impatient smartphone culture, this may be the most important takeaway from Newton's three letters on the growth of grace in the Christian life. Sync your spiritual expectations to the leisurely agricultural pace of God. Live simply and live patiently, knowing that God is growing you for the ages. Be patient and faithful in the ordinary means of grace.

Faithful pastor, don't fuss over the imperceptible growth in your flock. Let God's timing recalibrate your expectations for what maturity will look like in them. Although the progress is often unseen, and your pastoral labors never end, the Spirit-born fruit is growing. Celebrate even the smallest evidences of maturity you see. Christian, don't fuss over your current mood as a gauge of your spiritual health, but keep two eyes focused daily on the Christ who hung on a tree.

Remember, the growth of a believer is not like a mushroom, but like an oak, which increases slowly indeed but surely. Many suns, showers, and frosts, pass upon it before it comes to perfection; and in winter,

[39] *Letters* (Taylor), 34.
[40] W, 6:298.
[41] W, 1:642.

when it seems dead, it is gathering strength at the root. Be humble, watchful, and diligent in the means, and endeavor to look through all, and fix your eye upon Jesus, and all shall be well.[42]

Follow this Christ-centered plan and you will mature into a broad-spreading, deeply rooted tree, established for ages, flourishing forever.

---

[42] W, 2:141.

CHAPTER 8

SEVEN CHRISTIAN BLEMISHES

John Newton was a student of the Bible, of his own heart, and of the hearts of others. This led him to consider the many different contours and pitfalls of the Christian life all the way down to the various weaknesses of constitution and character flaws that stain Christ's witnesses in public. Newton had a category for character defects that did not rise to the level of blatant sins or gross violations of Scripture. In this chapter we address those types of flaws: personal habits that fall somewhere between character blemishes and "respectable" sins—the types of behaviors that make others wince. Even if these character traits don't fit into a clear sin category, they often are so deeply rooted they go unperceived by the offender.

Newton zeros in on seven types of Christians who broadcast these character flaws, using rather picturesque names in the tradition of John Bunyan. And while all of these portraits are of men, Newton assures us that "counterparts to the several characters may doubtless be found here and there among the women."[1]

He begins with a portrait of Austerus, a man of orthodox beliefs but stern character.

---

[1] W, 1:378–79.

Austerus: Orthodox (but Strict)

Austerus is a man who knows the truth, prizes the truth, and resists the wisdom or the promises of worldly indulgences. He is a man of firm faith, but the firmness of his faith gets projected onto others a little too severely. He lacks the courtesy and gentleness that should accommodate his orthodoxy. His closest friends can well attest to his genuine humility and love, but those in the marketplace, who do not know him well, observe a cold rigidity about him. "Instead of that gentleness and condescension which will always be expected from a professed follower of the meek and lowly Jesus, there is a harshness in his manner, which makes him more admired than beloved; and they who truly love him, often feel more constraint than pleasure when in his company."[2] Because he is bent toward strictness and severity, on the outside he seems to others to be proud, dogmatic, and self-important. It's not that he lacks any true humility, but he does lack a certain outward generosity in his relationships.

Cynicism is always out of place in the Christian life, but it finds a foothold in Austerus's life. With a suspicious spirit, many Christians who are like Austerus (including many pastors) heap problems on themselves by turning off others for lack of personal charitableness and gentle words.[3] Austerus is safe from a far greater danger in becoming so socially conformable and so gentle and so politically correct that he can no longer hold biblical convictions in the public sphere. No, he will not fail here. But there must be a "golden mean" between these two: a firm resolve when it comes to biblical convictions, and a kind posture in our dealings with other Christians, friends, neighbors, and even adversaries. A man can be admired for his biblical resolve and be admired for his Christlike gentleness.

Partly, Newton suggests, this austerity originates in the misuse of the law. Austerus believes God is glorified only by meticulous and calculated obedience, and yet he forgets that God is also glorified in the enjoyment of his good and perfect gifts. Austerus needs to remember that "the Lord is not a hard master; he gives us all things richly to enjoy; not to raise, and then disappoint our expectations, but, within the limits his wisdom prescribes, to gratify them."[4]

Austerus clings tightly to his orthodox theology, but he is a bit too self-

---

[2] W, 1:379.
[3] W, 6:272.
[4] W, 6:481–82.

concerned to heartily enjoy God's gifts with others. Both *overvaluing* and *undervaluing* God's good gifts are common mistakes for Christians.[5] In this case, Austerus could use more cheerful delighting in God's holy gifts, as well as more rejoicing in these good gifts in the presence of others. This would go a long way in helping to combat the strict, intimidating, and hard exterior he regularly projects.

Humanus: A Self-Sacrificing Life (with a Tireless Tongue)

As you can tell by his name, Humanus loves people. He is quite emotional, connecting well with others (today we would call him an "extrovert"), and there's nothing he wouldn't do for those in need. His love for others is genuinely motivated by a love for Christ, and in the name of Christ he will serve others tirelessly. If he sees someone in need, he will jump to respond and bring care. He is unflinchingly loyal. If you asked him to protect a safe containing your personal fortune, he would guard it faithfully.

But in getting into everyone's business, he is privy to a lot of personal secrets about the lives of his family and friends and neighbors. If he puts all the secrets he learns into a metaphorical vault, he leaves that door unsealed for others to see. Your gold may be safe with him, but your secrets aren't. As tirelessly as his hands serve others, his tongue tirelessly spreads information he should keep to himself. "Not that he would willfully betray you; but it is his infirmity: he knows not how to keep a secret."[6]

He is not a slanderer, he does not spread maliciousness about others, and he means no harm; it's just that he cannot keep silent. His mouth is as big as his heart, and he is prone to spout the private details of those he has sought to help, tainting his otherwise noble sacrifices. And worse, even with these private details, he's not good at keeping them accurate. The stories and words about others are a mix of private truth and invented misinformation streamed thoughtlessly out to others. His Christian friends cringe because they see how his streams of words unintentionally undermine his own reputation. Public consensus would label him a gossip.

The genuineness of Humanus's faith is evident in his example of pure and undefiled religion (James 1:27). He models a selfless and genuine Christian life. But often his pure and undefiled religion is spoiled by his careless words. Humanus must learn to bridle his tongue (James 1:26; 3:1–12). He

---

[5] *Letters* (Taylor), 258.
[6] *W*, 1:380.

must learn to keep secrets to himself (unless of course those secrets must be told to the authorities or to others in limited cases).[7] Writes Newton:

> In what they say of or to others, the tongues of believers are bridled by a heart-felt regard to truth, love, and purity. It is grievous to see how nearly and readily some professors of religion will venture upon the borders of a lie; either to defend their own conduct, to avoid some inconvenience, to procure a supposed advantage, or sometimes merely to embellish a story.[8]

Humanus falls into this last category. He exaggerates to embellish stories, and he embellishes stories to gain attention. Rather than continuing with this loose tongue, he should pray,

> Set a guard, O LORD, over my mouth;
>   keep watch over the door of my lips! (Ps. 141:3)

In the self-sacrifice of Humanus, the glory of Christ will shine in new splendor if he can, by the power of the Holy Spirit, learn to control his tongue.

Prudens: Generous in Private (but a Miser in Public)

Prudens is also a man willing to sacrifice for others, and his close friends can give you specific examples of when his open hand has served the poor and needy. The size of his gifts will not be impressive, but the meaning of his gifts may be greater than we realize. With his money, Prudens is scrupulous. When he's in the market, he quibbles and haggles every price down as low as possible. He wearies every merchant. He counts every penny. "For Prudens is a great economist; and though he would not willingly wrong or injure any person, yet the meannesses to which he will submit, either to save or gain a penny in what he accounts an honest way, are a great discredit to his profession."[9]

It's not illegal to bargain. It's not even ungodly to bargain. But bargaining tempts one toward an edginess that can undermine a Christian testimony in the marketplace. There are fair prices to be paid, but it's hard to see fair prices when the seller's motives are always held in distrust. Prudens squabbles over every price tag, and he certainly saves pen-

---

[7] W, 1:171.
[8] W, 6:384.
[9] W, 1:380–81.

nies for his troubles, but he comes across as "exceedingly hard, strict, and suspicious."[10]

In reality, Prudens lives a simple life, loves bargains, and really does save money to serve the poor. But he appears to the world like a Scrooge, and he should regularly stop and examine his heart for a remaining love of money.

Prudens is not really a miser, but he has a miser's tendencies. The miser, Newton writes, is one who simply forgets that money is a means and not an end. The miser wants more and more money in the pot, and cannot stand spending the money he has. "I consider covetousness as the most generally prevailing and ensnaring sin, by which professors of the gospel, in our commercial city, are hindered in their spiritual progress," Newton once wrote of the snares of London's financial district. "A disposition deeply rooted in our fallen nature, strengthened by the habits of business, the immense circulation of cash, the power of custom, and the fascinating charm of a balance-sheet, is not easily counteracted."[11] The love of money can sink its roots deep into every heart.

Yet of all people, the Christian is aware that it matters not how much money is left in his bank account after years of bargaining. What matters at the end of a Christian's life is how he used the money that passed in and out of his wallet. Was it used in a way that honored God and reflected gospel simplicity? Was it used to care for others? Or was it withheld to take advantage of others?[12]

Prudens must first be more careful to set his mind on things above, where Christ is, and put to death any remnant of miserly covetousness (Col. 3:1–5). In this sense, the solution is to become a spiritual hoarder, who is ever running his hands through gospel riches: "Jesus is mine: in him I have wisdom, righteousness, sanctification, and redemption, an interest in all the promises and in all the perfections of God."[13] Second, Prudens must continue to learn the freedom of glad, generous financial sacrifice. If he does learn to use his money more openly to lavish love on others, how he treats merchants in the market will be radically changed too. He can still bargain, but to gain a fair price, not to take advantage of others, and not in fear of being taken advantage of by everyone else. Then his glad generosity

---

[10] W, 1:381.
[11] W, 6:474.
[12] W, 6:473–74.
[13] W, 1:488.

will reveal itself in public, and his genuine Christian testimony will shine and reflect the glory of Christ more accurately to his heart.

Volatilis: Large-Hearted (but Always Late)

Volatilis is also large-hearted and loves to help. But he's also very hasty in his commitments, and often finds himself in schedule conflicts because he's permanently overcommitted. He finds it hard to say no, and that means he takes on too many requests and is always running from one engagement to another. Prudens is as cold and punctual as Volatilis is warm and late.

"He accepts, without a thought, proposals which are incompatible with each other, and will perhaps undertake to be at two or three different and distant places at the same hour. This has been so long his practice, that nobody now expects him till they see him."[14] Quickly he finds himself behind schedule and appears late, if he appears at all. His intentions are good, but his execution is flawed. The large heart he has to love and care for others is blemished by his inability to show up and follow through on his promises.

A commitment is a commitment. If a *man's word* is important, how much more important is a *Christian man's word*? Volatilis, Newton writes, "would do well to remember, that truth is a sacred thing, and ought not to be violated in the smallest matters, without an unforeseen and unavoidable prevention. Such a trifling turn of spirit lessens the weight of a person's character."[15]

Punctuality was an essential component to the gospel simplicity we addressed earlier. Gospel simplicity shows in single-minded dedication to the glory of God and requires speaking the truth in love, doing to others as they should do to you, and observing a strict punctuality in dealings. And punctuality was one reason Newton wrote so many letters. A letter received was an obligation for him to respond, and he believed it was "tolerably punctual" to respond within six to eight weeks.[16] And while the pressure to write back to so many letters may have been unrealistic in Newton's case, he was driven to respond to the volume of mail because his testimony was on the line. He wanted to minister grace to others, but he also wanted to maintain his Christian witness and punctuality.

Punctuality was part of Newton's life and factored into all his commit-

---

[14] W, 1:381.
[15] W, 1:382.
[16] W, 1:682. In a letter to a friend, Newton admitted at age seventy-four that his punctuality in correspondences declined in his later years (*Letters* [Ryland], 349).

ments. At age seventy-four he wrote a letter of advice to a young cousin, providing a lifetime of accumulated wisdom for years to come. Among other things, he said:

> Youth is the time to lay the foundation of good habits, which may be useful to us in future life. I much wish you to gain a habit of punctuality with respect to time, and the want of this is very inconvenient to the person who fails, and gives trouble to others; if you follow my advice, you will find the advantage long before you are so old as I am. I began to aim at this almost fifty years ago, and I have seldom, if ever, been five minutes behind my time, unless unavoidably prevented, for nearly fifty years past.[17]

In Newton's mind, this punctual record is the fruit of the gospel, and his timely appearances for every meeting and his timely correspondences are borne out of his gratitude for the amazing riches in Christ. It was in the shadow of Christ's love on the cross that Newton sought to maintain punctuality in his dealings. Volatilis needs to see how his tardiness spoils his love and agitates others.

Cessator: Heavenly Minded (but Earthly Disconnected)

Prudens may have been so concerned with keeping the change in his pocket that he failed to run his hands through his spiritual riches in Christ. Cessator is the opposite. He's so heavenly minded he finds himself disconnected from earth. He is quick to listen and very slow to act.

> Had he been sent into the world only to read, pray, hear sermons, and join in religious conversation, he might pass for an eminent Christian. But though it is to be hoped that his abounding in these exercises springs from a heart-attachment to Divine things, his conduct evidences that his judgment is weak, and his views of his Christian calling are very narrow and defective. He does not consider, that waiting upon God in the public and private ordinances is designed, not to excuse us from the discharge of the duties of civil life, but to instruct, strengthen, and qualify us for their performance.[18]

Of course a life aimed merely at success in business is the life of the fool, but this will not excuse Cessator's failure to work hard. He fails to see how

---

[17] *Letters* (Taylor), 177.
[18] *W*, 1:382.

the sermon on Sunday was given for him to engage his duties faithfully on Monday. And his family will suffer, Newton writes. His wife and children will soon discover that Cessator is detached from family life and quick to disappear into his books. His friendships strain. "He thanks God that he is not worldly-minded; but he is an idle and unfaithful member of society, and causes the way of truth to be evil spoken of."[19]

Cessator is only a hearer of the Word, not a doer (James 1:22–25). The utmost diligence in reading books and listening to sermons cannot justify the neglect of wife, children, friends, or work. In a letter on the art and craft of listening to sermons, Newton explained what's at stake here.

> Be cautious that you do not degenerate into the spirit of a *mere hearer*, so as to place the chief stress of your profession upon running hither and thither after preachers. There are many who are always upon the wing; and, without a due regard to what is incumbent upon them in the shop, in the family, or in the closet, they seem to think they were sent into the world only to hear sermons, and to hear as many in a day as they possibly can. Such persons may be fitly compared to Pharaoh's lean cows (Gen. 41); they devour a great deal; but, for want of a proper digestion, they do not flourish. Their souls are lean, they have little solid comfort, and their profession abounds more in leaves than in fruit. If the twelve Apostles were again upon earth, and you could hear them all every week; yet, if you were not attentive to the duties of the closet; if you did not allow yourself time for reading, meditation, and prayer; and if you did not likewise conscientiously attend to the concernments of your particular calling, and the discharge of your duties in relative life, I should be more ready to blame your indiscretion, than to admire your zeal. Every thing is beautiful in its season, and if one duty frequently jostles out another, it is a sign either of a weak judgment, or of a wrong turn of mind. No public ordinances can make amends for the neglect of secret prayer; nor will the most diligent attendance upon them justify us in the neglect of those duties, which, by the command and appointment of God, we owe to society.[20]

Cessator needs to hear these strong words.

Running from preacher to preacher as a hearer and not a doer will eventually harden one in certain dangerous ways, Newton writes. "Such unsettled hearers seldom thrive. They usually grow wise in their own con-

---

[19] *W*, 1:382.
[20] *W*, 1:222–23.

ceits, have their heads filled with notions, acquire a dry, critical, and censorious spirit; and are more intent upon disputing who is the best preacher, than upon obtaining benefit to themselves from what they hear."[21]

Gospel simplicity, a life lived for God's glory alone, sanctifies the ordinary to-dos of our lives like the philosophers' stone transforms any base metal into solid gold. The philosophers' stone may be a legend, but even so, it's a fitting metaphor for gospel simplicity. Newton wrote to his abolitionist friend William Wilberforce,

> Religion is not confined to devotional exercises, but rather consists in doing all we are called and qualified to do, with a single eye to his glory and will, from a grateful sense of his love and mercy to us. This is the alchemy which turns every thing into gold, and stamps a value upon common actions.[22]

And to a friend whose wife and family were buried under domestic cares, Newton wrote:

> A simple desire to please God, to walk by the rule of his word, and to do all to his glory; like the feigned philosopher's stone, turns all to gold, consecrates the actions of common life, and makes every thing that belongs to our situation and duty in civil and domestic life a part of our religion. When she is making or mending the children's clothes, or teaching them, and when her maid (if serious) is cleaning the kitchen, or a saucepan, they may be as well employed, as when they are upon their knees or at the Lord's Table. It is an unpleasant mistake to think all the time as lost which is not spent in reading, or hearing sermons, or prayer. These are properly called *means* of grace; they should be attended to in their proper season; but the *fruits* of grace are to appear in our common daily course of conduct. It would be wrong to neglect the house of God; it would be equally wrong to neglect the prudent management of her own house. It is chiefly as a mother and a mistress of a family, that she can let her light shine to his praise. I would not have her think that she could serve the Lord better in any other station, than in that in which his providence has placed her. I know that family cares are apt to encroach too much, but perhaps we should be worse off without them.[23]

---

[21] *W*, 1:220–21.
[22] Letters (Wilberforce), 106.
[23] *Letters* (Coffin), 159–60.

The busyness of business and the chaos of maintaining a busy home are situations equally governed by God. Our labors and the seeming hindrances in life are all from him, and they are for our ultimate good and his ultimate glory. Our labors are golden opportunities to apply the means of grace and to worship God in the kitchen or at the office.[24] Gospel simplicity guilds even the most ordinary tasks, when done for God's glory, into golden tokens of worship.

The Christian woman is called and equipped to be a faithful member of society, to care for the needs of a home, and to be an involved and loving mother. Likewise, the Christian man is called and equipped to be a faithful member of society, a diligent and productive employee, and an engaged and loving father. What they both need to appreciate are the many ways all their Christian books, sermons, prayers, fellowship, and participation in corporate worship are aimed at making them *better* husbands, wives, fathers, mothers, and employees.

Diligence in your calling is a matter of testimony. Cessator, in being a hearer only of the Word, and not a doer, has stained his Christian profession. This life (right now!) is our only chance to "hold forth the power of gospel truth in the midst of a crooked and perverse generation" (Phil. 2:15).[25] God has ordained his children to magnify the beauty of Christ both in how we treasure the word of hope and in how we live our involved and industrious lives before men. This is true worship.

Curiosus: Upright and Interested (but Nosy and Closed)

Curiosus is a Christian with a lot of wisdom and fellowship to offer his friends. He's also incredibly nosy. He likes to pry into the lives and details of others. "For this idle curiosity he is marked and avoided as a busy-body; and they who have the best opinion of him, cannot but wonder that a man, who appears to have so many better things to employ his thoughts, should find leisure to amuse himself with what does not at all concern him."[26] He means no harm by the questions, but his prying nature is a turnoff to others who feel used. He doesn't really know how his prying is perceived, but this prying weakens his Christian profession, and makes him avoided (and avoidable). People keep their distance, or if they get pulled into a discussion unsuspectingly, they give him as little information as possible.

---

[24] W, 6:49.
[25] W, 6:77.
[26] W, 1:383.

His problem is his idle curiosity. He is drawn to details that do not concern him. He knows no boundaries between what he *should know* and what he *should not know*. Such a man gets placed in the category of a busybody and a meddler (1 Tim. 5:13; 1 Pet. 4:15). (In our modern age of proliferated social media, Curiosus is less easy to spot, since he can now entertain his empty curiosities on his Facebook app.) However Curiosus manifests himself over the years, the solution remains the same for all generations. He needs to learn self-control over his curiosities in order to mind his "own affairs," so that he may "walk properly before outsiders" (1 Thess. 4:11–12). Newton has little more to say. Curiosus needs to stop it. His unnecessary and unhelpful meddling in the business of others' lives is a curiosity that stains his profession more than he realizes.

Querulus: Wrapped in Political Debates (and Politically Powerless)

This final portrait is the longest, the most detailed, and the only one of the seven to include no commendation. Newton's pointedness in this portrait is very obvious. It begins and ends on a critical note.

Querulus is always ready for a fight, and it's usually a fight related to some political bickering he doesn't know about until he reads the morning newspaper; and once he reads it, he throws his hands up, moans, and laments such blatant political failure and takes to the street corner (or blog or social media) to vent his frustrations. In politics, Querulus finds all sorts of things to debate, and all sorts of time to waste. He's too far away from the political debates to have all the information necessary to comprehend the issues. Yet he's quick to voice his cure for political ills. Were he a mere citizen, the political debates would be understandable, but he's a Christian! And because Querulus is a Christian, his coffee-shop political debates are "worse than weakness"; they are a waste of time, a form of worldliness, an activity you would expect from a non-Christian who can hope in nothing beyond the gears of politics turning in his desired direction.

Christian hope rests in the first and ultimate sovereign cause of all things: "The LORD reigns" (Pss. 93:1; 96:10; 97:1; 99:1). This phrase should be printed as the lead story with bold black headlines at the top of every daily newspaper.[27] It was Newton's firm resolution on politics and

---

[27] *Letters* (Campbell), 175–76.

politicians. "There is a peace passing understanding, of which the politicians cannot deprive us."[28]

This position on politics worked itself out in a number of global conflicts. In the spring of 1799, as the French Revolutionary Wars reinflamed and Britain pressed on to defeat Napoleon, Newton wrote a friend, "O what a mercy to see all power in heaven and earth exercised by him who was nailed to the cross for sinners."[29] Nothing in the world of politics or war was outside of the crucified Christ's supremacy. Such a conviction of God's reign over world affairs should shape how every Christian engages in political debate. Two years later Newton wrote the same friend:

> The wrath of man, so far as it is permitted to act, shall praise him [God]. . . .
> It is the same now with [Napoleon] Bonaparte. When I heard of his unexpected escape from Syria, and arrival in France, I instantly concluded that the Lord had some important business for him to do. And when he has done his work, he will be laid aside, as many who have been in services not so fit for the godly.[30]

Biblically speaking, Sennacherib's *blasphemies* executed God's will no less than Hezekiah's *prayers* (2 Kings 18:13–19:37; 2 Chron. 32:1–23). And when Sennacherib could do no more, "he was thrown aside like an old broom, when the dirty work for which he was commissioned was performed."[31] In March 1793, at the start of the French Revolutionary Wars, Newton wrote, "The whole compass of my politics lies in Psalm 76:10":

> Surely the wrath of man shall praise you;
>   the remnant of wrath you will put on like a belt.[32]

The wrath of men and the enterprises of kings are always governed by God *for his praise and his purposes*, although only those enlightened by Scripture and the Holy Spirit "can perceive his interference."[33] Christ reigns over all.

> He who loved you and died for your sins, is the Lord of glory. All power in heaven and in earth is committed unto him. The Lord reigneth, let the

---

[28] *Letters* (Bull 1847), 163.
[29] Letters (More), 80.
[30] Letters (More), 154.
[31] *Letters* (Campbell), 12.
[32] Letters (Palmer), 73.
[33] W, 4:22, 430.

earth be never so unquiet. All creatures are instruments of his will. The wrath of man, so far as it is permitted to act, shall praise him, shall be made subservient to the accomplishment of his great designs; and the remainder of that wrath, of all their projected violence, which does not coincide with his wise and comprehensive plan, he will restrain.[34]

At this point we must ask how Newton could be so opposed to a Christian in political debate when he was so key in fortifying William Wilberforce's political career, which eventually ended the British slave trade. Here's the key:

> Querulus wastes much of his precious time in declaiming against the management of public affairs; though he has neither access to the springs which move the wheels of government, nor influence either to accelerate or retard their motions. Our national concerns are no more affected by the remonstrances of Querulus, than the heavenly bodies are by the disputes of astronomers. . . . If a Christian be placed in a public sphere of action, he should undoubtedly be faithful to his calling, and endeavor by all lawful methods to transmit our privileges to posterity: but it would be better for Querulus to let the dead bury the dead. There are people enough to make a noise about political matters, who know not how to employ their time to better purpose.[35]

Querulus is politically powerless; Wilberforce was a gear in the mechanics of politics. This marks a key distinction. Newton was not opposed to Christians in politics; he was opposed to ordinary Christians who engaged in unproductive political debate on the street corner with inadequate information and no political power to enact real change. For this reason Newton refrained from talking politics.[36] Christians need to know the difference, and Querulus needs to know how his bent toward polarizing politics gets in the way of his testimony.

In all his political debating, Querulus forgets to pray for his country. Newton puts the point bluntly: "Our Lord's kingdom is not of this world; and most of his people may do their country much more essential service

---

[34] *W*, 5:267.
[35] *W*, 1:383–84.
[36] "I neither condemn nor justify the measures of government. I am not sufficiently acquainted with matters of *fact*, or matters of *right* to qualify me to judge. And if I were, they are not my proper concern, nor could my influence affect them. But I wish that I and my people may be known as *the quiet of the land* (Ps. 35:20)" (Letters [Palmer], 110).

by pleading for it in prayer, than by finding fault with things which they have no power to alter." A nation's safety lies more in the prayers of its people than in the fleets of its navy.[37]

This explains why Newton largely steered clear of politics himself. "From poison and politics, good Lord deliver me. I think a political spirit as hurtful to the life of God in the soul as poison is to the bodily frame."[38] "It is well both for ministers and private Christians to have as little to do with politics as possible."[39] To one such pastor he said in a letter:

> My dear Sir, my prayer to God for you is, that he may induce you to employ the talents he has given you, in pointing out sin as the great cause and source of every existing evil, and to engage those who love and fear him, instead of losing time in political speculation, for which very few of them are tolerably competent, to sigh and cry for our abounding abominations, and to stand in the breach, by prayer, that, if it may be, wrath may yet be averted, and our national mercies prolonged. This, I think, is the true patriotism, the best, if not the only way, in which persons in private life may serve their country.[40]

To another pastor he wrote:

> I am or would be of no sect or party, civil or religious; but a lover of mankind. It is my part to mourn over sin, and the misery which sin causes, to be humbled for my own sins especially, to pray for peace, and to preach the gospel. Other things I leave to those who have more leisure and ability, and I leave the *whole* to him who does all things well![41]

Newton made a similar point in a letter likening national sin to Britain's mounting national debt.

> Some people are startled at the enormous sum of our national debt: they who understand spiritual arithmetic may be well startled if they sit down and compute the debt of national sin. *Imprimis*, Infidelity: *Item*, Contempt of the Gospel: *Item*, The profligacy of manners: *Item*, Perjury:

[37] *Letters* (Campbell), 13.
[38] *Letters* (Campbell), 11.
[39] *Letters* (Campbell), 12.
[40] W, 6:588–89. See also John Newton, *365 Days with Newton*, ed. Marylynn Rouse (Leominster, UK: Day One, 2006), 96.
[41] *Letters* (Ryland), 296.

Item, The cry of blood, the blood of thousands, perhaps millions, from the East Indies (slavery).[42]

Slavery affords an interesting look into Newton's thinking. As Wilberforce pushed his way politically toward abolishing slavery in Parliament, Newton was compelled to preach at least two sermons against the slave trade: "I considered it not in a political but in a moral view, from Jeremiah 2:34–35," he explained to a friend, because if abolition fails to pass,

> I shall fear not only for the poor slaves, but for ourselves. For I think if men refuse to vindicate the oppressed, the Lord will take their cause into his own hands. And the consequences may be dreadful both abroad and at home, whatever mischiefs may arise from hurricanes, insurrections, etc. etc., I shall attribute to this cause.[43]

So we must qualify whatever Newton has said about politics with this *moral* category. There's a time and season for a preacher to address the nation's immoralities, even if such an act appears to some to be politically motivated activism. Would Newton preach against the proabortion movement and the prohomosexual agenda today? Would he support grassroots political engagement motivated by Christian moral convictions? I would guess so, but I'm also certain Newton would eagerly warn us about the political bickering of Querulus and the blistering, politically motivated sermons that declare to the world, "The greatest need for this nation is a power shift in political parties." This is a false hope. Rather, the church should protect her contemporary opportunity to proclaim to the world, "The greatest problem we face as a nation is our sin, and the only ultimate solution is Christ crucified."

As for Querulus, "his zeal is not only unprofitable to others, but hurtful to himself. It embitters his spirit, it diverts his thoughts from things of greater importance, and it prevents him from feeling the value of those blessings, civil and religious."[44] He becomes hardened by controversy and

---

[42] *W*, 2:86. Newton: "I wish to watch, and pray, and mourn for the abounding of sin, and the abounding woes with which sin has filled the world. Nor would I forget my own sins, which contribute to fill the national cup" (*Letters* [Bull 1847], 301).

[43] *Letters* (Bull 1847), 262–63, 265. Newton was slow to add his own public voice to the work of abolition. Forced off the seas and out of the slave trade by an epileptic seizure in 1754, Newton would not address slavery in public for another thirty-four years when he published a pamphlet "Thoughts upon the African Slave Trade" (1788), an influential detailed account of the brutality he witnessed firsthand.

[44] *W*, 1:384–85.

embittered by deadlock, and unwittingly misdirects others away from the root of a nation's problems (sin) and away from a nation's only hope (Christ).

Stench or Sweet Aroma?

This chapter should sting. If it doesn't, I think Newton would be concerned. Even if one of the portraits does not jump out, characteristics in the various portraits should poke at personal traits we perceive in ourselves. This was Newton's intent. In these portraits he does not say all Christians will find a perfect match. We know Newton well enough to remember how careful he is with unqualified diagnoses. Through this list of portraits, Newton intends to help us all locate a character flaw in our lives that may tarnish the glory of Christ in our interactions with the world. This is an act of pastoral love. Of course "some are offended at the minister who detects any part of their character which is defective; but a Christian is thankful when his defects are discovered to him."[45]

In these seven portraits Newton is dealing not with the profane sins, but with the more "respectable" sins, the ones that prove to be an unnecessary turnoff to others. Though not a matter of life and death of the Christian life, these character traits unnecessarily push people away, rather than emit the sweet aroma of Christ (2 Cor. 2:14–17).

In all these portraits, Pastor Newton is eminently concerned about the testimony of his congregation in the small town of Olney and in the busy city of London. If his people are stiff and cold in how they engage others (Austerus), if they spew secrets and embellish stories (Humanus), if they prove to be cruel bargainers in the marketplace (Prudens), if they always show up late (Volatilis), if they are disconnected from the realities of daily life (Cessator), if they are nosy (Curiosus), and if they get red-faced in street-corner political debates (Querulus), these character traits will unnecessarily smudge the local church's collective testimony in their city (Phil. 2:14–18). To close this chapter I'll let Pastor Newton explain this smudging effect in three excerpts, the first two from sermons, and the third from a letter.

> It will be in vain for ministers to declare that the doctrines of grace (Calvinism) are doctrines according to godliness, unless, our testimony is supported by the tempers and conduct of our people: the world will prob-

[45] *Letters* (Campbell), 159.

ably judge, rather by what they see in you, than by what they hear from us. Nor will it suffice that they cannot say you are an adulterer, a drunkard, a miser, or a cheat. If you espouse our doctrine, they will expect you to be humble, meek, patient, and benevolent; to find integrity in all your dealings, and a punctual discharge of your duty in every branch of relative life.[46]

Most people are most likely to be convinced by what they observe of you, than by what they hear from us. We assure them that our Gospel teaches those who receive it to renounce all ungodliness and worldly lusts, to live soberly, righteously, and godly (Titus 2:12); to be temperate in prosperity, patient under affliction; to fill up their several relations in life with integrity and diligence; to be cheerfully submissive to the will of God under all changes; to be meek, gentle, and benevolent, forbearing and forgiving; in a word, to do, in all cases, to others, as we would they should do unto us (Matt. 7:12). Happy for us, if, when we look around upon our hearers, we can with confidence say, "Ye are our epistles, known and read of all men" (2 Cor. 3:2).

If any ask us concerning the tendency of our doctrines, shall we send them to you, that they may notice, not only your serious and constant attendance upon public worship, but the good order of your families, your behavior as husbands or wives, parents or children, masters or servants; your punctuality in business and to all your engagements and promises, and the tenderness you discover to the characters and concerns of your neighbors? Shall we send them to you when you are in trouble, when you are visited with sickness and strong pain, or when the desire of your eyes is taken away with a stroke (Ezek. 24:16), that they may see with their own eyes and be satisfied, that you have neither followed cunningly-devised fables, nor contented yourselves with mere lifeless notions of the truth; but that your religion is real and powerful, and not only inspires you with a good hope respecting a future state, but is the source of your comfort, and the spring of your conduct, in the present life? May we venture, my friends, to make this appeal? Then, undoubtedly, you are wise to win souls.[47]

A minister's hands are strengthened when he can point to his people as so many living proofs that the doctrines he preaches are doctrines according to godliness; when they walk in mutual love; when each one, in their

---

[46] W, 4:205.
[47] W, 5:217–18.

several places, manifests an humble, spiritual, upright, conduct; when they are Christians, not only at church but in the family, the shop, and the field; when they fill up their relations in life, as husbands or wives, masters or servants, parents or children, according to the rule of the word; when they are evidently a people separated from the world while conversant in it, and are careful to let their light shine before men, not only by talking, but by acting as the disciples of Christ.[48]

The reception of the gospel in others and the legitimacy of doctrine are at stake in the lives of Christians. But this is only a start to give us a flavor for how Newton sought to explain this truth in eighteenth-century England. In every age the church must evaluate how certain flaws, or character blemishes, or "respectable sins" unnecessarily undermine the testimony of the gospel in culture. Such matters should continue to concern the most deeply committed Reformed pastors and congregations.

---

[48] *W*, 1:703.

CHAPTER 9

THE DISCIPLINE OF TRIALS

John Newton claimed to have endured only "light and few" afflictions throughout his life, but if we compare a typical twenty-first-century experience with his eighteenth-century existence, we uncover a few particularly challenging afflictions that shaped Newton's truly difficult life.

Throughout his later adulthood, Newton could easily recollect old memories of unspeakably sadistic brutality shown toward black slaves, vivid scenes of torture burned permanently into his memory.[1] The memories hit close. While he himself was attempting to grab at the lucrative slave-trade wealth in West Africa, in a twist of fate, Newton got entrapped and enslaved in Guinea, becoming "the servant, the scorn, and the pity of slaves." Newton described this eighteen-month trial as his "African Egypt." He found himself "lost in the wilds of Guinea," and subjected to the bitterness of one black African tribal princess who treated Newton worse than a slave (1746–1747).[2] Under such savage oppression (physically and emotionally), Newton drew the scorn and pity of other slaves who witnessed his grisly state. It was the kindness of the most compassionate of these slaves that likely preserved Newton's life.

His time on Plantane Island was the darkest and lowest point in his life. There he sunk to the bottom of the socioeconomic sewer: scorned, bled of human dignity, and scarcely fit to be a slave himself. By his own

---

[1] Aitken, 23–24.
[2] Aitken, 57–67.

folly, Newton found himself "depressed to the lowest degree of human wretchedness," living in a dunghill and a howling wilderness (Deut. 32:10; 1 Sam. 2:8). He was trapped beyond all hope of escape or redemption. And he would never forget it. The despairing trauma of imprisonment was felt so deep, Newton wrote, the painful memories were etched into "every waking hour" of his last fifty years on earth, and the episode was later etched into his tombstone.[3] Newton eventually escaped this slavery and found his way back to England on a ship called the *Greyhound*, but it was on the voyage home that Newton nearly died at sea in the merciless storm (1748).

Young John's life as a sea traveler was stressful, and could fill several pages, but Newton's life at home held trouble as well. His mother died about two weeks before John's seventh birthday. About a month after John turned twenty-five, his father drowned in a swimming accident. And in the fall of 1754, a random epileptic seizure hit John's life and ended his career on the sea. He was newly married and now unemployed. And this is only a sampling of the first three decades of John Newton's life, a series of near-death experiences and bitter hardships.

On dry land, Newton's troubles would continue. His appointment to ministry in the Anglican Church was dragged out for six frustrating years. Then after his appointment, his new role as a pastor multiplied Newton's trials as he cared for the burdens of his poor flock in Olney. Once married, the Newtons never had biological children (infertility the most likely cause[4]), and one of their two adopted daughters, Eliza, died from tuberculosis at age fourteen (1785). Their other adopted daughter, Betsy, would face adult-onset depression severe enough to get her institutionalized at Bedlam. Speaking of depression, Newton endured a long and painful friendship with William Cowper, a suicidal man institutionalized several times during his twenty-seven-year bout with despair, something Newton called "a very great trial to me." In Cowper's case, Newton's pastoral attentiveness was quite literally a matter of life and death. But as we will see later, his most difficult and painful trial would come later.

Perhaps this brief outline of his trials explains why Pastor Newton was so eager to respond to the letters of the suffering.

---

[3] *Letters* (Campbell), 172; *Letters* (Ryland), 380–81. The phrase on his tombstone ("a servant of slaves in Africa") is clearly a synonym for this "African Egypt" (*Letters* [Bull 1847], 300).
[4] Aitken, 141–42.

Trials: God's Design

Newton firmly trusted in God's sovereign power over all things, and he was quick to dismiss all hints to the contrary. No afflictions in the Christian life are accidental. No trials in the Christian life are the product of coincidence. None. And from this firm conviction, Newton never wavered. "Though he put forth his hand, and seem to threaten our dearest comforts," Newton wrote of God's presence in trials, "yet when we remember that it is *his* hand, when we consider that it is *his* design, *his* love, *his* wisdom, and *his* power, we cannot refuse to trust him."[5] Over and over again, this is his point. Every affliction in the life of the believer is designed by God and sovereignly implemented by him.

If the Christian's trials are designed by God (and they are), and if the Christian's salvation is secure in Christ (and it is), then no trial is the experience of God's punitive wrath poured out on us for our sins. "There is no sting in your rod, nor wrath in your cup."[6] Christ was crushed under the searing sting of God's white-hot wrath so we would never experience it. Christ's suffering was punitive; Christian suffering is restorative. The cup Christ drank was filled with wrath; the cup of suffering God calls his children to drink during the Christian life is "only medicinal to promote their chief good."[7]

Trials: Designed for Good

God's sovereign power over every trial in the Christian life is an important theme we will return to later. For now we will simply look at the effects of this sovereignty as "good medicine" for the Christian life. God uses disease and sickness and poverty and all the large and small pains of life *for our good*. Like heavy weights on a grandfather clock, trials are necessary for the Christian life to operate properly.[8] God "will suffer nothing to grieve us, but what he intends to employ as means for our greater advantage."[9] Christ is the Author and Perfecter of our faith, and he weaves trials into the storyline of our lives for a twin benefit: his glory and our good.

The end of the Christian life is one port (Zion), and every Christian is like a vessel on the open seas. Our destination is the same, but we all take

---

[5] *W*, 6:33.
[6] *W*, 6:72.
[7] *W*, 2:24.
[8] *Letters* (Ryland), 177.
[9] *W*, 2:432; see also 1:170; 6:5.

slightly different courses to get there, and Christians will endure vicious storms along the way, some more than others, depending on the route God has intended. All these light and momentary afflictions on the open sea of the Christian life are working together by God in our lives to prepare for us "an eternal weight of glory beyond all comparison" (2 Cor. 4:17). The pain we experience now cannot compare with the glorious end in store for us (Rom. 8:18). "God in Christ is our Father and our Shepherd. Heaven is our home; and all things we meet by the way are appointed and overruled in a subserviency to our sanctification and happiness."[10] In Newton's letters I count ten specific answers for why this is the case.

Trials Smoke Out Idols

In one biting metaphor, Newton writes that indwelling sin in the Christian life lies dormant until trials strike.

> There are abominations which, like nests of vipers, lie so quietly within, that we hardly suspect they are there till the rod of affliction rouses them: then they hiss and shew their venom. This discovery is indeed very distressing; yet, till it is made, we are prone to think ourselves much less vile than we really are, and cannot so heartily abhor ourselves and repent in dust and ashes.[11]

The brood of vipers living in the heart are "bosom sins," deep-seated depravities that form habits and go unnoticed and unopposed. The idol of comfort, for example, lies fast asleep under the rock until the whip of affliction slaps down with force into our lives, rousing the vipers. Afflictions awaken us to our sins because they often push our idols out of reach.

In other words, trials are designed to prevent us from living at peace with our idols and remaining sin. Much of our sin appears hidden and dormant until the whip-snap of affliction rouses the indwelling sin to stand up and show itself, or stand up and hiss, or stand up and strike. It is more necessary for us to see the sins remaining in our hearts and to flee to Christ for grace than it is to live blissfully ignorant of the cancers in our soul. And we know this, Newton explains, because God sends afflictions into our lives. Trials are medicines of kindness applied to serious diseases called indwelling sins.

---

[10] *Letters* (Jones), 85.
[11] W, 2:199.

I suppose a doctor would not long attend upon a patient who should insist upon choosing his own medicines, especially if he should object to every medicine that was either unpleasant to the taste or in its operation, for there are few efficacious medicines that are otherwise. Dangerous and inveterate diseases are seldom cured by cakes and comfits [candies].[12]

No. Indwelling sins are more readily smoked out with noxious trials than with powdered donuts. God would not send the pain if he did not intend to rouse the vipers and drive them out. The Christian life includes God's intention that we not only comprehend our sins theoretically, but feel them actually. Trials make us *feel* the power of the sins residing in our hearts, and such awareness is essential to the cure.

Trials Drive Christians to Pray

Normally our prayer lives are unimpressive. Sin degenerates the beauty of prayer into a painful chore. The glorious privilege of prayer becomes for us a "mere task" we ignore at the slightest excuse. The chief pleasure of prayer comes in the finishing of it. Instead of enjoying the blessed communion with the Almighty, we are dragged before God like a slave and we run away from prayer like a thief.[13] Or we fall into the trap of mindless praying. We slip into rote prayers when life becomes comfortable.

Mindless and habitual prayers are never less suited than when the circumstances of our lives crumble around us. Trials breathe new desperation—new life—into our prayers. Suffering pours new language into our longings. Newton writes, "Experience testifies, that a long course of ease and prosperity, without painful changes, has an unhappy tendency to make us cold and formal in our secret worship."[14] Easy lives weaken our communion with God.

Trials give new life to prayer,
Trials lay us at his feet,
Lay us low and keep us there.[15]

Writing to one couple facing possible trials in the near future, Newton reminded them that sometimes God uses trials to shake us from making

---

[12] *Letters* (Coffin), 44–45.
[13] *W*, 1:441.
[14] *W*, 2:22.
[15] *Letters* (Bull 1847), 284.

the mistake of assuming marital comfort is the ultimate security. It's not. And serious sickness in our spouse is one quick way God drives us to himself. "When he makes two persons happy in a mutual affection, he sees now and then a need-be to put their faith and patience to a trial, and to quicken them to prayer by touching them where they are most sensible; hereby he humbles us for the idolatry, unbelief, and ingratitude of our hearts."[16]

By showing us the insufficiency of our human comforts, God drives us to our knees in trials and prepares us for praise when deliverance arrives. Newton learned this lesson from Psalm 116:1–2.

> Trouble excites prayer, prayer brings deliverance, deliverance produces praise, and likewise teaches and encourages us where to go for help next time—yea, as long as we live. We do not come to the Lord upon a mere peradventure whether he will hear us or not, for he has heard us often; nor can we, nor need we say, that if he will help us but this one time, we will not trouble him again. We shall always need his assistance, and he is always ready to afford it. While we live in this poor world, trials of one kind or another will come in succession.[17]

Trials will hit our lives, not to keep us on our toes, but to keep us on our knees in humble dependence on God.

Trials Call Back Wandering Souls

Our Lord knows when we are wandering from him, and when we are, trials snatch our attention quickly. When life is easy and prosperous, we are especially tempted to forget our Savior, and our wandering hearts cause many trials in life. Newton speculated, "If we could keep up a more constant sense of our dependence upon the Lord, and that we, and all that we call ours are in his hand, we should perhaps be exempted from many trials, which now our proneness to forget renders necessary."[18] No matter how comfortable we make our lives, trials in the Christian life "are necessary to discipline us, and to keep us from wandering."[19]

Wandering away from God in self-sufficient neglect is incredibly dangerous. We are apt to sleepwalk right into Satan's trap.

---

[16] W, 6:73.
[17] Letters (Bull 1847), 277.
[18] Letters (Taylor), 140.
[19] W, 5:540.

Every day almost I meet with occasions of admiring the wisdom, care, and faithfulness of our Great Shepherd intimating and adjusting his dispensations exactly to our need and state. When the enemy is spreading a snare for our feet, when our deceitful hearts are beginning to start aside, when we have perhaps actually taken some steps in that path, which if persisted in might terminate in apostasy. Oh! Then how gracious, how seasonable, how salutary are those tokens of love (called affliction in the language of mortals), which he sends to break the snare, to check our progress, and to recall our wandering feet into the path of duty and peace.[20]

For hearts prone to wander, God's tokens of love (trials) are safety checks along the believer's path, calling the Christian back to the path of gospel awareness and the safety of true obedience.

Trials Humble Proud Hearts

Trials are intended to humble us and launch a frontal assault on our pride. To one pastor, Newton warned of the temptations to pride in the ministry. "It requires much discipline to keep pride down in us, even considered only as Christians, more as ministers, still more as ministers conspicuous for ability and usefulness; and, when the appendages of family and influence are added, the temptations to self-importance are still increased."[21] The minister, in order to be useful for others, must be emptied of himself, and he is emptied of his self-centeredness by trials. Thus, trials are aimed at setting us free from the shackles of our own self-righteousness and self-importance. "Messengers from Satan, and thorns in the flesh, are *gifts* and mercies if they preserve us from being exalted above measure" (2 Cor. 12:7–10).[22] One of Newton's most popular hymns opens with this plea for spiritual maturity:

> I ask'd the Lord, that I might grow
> In faith, and love, and ev'ry grace,
> Might more of his salvation know,
> And seek more earnestly his face.

In answer to this prayer came trials, and the hymn concludes with the Lord's explanation why:

---

[20] *Letters* (Bull 1869), 414.
[21] *Letters* (Bull 1869), 415.
[22] *Letters* (Campbell), 55.

These inward trials I employ,
From self and pride to set thee free;
And break thy schemes of earthly joy,
That thou mayst seek thy all in me.[23]

If we are to live a *holy life*—a truly *joyful life*—we must learn to live a *self-less life*. Our grip on self-interest and on the idols of this world that promise security is rarely loosened without the assistance of trials. "A smith, when about to make a poker, puts his iron into the fire. The Lord, when he means to make his people more holy, puts them into the furnace."[24]

Trials remind us that our idolatrous securities and our self-centered sufficiencies only bring spiritual weakness, not strength. "While we have such a depraved nature, and live in such a polluted world; while the roots of pride, vanity, self-dependence, self-seeking, are so strong within us, we need a variety of sharp dispensations to keep us from forgetting ourselves."[25] Trials kick out from under us the false securities we rest on.

> The Lord permits us to feel our weakness, that we may be sensible of it; for though we are ready in words to confess that we are weak, we do not so properly know it, till that secret, though unallowed, dependence we have upon some strength in ourselves is brought to the trial, and fails us. To be humble, and, like a little child, afraid of taking a step alone, and so conscious of snares and dangers around us, as to cry to him continually to hold us up that we may be safe, is the sure, the infallible, the only secret of walking closely with him.[26]

Trials are redemptive; they redeem us from our pride; they free us from ourselves.

Trials Kill Worldliness

When Newton learned that a Christian acquaintance had lost her house and all her worldly possessions in a fire, he went out to meet her and found her in tears.

"Madam, I am come to congratulate you," Newton said with a smile and the characteristic blunt wit he sometimes employed with his friends.

---

[23] W, 3:608.
[24] *Letters* (Campbell), 176.
[25] *Letters* (Bull 1869), 83.
[26] W, 1:693.

"What!" she replied, "upon the destruction of my property?"

"No, but to hail you on your possessing property which nothing can destroy," said Newton. In recalling the event to a friend, Newton said, "This awakened a surprise and a smile in her tears, like a sunshine in the showers of April."[27]

When rust and moth and robbers eliminate our securities, when cancer arrives, or when we find ourselves speechless in the company of a suffering friend, in this place we *feel* deep in our bones that this world cannot be the eternal rest our hearts long for. Trials remind us of the vanity of this life, and the vanity reminds us that this world is fallen, and the fallenness reminds us that it is a deeply unsatisfying world. For all the entertainment and the joy offered here, trials make us uneasy and set our hearts on things above, where Christ is (Col. 3:1–4). "Let us adore the grace that seeks to draw our hearts above!"[28] Our treasure is not in this world, and the Christian life is about turning away from the treasures on earth that promise powerlessly what only Christ can give. When life is easy, we start to unpack our bags and make a nice home for ourselves here in this world. Sometimes, in the wisdom of God, the house blocking our view of Christ will be burned to the ground. The loss is gain.

The Israelites reviewed the lesson of gainful loss many times as they wandered the wilderness waiting for their new home. Before he extracted them from Egypt and shepherded them toward the Promised Land, God allowed them to endure the awful pain of Egyptian slavery.[29] Drawing from the exodus typology for the Christian life, Newton believed the same distaste for this world is essential preparation as we anticipate the new heavens and the new earth. "It is happy for us if we have suffered enough to make us desire a better country."[30] It is good for our lives to be emptied of selfish comforts to make room for what is greater. "Self-will, self-dependence, the affections cleave to the dust. Affliction shows them what they are, what the world is, and makes them look upward and long for their rest."[31] "A considerable part of our trials are mercifully appointed to wean us from this propensity [worldliness]; and it is gradually weakened by the Lord's showing us at one time the vanity of the creature, and

[27] Letters (Jay), 306. See also *Letters* (Campbell), 65–66; W, 2:31–32; *Letters* (Bull 1869), 224–25.

[28] W, 3:484.

[29] W, 6:223.

[30] W, 6:223.

[31] John Newton, *365 Days with Newton*, ed. Marylynn Rouse (Leominster, UK: Day One, 2006), 246.

at another his own excellence and all-sufficiency."[32] The house burns to make way for a clearer sight of Christ. To live in the world without world-separating and Christ-magnifying trials would be ruinous to our souls. For redeemed sinners who are lured toward worldliness, trials are a sort of death, a redemptive death, a death to spare us from a worse death. *Nisi periissem, periissem*—unless I had died, I would have died.

Trials Are Ice Water on Sleepy Souls

The Christian life is one of sobriety and wakefulness (1 Thess. 5:6). Drawing from Bunyan's allegory *The Pilgrim's Progress*, Newton believed we walk this life in danger of spiritual laziness. We use spiritual adrenaline to fight spiritual pits, spiritual dragons, and spiritual battles, but often we overlook the spiritual sleepiness of that place Bunyan called "The Enchanted Ground." This is a stretch of path deceptively placed near the end of the pilgrimage, beckoning the pilgrim to stop, to relax, to spiritually retire, and thus to fall into the snare of spiritual slumber, spiritual inactivity, and spiritual susceptibility. This enchanted ground is pleasurably inviting but spiritually deadening. When the Christian lies down on the ground for a little spiritual nap, the lightning bolt of affliction pierces the bogus peace, the illusion is broken, and he finds himself stranded in a desolate wilderness, bloodshot eyes wide awake and now looking to return to the right path.[33] "With such hearts as we have, and in such a world as we live in, much discipline is needful to keep us from sleeping upon the enchanted ground."[34] "We live on an enchanted ground, are surrounded with snares, and if not quickened by trials, are very prone to sink into formality or carelessness. It is a shame it should be so, but so it is, that a long course of prosperity always makes us drowsy."[35]

Trials are medicines measured out with care and prescribed by our wise and gracious Physician. He proportions the frequency and the weight of each dose exactly to what the case requires.[36] Many of his people are sharply exercised with daily, unrelenting financial trials and poverty. Others face lifelong, incurable trials in their families.

> They who have comfortable firesides, and a competence for this world, often suffer by sickness, either in their own persons, or in the persons

---

[32] W, 1:214.
[33] W, 6:445.
[34] W, 6:488. See also Letters (Wilberforce), 137.
[35] *Letters* (Taylor), 43.
[36] *Letters* (Bull 1847), 178.

of those they love. But all of these crosses are mercies if the Lord works by them to prevent us from cleaving to the world, from backsliding in heart or life, and to keep us nearer to himself. Let us trust our Physician, and he will surely do us good. And let us thank him for all his prescriptions, for without them our soul-sickness would quickly grow upon us.[37]

Trials Sweeten Promises

The Bible is studded with promises for sufferers. Passages like Isaiah 41:10 and 43:2 are stars in a constellation of promises blazing before the eyes of the suffering reader.

> How grand and magnificent is the arch over our heads in a starry night! But if it were always day, the stars could not be seen. The firmament of Scripture, if I may so speak, is spangled with exceeding great and precious promises, as the sky is with stars, but the value and beauty of many of them are only perceptible to us in the night of affliction.[38]

These abundant promises in Scripture sparkle like diamonds on the pages of Scripture to those in the darkness of suffering, and these promises are snatched up and prized when the dark trials crash into our lives. In pain, those promises become for us more than lines in a book. Trials open Scripture and offer us deep experiences of joy and glory. Trials help us "find peace and comfort within when things are disagreeable and troublesome without."

> We are enabled to set to our seal that God is true; then we learn how happy it is to have a refuge that cannot be taken from us; a support that is able to bear all the weight we can lay upon it; a spring of joy that cannot be stopped up by any outward events. A great part of the little we know of our God, his faithfulness, his compassion, his readiness to hear and to answer our prayers; his wisdom in delivering and providing when all our contrivances fail; and his goodness in overruling every thing to our soul's good; I say, much of what we know of these things, we learnt in our trials, and have therefore reason to say, It was good for us to be afflicted (Ps. 119:71).[39]

---

[37] *Letters* (Taylor), 43–44.
[38] *Letters* (Taylor), 151.
[39] *W*, 6:36.

Trials Prove Grace

To some extent, every Christian faces the nagging question: Am I really a Christian? Or am I self-deceived? This question can debilitate the soul if it goes unanswered for long. But a little sense of the question is helpful. And it's in the midst of trials when all around us gives way and billows of trials crash into our lives—when we are left with nothing more than our faith, our Christ, and our Bibles—that we see with unclouded vision just how tightly we cling by faith. Suffering proves the reality of grace in our lives, because it strips away all the artificial supports we try to lean on. If we trust in cleverly devised fables or worldly comforts and securities, trials will expose those false supports. "By trials our graces are proved, exercised, and strengthened, and the power and goodness of the Lord towards us are more manifested and glorified."[40]

By default we grow confident and secure in ourselves and in the world around us over time, and those false securities must be shaken. Trials are earthquakes to test our foundations and assure our souls of God's design in our lives.

> When faith and knowledge are in their infancy, the Lord helps this weakness by cordials and sensible comforts; but when they are advanced in growth he exercises and proves them by many changes and trials, and calls us to live more directly upon his power and promises in the face of all discouragements, to hope even against hope, and at times seems to deprive us of every subsidiary support, that we may lean only and entirely upon our beloved.[41]

Trials crumble away all the false securities and prove the work of God in our hearts.

Trials Teach Compassion

In our personal trials God shows us compassion and prepares us to serve those who suffer. This is especially true for ministers. Your trials, Newton told one pastor, "are not for your own sake alone," but to make your sermons "more varied, experimental and consolatory to your people, and to qualify you with wisdom, tenderness, sympathy and promptitude, in speaking a word in season to them that are weary."[42] This is true for the

---

[40] *Letters* (Taylor), 100. See also W, 1:525; 2:218.
[41] *Letters* (Bull 1869), 81.
[42] *Letters* (Ryland), 200. Speaking to Christian leaders and counselors, John Piper applied Newton's point. "It is true that we must be personally bold and afraid of no man but courageous as we contend for the truth. If we are simply nice, concerned, genuinely curious, attentive, supportive, and affirming, we may

ministry of every believer. Trials make us more compassionate and sympathetic to our suffering brothers and sisters.

Trials Produce Confidence in God

One of Newton's favorite metaphors for those who endured severe suffering was the burning bush unconsumed (Ex. 3:2). Like those in poverty or those who lose a house, some Christians are called to endure a disproportionate amount of suffering. Such Christians are a spectacle of grace in the church, like flaming bushes unconsumed, and cause us to ask, like Moses: "Why is the bush not burned?" The strength and stability of these believers can be explained only by the miracle of God's sustaining grace. The God who sustains Christians in unceasing pain is the same God—with the same grace—who sustains me in my smaller sufferings. We marvel at God's preserving grace and grow in our confidence in him as he governs our lives.

Love Tokens

It is no surprise Newton fought against the unbelief that rejected trials. We are naturally so shortsighted we cannot see the *worse things* our trials *prevent*, nor the *best things* our trials are *producing*. Indeed, "I have reason to praise him for my trials, for, most probably, I should have been ruined without them."[43] In these ways trials and suffering in the Christian life are intentional and will bear eternal fruit.

Suffering and affliction are truly among our chief mercies, counterintuitive gifts for the Christian life.

> Years of health are mercies—intervals of sickness are mercies likewise—to the flesh they are not joyous but grievous; but there is a *need-be* for them, and peaceful fruits of righteousness to be gathered from them, if not immediately yet *afterward* (Heb. 12:11). Afflictions are either small daily medicines which our Physician and best friend sees that our spiritual maladies require, or they are furnaces to prove and purify our graces; or, lastly, they are occasions which his providence appoints for the clearer

---

win a hearing with suffering people, but we will never lead them to life. Grace means courage and clarity. But it is just as true that our boldness must be brokenhearted boldness, that our courage must be a contrite and lowly courage, and that we must be tender contenders for the truth. If we are brash and harsh and cocky and clever, we may win a hearing with angry and pugnacious people, but we will drive away those who suffer" (John Piper, "Counseling with Suffering People," *The Journal of Biblical Counseling* 21, no. 2 [Winter 2003]: 24–25).

[43] *Letters* (Bull 1847), 234.

manifestation of his power and love to us, in us, and by us. When he darkens our sky, and brings a cloud over us, it is a ground on which he designs to paint his covenant rainbow. The rainbow is a beautiful and wonderful appearance, but it is never seen in fair weather. If we had gone to heaven as upon a carpet, without meeting one rough step or strong blast all the way, still we should have been losers.[44]

Such is the perspective of a man who sees God's gracious hand behind every trial in the Christian life (Heb. 12:10–11). All suffering in the Christian life has an aim and an end, "an eternal weight of glory beyond all comparison" (2 Cor. 4:17). Every moment of our suffering is a "love token," proof of God's favor, proof of his enduring love, proof of his fatherhood over us, proof of his divine claim on us, proof of his friendship to us, and proof of our preciousness to him.[45] The same Christ who was pierced for sinners is the Christ who governs and rules over every trial, measuring every sting with "a love which can give no unnecessary pain to those for whom he died upon the cross."[46]

Trials: Satan's Lies

And yet while every trial in the life of the Christian is designed for ultimate good (Rom. 8:28), sometimes those trials are the result of the Lord allowing Satan "to rage" on our lives, a taste of what Job experienced. Whether or not he is an instrument of our pain, Satan loves to fish in troubled waters, "to assault believers when under the pressure of great trials," and to convince us of deadly lies that threaten to undo all the good God has designed.[47] When trials hit, Satan deceives. And here are four of his evil designs, according to Newton:[48]

1. *Futility.* Satan aims to persuade the believer that God has no design in suffering, that the suffering is vain, and that God is essentially powerless to stop it. Satan despises the idea that his power and influence on us are governed by God for our good.

2. *Complaint.* Satan tempts us to charge God with "impatient" speeches, to complain and to decry God, which is "like letting in wind upon a smothering fire, which will make it burn more fiercely." When the believer

[44] *Letters* (Jones), 115.
[45] W, 3:456–57.
[46] *Letters* (Taylor), 142, 192.
[47] *Letters* (Taylor), 199.
[48] W, 1:232–35.

complains in the trial, it only aggravates the pain and makes the trial unnecessarily more painful to endure (Job 1:22).[49]

3. *Profanity*. Satan hatches blasphemous thoughts of God in the mind of the believer during the trial to make it appear that these come from the heart of the believer, causing the believer to be disillusioned by the blasphemy. "When a child of God is prompted to blaspheme the name that he adores, or to commit such evils as even unsanctified nature would recoil at; the enemy has done it."

4. *Distraction*. When Christ was most in pain, he prayed most earnestly, and we must battle for such fervency in prayer when trials hit. Satan uses trials to drive a wedge between the believer and the throne of grace, our stronghold in the storm of trials. To one suffering friend, Newton closed a letter with this advice: "Above all, keep close to the Throne of Grace. If we seem to get no good by attempting to draw near him, we may be sure we shall get none by keeping away from him."[50] Satan's attempt to pry us away from the throne of grace in our trials is his effort either to stop our prayers or to frustrate them. Our prayers seem most feeble and short and empty when the trials come, but we must press toward the throne and not run away. Satan entices us to think our short and feeble prayers are ineffectual and vain, and yet "short, frequent, and fervent petitions, which will almost necessarily arise from what is felt when temptation is violent, are best suited to the case."[51]

In other words, Satan's work amid trials is to further aggravate the pain with disillusionment and hopelessness in God. At root, he must first convince the believer that the trial is not from God. Naturalism, secularism, materialism, theological liberalism, open theism, the prosperity gospel, and a host of other modern ideologies cannot comprehend God's intentional, sovereign, loving design over the tragedy of human suffering.[52] The

---

[49] Timothy Keller: "One of the reasons many of you are in a great deal of distress now is because you refuse to see the frustrations, pressures, stresses, and the disappointments of your life as having an order to them, as being part of God's order, his training. John Newton, the great hymn writer, said he never had much trouble when God would alter his life; he only had a lot of trouble when God would alter his day" (sermon, "The Only Wise God" [November 22, 1992]).

[50] *W*, 2:148. Keller, building off Newton's quote, writes: "Suffering drives us toward God to pray as we never would otherwise. At first this experience of prayer is usually dry and painful. But if we are not daunted and we cling to him, we will often find greater depths of experience and, yes, of divine love and joy than we thought possible" (Timothy Keller, *Walking with God through Pain and Suffering* [New York: Dutton, 2013], 192).

[51] *W*, 1:235.

[52] Keller: "Christianity teaches that, contra fatalism, suffering is overwhelming; contra Buddhism, suffering is real; contra karma, suffering is often unfair; but contra secularism, suffering is meaningful. There is a purpose to it, and if faced rightly, it can drive us like a nail deep into the love of God and into more stability and spiritual power than you can imagine" (*Walking with God through Pain and Suffering*, 30; see also 11–84).

truth is that God designs trials for Christians, and those trials, says Newton, "are not the tokens of God's displeasure, but fatherly chastisements,
and tokens of his love, designed to promote the work of grace in their
hearts, and to make them partakers of his holiness."[53] In the furnace, we
must be aware of Satan's designs aimed at unnecessarily aggravating the
pain and embittering us toward God. In trials, we battle for the truth, battle
for trust, battle to embrace trials.

"My Carriage Is Broken!"

Even while we fight the good fight of faith, our gut response to loss often will
start with bickering and whining. One of Newton's most famous stories comes
in another meeting he had with a woman who lost her material wealth.

> I went one day to Mrs. G——'s, just after she had lost all her fortune. I could
> not be surprised to find her in tears: but she said, "I suppose you think I
> am crying for my loss, but that is not the case: I am now weeping to think
> I should feel so much uneasiness on the account." After that I never heard
> her speak again upon the subject as long as she lived. Now this is just as it
> should be. Suppose a man was going to York to take possession of a large
> estate, and his chaise [carriage] should break down a mile before he got
> to the city, which obliged him to *walk* the rest of the way; what a fool we
> should think him, if we saw him wringing his hands, and blubbering out
> all the remaining mile, "My chaise is broken! My chaise is broken!"[54]

Hope of our eternal wealth recasts every inconvenience and pain experienced in this life. Every trial in the Christian life is carefully measured out
and applied by necessity. Every trial is "a need-be," Newton often said.[55] They
are all either "salutary medicines," or "honorable appointments," to put us
in circumstances that best qualify us to honor our Savior.[56] That means one
of the great miracles in the Christian life is when God equips Christians not
only to *not* blubber about them, but also to submit and endure trials and
even to value and embrace them.

John Newton condensed into one sentence what Timothy Keller calls
"an ocean of biblical theology in a thimble."[57] Writes Newton, "All shall

---

[53] W, 4:239.
[54] W, 1:107–8.
[55] W, 1:249, 443; 2:178; 6:99, 264.
[56] W, 6:338.
[57] Keller, *Walking with God through Pain and Suffering* , 267.

work together for good: everything is needful that *he sends*; nothing can be needful that *he withholds*."[58] All of the *sending* and the *withholding* in our lives is managed by God for our ultimate flourishing. But do we believe it? "How happy are they who can resign all to him, see his hand in every dispensation, and believe that he chooses better for them than they possibly could for themselves!"[59] The truth is that our peace depends on our sin being subdued, and Christ subdues our sin through the wisely chosen medicine called "trials." Therefore,

> look upon him as a physician who has graciously undertaken to heal your soul of the worst of sicknesses, sin. Yield to his prescriptions, and fight against every thought that would represent it as desirable to be permitted to choose for yourself. When you cannot see your way, be satisfied that he is your leader. When your spirit is overwhelmed within you, he knows your path: he will not leave you to sink.[60]

Newton's unshaken confidence in Christ emerges in these words.

In metaphors like the carriage, Newton stresses how temporal losses in life make our eternal riches more real to us. All our trials are disciplinary, and as disciplinary, all our trials are designed for our good; since they are designed for our good, we must learn to subject ourselves to them. Even in the most painful wounds left by the malice of others, such pains are intended in the Christian life to bring about ultimate good (Gen. 50:20).[61]

---

[58] *W*, 2:147. Not only in his recent book on suffering, but throughout his preaching ministry in Manhattan, Keller has frequently stressed Newton's point. "John Newton says, 'Everything is necessary that he sends. Nothing can be necessary that he withholds.' Sometimes I wonder how anybody gets through life without memorizing that little saying" (sermon, "The Only Wise God"). "John Newton put it so perfectly. I try to say it every year or so, but that's probably not enough. Memorize this: 'Everything is necessary that he sends. Nothing can be necessary that he withholds.' If it's in your life, you need it, even if it's bad. If it's not in your life, you don't need it, even though you think you do. Why? Because there is an order to your life. Your Father hates to see brokenness and tragedy, but he is monitoring it. He's letting it into your life in stages in ways that actually will teach you the things he wants you to learn" (sermon, "How To Handle Trouble" [September 26, 1993]). "'Everything is necessary that he sends. Nothing can be necessary that he withholds.' The premise is the things that really hurt you and really kill you are foolishness, pride, selfishness, hardness of heart, denial of your flaws and weaknesses, and the belief that you don't need God. Those are the only things that can hurt you in the long run. Those are the only things that can hurt you in the totality of your life. In the short run, selfishness feels great. In the long run, it will destroy you. . . . Any bad thing (and the bad things God hates), God will bring in only to cure you of the things that can really destroy you in the long run, in the totality. . . . One of the main reasons, I think, why a lot of Christians are continually overthrown is not because bad things are happening to them. At least fifty-percent of their discouragement and their despondency is the surprise that the bad things have happened to them. Do you see the distinction?" (sermon, "A Christian's Happiness" [July 6, 1997]).

[59] *W*, 1:456.

[60] *W*, 2:147.

[61] In a curious reference from his life, reminiscent of Jacob meeting his brothers, Newton later returned to Africa to face the woman who oppressed him for two years. "Her name sounds like the letter P, or, I believe rather like the two letters PI. When I went there as a captain of a ship, I sent my long boat ashore for her. They soon brought her on board. I desired the men to fire guns over her head, in honor of her,

Newton is not afraid to say that Christians are to rejoice in trials, and thank God for them.[62]

The Sovereign Dispenser of Trials

Again, afflictions and trials are never coincidental in the Christian life. Not ever. "Afflictions spring not out of the ground, but are fruits and tokens of Divine love, no less than his comforts; that there is a need-be, whenever for a season [one] is in heaviness."[63] When his daughter Eliza endured deep depression, Newton wrote: "My trial is great, but the all-sufficient Lord is my support. I am sure this affliction did not spring out of the ground. I trust the event will be to his glory and our good."[64] And as Newton's sister-in-law (Mrs. Cunningham) lay dying, he wrote:

> We have two comforts—first, to know that afflictions spring not out of the dust, but they are appointed by him who does all things well, and who is all-sufficient to make up every loss. And secondly, with respect to Mrs. Cunningham, we know that our loss will be her gain. Jesus is her Shepherd and Savior, her sun and shield, she knows his name, and puts her trust in him. Even now he supports her, and enables her to look forward with comfort; and whenever she leaves this world she will be happy in and with him forever. Therefore I trust we shall not sorrow as them that have no hope; nor complain, because the Lord has done it. Yet it will be a trial.[65]

Newton lives with the rhetorical question ringing in his ear: Does disaster strike, unless the Lord has done it? (Amos 3:6). The Lord's doing—his mysterious will—will not make the pain less painful, but it puts the pain into eternal perspective. He is wise, and we are not. He sees the whole path of our lives; we cannot. Therefore it would be foolish for us to plan our lives or determine what is good for us. To a friend with a sick wife, Newton wrote:

> But I am so short sighted as to events and consequences, that in any supposable case, I seem to tremble at the thought of having my own choice,

because she did not intend it. She seemed to feel it like heaping coals of fire upon her head. I made her some presents, and sent her ashore. She seemed to feel most comfortable when she had her back to my ship" (*Letters* [Campbell], 181).
[62] W, 1:227.
[63] W, 1:443.
[64] *Letters* (Bull 1847), 305.
[65] Letters (Barlass), 601.

even if it were allowed me to choose. In my better judgment I am pleased
to think, that infinite wisdom and goodness have engaged to manage for
me. I am sure that afflictions do not happen at random, nor spring out of
the ground; that the Lord takes no pleasure in afflicting us. . . . You may be
assured he will not try you beyond what he will enable you to bear. If it be
for your good, especially for your chief good, *his glory*, she shall recover;
he will restore her, though a hundred physicians had given her up.[66]

Christians can embrace trials for one reason: Christ reigns supreme
over the trials for our eternal good. If Christ reigns over all the situations
and circumstances of our lives (and he does), and if we suffer the sting of
affliction (and we do), then it can only be explained by understanding the
necessity of trials. "Faithful are the wounds of that friend who was himself
wounded and slain for us, and who now reigns over all."[67] Christ is sovereign over trials: he is

the Supreme Disposer of all that concerns us, that he numbers the very
hairs of our heads, appoints every trial we meet with in number, weight,
and measure, and will suffer nothing to befall us but what shall contribute to our good;—this view, I say, is a medicine suited to the disease, and
powerfully reconciles us unto every cross.[68]

"What a comfort to be assured that our afflictions do not happen to us at
random, but are all under the direction of infinite wisdom and love, and all
engaged to work together for good to them that love the Lord."[69] No pain or
suffering is felt in life that is not sovereignly coordinated by the plan and
will of God for our lives. "Diseases hear his voice," said Newton of Christ.[70]
So also the wind and the waves. No storms, no pain, no disease, no depression, no poverty, and no disability will ever enter our lives contrary to the
overruling purpose and design of Christ.

Stinging Unbelief

If Christ reigns over every trial and pain, our submission is imperative. When
trials hit, our unbelief can lead us to respond wrongly, only furthering the

---

[66] *Letters* (Ryland), 185.
[67] Letters (Palmer), 137.
[68] *W*, 6:5.
[69] Letters (Wilberforce), 39.
[70] *W*, 6:72. See also *Letters* (Bull 1847), 256.

damage and causing unnecessary pain. Even in affliction the believer can overflow with joy (2 Cor. 6:10; 7:4). All our unhappiness is triggered by unbelief. In other words, "The heaviest part of our trials is owing, not so much to the dispensations which cause them, as to the self-will and unbelief of our hearts; and our relief depends more upon the cure of our wrong inward dispositions, than upon any change of our outward circumstances."[71]

Newton never discounts the sharp pinch we feel in trials. But in that pain, the Christian's grief must be moderated by faith, by his trust in the all-powerful and all-wise King who manages all the details of his life (Mic. 4:9). When trials hit, *grief* exists alongside faith; but *excessive grief* is the product of unbelief.[72] Likewise, it's possible to kick against trials and prolong the pain and aggravate the sting.

Under the sovereign design of God, all trials can be embraced because "your peace does not depend upon any change of circumstances which may appear desirable, but in having your will bowed to the Lord's will, and made willing to submit all to his disposal and management."[73] The mature Christian, Newton writes, "will not only submit to trials, but rejoice in them, notwithstanding the feelings and reluctance of the flesh."[74] The voice of our reluctant flesh will always be heard when the trials arrive, and only faith can point us forward.

> For if I am redeemed from misery by the blood of Jesus; and if he is now preparing me a mansion near himself, that I may drink of the rivers of

---

[71] *W*, 5:622; *Letters* (Bull 1847), 233–34.

[72] Newton: "There is something fascinating in grief: painful as it is, we are prone to indulge it, and to brood over the thoughts and circumstances which are suited (like fuel to fire) to heighten and prolong it. When the Lord afflicts, it is his design that we should grieve: but in this, as in all other things, there is a certain moderation which becomes a Christian, and which only grace can teach; and grace teaches us, not by books or by hearsay, but by experimental lessons: all beyond this should be avoided and guarded against as sinful and hurtful. Grief, when indulged and excessive, preys upon the spirits, injures health, indisposes us for duty, and causes us to shed tears which deserve more tears" (*W*, 2:26). To another friend, Newton wrote something similar, "There is something fascinating in grief: though we feel it hurts our peace, and may know, that when it is great, and long continued, it threatens the very root of our usefulness, we are apt to indulge it, and to brood over sorrow till it gives a tincture to the whole frame of our spirit, and, perhaps, makes a lodgment in us, too deep to be removed. We say, indeed, the Lord is wise and good, and does all things well; and, for our principles' sake, we avoid positive complaint; but folded hands, downcast looks, and reiterated sighs, are deemed very allowable, as they doubtless are for a time; but, if for a long time, they become ensnaring and injurious. I pray the Lord to make you heartily willing to be wholly set at liberty from this insinuating and plausible source of pain; this willingness is half the matter, and will marvelously facilitate the cure. Dally no more with grief; try to cut short all recollections that feed the anguish of the mind" (*Letters* [Ryland], 193–94). To another friend, grieving at the loss of a beloved minister, he wrote, "Your loss is great. The first emotions of grief were unavoidable, and he who knows our frame allows us, that these things for the present are 'not joyous but grievous.' But neither shall I commend you if you indulge a continuance and excess of grief" (*Letters* [Taylor], 238; and *Letters* [Bull 1869], 409. See also *Letters* [Bull 1869], 281).

[73] *W*, 2:149.

[74] *W*, 2:35.

pleasure at his right hand for evermore (Ps. 16:11); the question is not (at least ought not to be), how may I pass through life with the least inconvenience? But, how may my little span of life be made most subservient to the praise and glory of him who loved me, and gave himself for me?[75]

This mindset is a key point in understanding Newton on trials: "God has greater ends in view by sending trials, than the mere personal good of the individual tried. Yes, his own glory" (John 9:1–3; 11:1–4).[76]

The Immediate Aim of Suffering

The *ultimate aim* of trials is to prepare us for eternal joy in Christ. But we still have not yet arrived at the *immediate aim* of trials. To find this answer we must return again to one of Newton's treasured passages, the words spoken by Christ to the apostle Paul:

> But he [Jesus] said to me, "My grace is sufficient for you, for my power is made perfect in weakness." Therefore I will boast all the more gladly of my weaknesses, so that the power of Christ may rest upon me. For the sake of Christ, then, I am content with weaknesses, insults, hardships, persecutions, and calamities. For when I am weak, then I am strong. (2 Cor. 12:9–10)

When Newton reads "my grace is sufficient," he translates this as the all-sufficient grace of Jesus Christ. This amazing grace, offered to those who are weak in their suffering, pours out from the person of Jesus Christ.

The immediate value of suffering is its potential to draw us *toward* Christ and into a fuller experience of our union with him. Trials are a doorway into deeper communion with Christ as we share in his sufferings (Rom. 8:17; 2 Cor. 1:5; 4:10; Phil. 3:10; Col. 1:24; 1 Pet. 4:13). "He has sanctified poverty, pain, disgrace, temptation, and death, by passing through these states: and in whatever states his people are, they may by faith have fellowship with him in their sufferings, and he will by sympathy and love have fellowship and interest with them in theirs."[77] Certainly, trials are the hammer blows that chisel off sins and idols and worldliness from the sculpture of grace God is fashioning in us. But most importantly, in each

---

[75] W, 2:35.
[76] *Letters* (Campbell), 163.
[77] W, 2:21.

trial, we are drawn to find our all-sufficiency in Christ. Newton put the constrictive power of trials perhaps most famously in the lines of a hymn mentioned earlier. Trials are God's gracious response to the prayer for maturity. The Lord says at the end of the hymn,

> These inward trials I employ,
> From self and pride to set thee free;
> And break thy schemes of earthly joy,
> That thou mayst seek thy all in me.[78]

In these lines we find the immediate value of trials. Trials come into our lives for our good—the good of emptying us of ourselves. Trials humble us; they set us free from pride. Trials break us off from seeking our identity and highest joys in this world. Part of why trials make Christ beautiful to our eyes is that trials break off all our worldly securities, and in the moment of suffering, we see that wealth and notoriety and possessions and lust and all the other allurements of the world are emptied of their appeal, and we are left, like the bankrupt prodigal, running home. "When great trials are in view," Newton writes,

> we run simply and immediately to our all-sufficient Friend, feel our dependence, and cry in good earnest for help; but if the occasion seems small, we are too apt secretly to lean to our own wisdom and strength, as if in such slight matters we could make shift without him. Therefore in these we often fail.[79]

Trials remove every false support in our lives to make it possible for us to deepen our delight in Christ. "A considerable part of our trials are mercifully appointed to wean us from this propensity; and it is gradually weakened by the Lord's shewing us at one time the vanity of the creature, and at another his own excellence and all-sufficiency."[80] "When forced from one creature-comfort perch upon another, the Lord mercifully follows us with trials, and will not let us rest upon any. By degrees our desires take a nobler flight, and can be satisfied with nothing short of himself."[81] And when all of this is happening, trials draw us to seek mercy and greater delights from

[78] *W*, 3:607–8.
[79] *W*, 1:622.
[80] *W*, 1:214.
[81] *W*, 2:219.

Christ, because, "as sufferings abound, consolations also abound by Jesus Christ" (2 Cor. 1:5).[82] The more pain we feel, the more aware we become of our weakness and Christ's all-sufficiency. Joy in Christ is the key to enduring trials.

> Natural fortitude, and cold reasonings, more conformable to the philosophy of the heathens, than to the spirit of the gospel, may stifle complaints; but to rejoice in tribulation, and in every thing give thanks, are privileges peculiar to those who can joy in God through our Lord Jesus Christ, by whom they have obtained reconciliation.[83]

Only by delighting ourselves in Christ can we embrace the trials of life. "Oh, the name of Jesus, when we can speak of him as ours; this is the balm for every wound, cordial for every care; it is as ointment poured forth, diffusing a fragrance through the whole soul, and driving away the hurtful fumes and fogs of distrust and discontent!"[84] There is no wasted pain in the Christian life if that pain draws us closer to Christ, for Christ is never more all-sufficient for us than when Christ is all we have. The *ultimate aim* of suffering is to ready us to worship Christ eternally (sight). The *immediate aim* of suffering is to draw us closer to Christ in communion (faith). To live in trials is Christ.

Metaphors for God's Presence

Before we leave this theme of trials, Newton would want us to sharpen one final point. It should be clear by now that the Christian's trials cannot be explained as the experience of Christ's forsaking and withdrawing from us. Christian trials are not the wrath of a holy God, but the loving discipline of a tender Father drawn close. Never is Christ more active in the Christian life than when we discover our greatest need for help. When the Lord puts us in the furnace to purify us and to remove the dross of sin and false securities and idolatries, he is not discarding or abandoning us. Quite the opposite, Newton assures us:

> The innumerable comforts and mercies with which he enriches even those we call darker days, are sufficient proofs that he does not willingly

---

[82] W, 2:31.
[83] W, 6:424–25.
[84] W, 6:33–34.

grieve us: but when he sees a need-be for chastisement, he will not with-hold it because he loves us; on the contrary, that is the very reason why he afflicts. He will put his silver into the fire to purify it; but he sits by the furnace as a refiner, to direct the process, and to secure the end he has in view, that we may neither suffer too much nor suffer in vain.[85]

There is a furnace for every Christian. Pain is a form of discipline. It is needful. But God regulates the furnace, and he never closes the door and walks away. "The Lord has been pleased to put us in the fire," to be sure, "but, blessed be his name, we are not burnt."[86] Every trial has a temperature setting and a duration intended for our ultimate good.

Likewise, Christ is a skilled surgeon. "Faithful are the wounds of our infallible Friend; he sometimes cuts deep, but never too deep, nor in the wrong place, nor at the wrong time, and he is near to heal. Perhaps the pain may be felt for a season; but it will subside as the cure advances, till at length nothing will remain but a scar."[87] Trials will overwhelm us if we think of them as the result of God's oversight, forgetfulness, or abandon-ment. All our sufferings are the incisions of a divine surgeon, perfectly suited to our ultimate spiritual needs. The pain God brings into our lives by his sovereign power has an end and an aim in our flourishing.

Christ is not like a stoic king but more like a compassionate mother at-tending her newborn. "Sooner shall the most tender mother sit insensible and inattentive to the cries and wants of her infant," Newton writes, "than the Lord Jesus be an unconcerned spectator of his suffering children."[88]

No, with the eye, and the ear, and the heart of a friend, he attends to their sorrows; he counts their sighs, puts their tears in his bottle; and when our spirits are overwhelmed within us, he knows our path, and adjusts the time, the measure of our trials, and every thing that is necessary for our present support and seasonable deliverance, with the same unerring wisdom and accuracy as he weighed the mountains in scales and hills in a balance, and meted out the heavens with a span.[89]

The combined force of these metaphors points to a profound real-ity. Newton was fully convinced that the hands guiding storms and trials

---

[85] W, 2:21.
[86] W, 6:62.
[87] Letters (Taylor), 140.
[88] W, 2:20.
[89] W, 2:20.

into our lives are the same hands pierced by nails to redeem our souls. The Christ crushed in agonizing pain for sinners is the same Christ who governs and rules over every trial, measuring every sting with "a love which can give no unnecessary pain to those for whom he died upon the cross."[90] If Christ bore for us the searing agony of God's wrath, the same Christ will never send into our lives one pinch of pain beyond what is absolutely necessary for our ultimate flourishing. Whatever pain is *necessary*, our crucified Savior will dispense. Whatever pain is *unnecessary*, our crucified Savior will withhold. Such careful and loving providence is proven by the pain he bore for us on the cross.

Newton's Great Trial

Most of our trials are experienced in various daily pains: little frustrations, failures, pressures, stresses, disappointments, and the like. But there are times when massive trials hit, and hit hard.

John Newton fell in love immediately when he met Mary Catlett (or Polly) for the first time. He was an immature seventeen-year-old boy; she was a mature thirteen-year-old. Against all odds, they would later marry and enjoy over forty years of love and faithful companionship. Their beautiful love story was preserved when John edited and published his letters to Polly after her death, and was later brought to life in a 430-page biographical novel by Grace Irwin.[91] After reading the novel, English professor Clyde Kilby asked, "Is there anywhere a more beautiful love story than that of John Newton and Mary Catlett?"[92]

Perhaps not. Polly was his right hand, John Newton often said, and only death could separate them. Their sad moment of parting came on the night of December 15, 1790. John was at Polly's bedside as she neared the end of a long and painful battle with cancer. Holding a candle in the evening darkness, John watched and prayed as Polly's breathing became increasingly labored. Finally, late in the evening, she passed peacefully to heaven.

For the remainder of his life, John Newton would refer to the loss of his beloved wife as "my great trial"—a necessary trial—but one that hurt deeply, and one he said he would not experience again for all the wealth of the Indies. Those things in life that bring the most comfort are the things

---

[90] *Letters* (Taylor), 142, 192. See also *Letters* (Bull 1847), 124; W, 2:178.
[91] For the letters from John to Polly, see W, 5:303–644. For the novel, see Grace Irwin, *Servant of Slaves: A Biographical Novel of John Newton* (Grand Rapids: Eerdmans, 1961).
[92] Front cover of Irwin, *Servant of Slaves.*

that, when taken away, leave the harshest sting. And the loss of his beloved Polly stung every day of his widowed life for the next seventeen years (or 6,214 days). Daily he thought of her, and annually he observed the date of her death as a solemn day of reflection.

On the one-year anniversary of her passing, Newton was afforded a moment to testify of God's all-sufficient promises in a letter to a friend who faced the sickness, and likely death, of a son. The trial of Newton, still fresh in his memory, led him to pen this testimony—a rather grisly, but faith-filled witness of God's sustaining grace in suffering.

> I have not only *read* these gracious promises [in Scripture], and *believe* them to be true, but I have *tried* them, and *found* them to be true. I never was, strictly speaking, a father, though I think I have come tolerably near the feelings of one; but I have been a husband, and I think, in that rela- tion, I have known all the tender feelings, both pleasing and painful, of which the human heart is susceptible. . . . At length, the trial which I most dreaded came upon me. Suspense was long; sensations were keen. My right hand was not chopped off at a stroke (I would be thankful, however, that it was not). It was sawn off by slow degrees; it was an operation of weeks and months; almost every following week more painful than the preceding. But did I sink? Did I despond? Did I refuse my food? Did sleep forsake my eyes? Was I so troubled in mind or weakened in body that I could not speak? Far, far from it. The Lord strengthened me, and I was strong. No part of my public service was interrupted; and, perhaps, I never preached with more energy than at that period. . . . I felt as much as I could well bear, but not too much; and to this hour I only stand because I am upheld. Were I left a little to myself, there is enough in my heart still to make me very wretched under a sense of my loss.[93]

[93] *Letters* (Bull 1847), 257–59.

CHAPTER 10

THE GOAL OF BIBLE READING

In this chapter we focus on only one means of grace—Bible reading. The emphasis is not intended to diminish or overlook Newton's wise instruction on prayer[1] or fasting or the Lord's Supper, or any of the other means of grace (or what he called *medicines*), but to put the emphasis appropriately where he places it—on Scripture. Since all the disciplines for Newton center on Christ, all the disciplines in the Christian life ultimately center on the

---

[1] To cite just one example, Newton writes: "I sometimes think that the prayers of believers afford a stronger proof of a depraved nature than even the profaneness of those who know not the Lord. How strange is it, that when I have the fullest convictions that prayer is not only my duty—not only necessary as the appointed means of receiving these supplies, without which I can do nothing, but likewise the greatest honor and privilege to which I can be admitted in the present life—I should still find myself so unwilling to engage in it. However, I think it is not prayer itself that I am weary of, but such prayers as *mine*. How can it be accounted prayer, when the heart is so little affected—when it is polluted with such a mixture of vile and vain imaginations—when I hardly know what I say myself—but I feel my mind collected one minute, the next, my thoughts are gone to the ends of the earth. If what I express with my lips were written down, and the thoughts which at the same time are passing through my heart were likewise written between the lines, the whole taken together would be such an absurd and incoherent jumble—such a medley of inconsistency, that it might pass for the ravings of a lunatic. When he points out to me the wildness of this jargon, and asks, is this a prayer fit to be presented to the holy heart-searching God? I am at a loss what to answer, till it is given to me to recollect that I am not under the law, but under grace—that my hope is to be placed, not in my own prayers, but in the righteousness and intercession of Jesus. The poorer and viler I am in myself, so much the more is the power and riches of his grace magnified in my behalf. Therefore I must, and, the Lord being my helper, I will pray on, and admire his condescension and love, that he can and does take notice of such a creature—for the event shows, that those prayers which are even displeasing to myself, partial as I am in my own case, are acceptable to him, how else should they be answered? And that I am still permitted to come to a throne of grace—still supported in my walk and in my work, and that mine enemies have not yet prevailed against me, and triumphed over me, affords a full proof that the Lord has heard and has accepted my poor prayers—yea, it is possible, that those very prayers of ours of which we are most ashamed, are the most pleasing to the Lord, and for that reason, because we *are* ashamed of them. When we are favored with what we call enlargement, we come away tolerably satisfied with ourselves, and think we have done well" (*Letters* [Jones], 109–11).

revelation of Christ in God's holy Word. And because 2 Corinthians 3:18 and 4:6 operate as the *medulla* of the Christian life, under this heading of Bible reading we begin tying together several themes already touched on: the all-sufficiency of Christ, the daily need for communion with Christ, and Christ's sanctifying glory.

Approaching Scripture

Proper Bible reading begins before we open the book. It begins in our approach. In a pair of sermons titled "On Searching the Scriptures" (John 5:39), Newton explains *how* four elements inform our approach to the Bible—*sincerity, diligence, humility,* and *prayer.*

As we might expect, Newton introduces his approach with the language of *sincerity.*

> I mean a real desire to be instructed by the Scripture, and to submit both our sentiments and our practices to be controlled and directed by what we read there. Without this, our reading and searching will only issue in our greater condemnation, and bring us under the heavy doom of the servant that knew his master's will and did it not.[2]

If we read the Bible for self-justification or to prove ourselves right, or if we have no intention of changing our lives based upon what we read, we've already failed in our approach. The Bible was given to teach us, reprove us, and correct us (2 Tim. 3:16), and none of these transformations are possible unless we approach the Bible in submission to what will change us, teach us, reprove us, and correct us.

The second element of our approach is *diligence.* Many readers of the Bible are simply ignorant of the precious value of the eternal wisdom they hold in their hands. They lack care, and they need to be urged to search this book of treasure with greater diligence (John 5:39).

> The word which is rendered *search,* ἐρευνάω, is borrowed from the practice of miners: it implies two things, *to dig* and *to examine.* First, with much labor they pierce the earth to a considerable depth; and when they have thus found a vein of precious ore, they break and sift it, and suffer no part to escape their notice. Thus must we join frequent assiduous reading, with close and awakened meditation; comparing spiritual things with spiritual,

---

carefully taking notice of the circumstances, occasion, and application of what we read; being assured, that there is a treasure of truth and happiness under our hands, if we have but skill to discover and improve it.[3]

By applying these first two approaches together—*sincerity* and *diligence*—we will avoid wasting our lives.[4] "Let us not be like fools, with a prize, an inestimable prize, in our hands, but without heart or skill to use it."[5]

Third, we must approach the Bible with *humility*. God gives grace to the humble, and he resists the proud (James 4:6; 1 Pet. 5:5). We do not come to the Bible with confidence in our powers of interpretation; we approach with humble dependence on the God who is eager to reveal himself. False teaching is spread by a vain interpreter who has

> undertaken by his own strength and wisdom to decide authoritatively on the meaning of Scripture; without being aware of the ignorance, prejudice, and weakness, which influence his judgment in religious matters; without knowing the utter inability of the natural man to discern the things of God, and without attending to those means the Scripture itself has appointed for the redress of these evils.[6]

And so we approach the Bible with deep reverence and humility in proportion to our self-distrust when handling eternal truths.

Finally, we approach the Bible in *prayer*. Sincerity, diligence, and humility are all gifts from God, and therefore a right approach to Scripture presses us toward prayer. "Prayer is indeed the best half of our business while upon earth, and that which gives spirit and efficacy to all the rest. Prayer is not only our immediate duty, but the highest dignity, the richest privilege we are capable of receiving on this side of eternity."[7] One of Newton's hymns captures what we participate in when we pray:

> Thou art coming to a King,
> Large petitions with thee bring;
> For his grace and pow'r are such,
> None can ever ask too much.[8]

---

[3] *W*, 2:325.
[4] *W*, 2:326.
[5] *W*, 2:336.
[6] *W*, 2:327.
[7] *W*, 2:328.
[8] *W*, 3:341. Timothy Keller frequently cites this from Newton in his messages: "If you're pessimistic about what God can do in your life and what God can do through you, you are not treating him as a King. Can you

We pray rightly when we pray largely. We approach God as a King only when we pray for things that an all-sufficient King alone can offer, which includes accurate understanding of his Word. Therefore, in light of these prayer privileges, all theological education, our work in the original languages, and our access to commentaries will only stoke our pride if we fail to approach the Bible with true sincerity and humility, evidenced in dependent prayer.[9] With that in mind, Newton can say that the prayerless are "utterly unqualified to 'search the Scripture.'"[10] Only the prayerful—those whose prayers are properly King-sized—are rightly positioned to dig into and discover and be changed by the magnificent wisdom of God and the precious things of Scripture (Ps. 119:18; James 1:5).

Christ in the Old Testament

One King-sized prayer could include this aim: finding the glory of Christ in the Old Testament. By opening the Bible we discover that Christ is "the main design and subject" to the entire Bible, and he can be found in every *book* and on almost every *page* of the Bible.[11] Christ should inform our interpretations of Old Testament *prophecies*, *types*, and *ceremonies*. The prophecies of Christ include promises that Jesus would be born to a virgin in Bethlehem 490 years after the command to rebuild Jerusalem; his ministry would begin in Galilee; and he would be despised and rejected of men, betrayed by one of his disciples, and sold for thirty pieces of silver.[12]

Newton divides the *types* of Christ in the Old Testament between *personal types* and *relative types*. The first category includes Adam, Enoch, Melchizedek, Isaac, Joseph, Moses, Aaron, Joshua, Samson, David, and Solomon as types or figures of Christ in his person or humiliation or exaltation. Of relative types he includes the ark of Noah, the rainbow, the manna, and the brazen serpent.[13]

The same is true of the Old Testament religious ceremonies, each pointing forward to a consummate fulfillment in Christ.

The ark of the covenant, the mercy-seat, the tabernacle, the incense, the altar, the offerings, the high priest with his ornaments and garments, the

serve him? Can you obey him? Can you kiss him? Can you rejoice with trembling? There is no refuge from him, but there is a tremendous refuge in him. Blessed are those who find refuge in the King" (sermon, "Jesus Our King" [December 12, 1993]).
[9] W, 2:329–30.
[10] W, 2:328.
[11] W, 2:330.
[12] W, 2:331–32.
[13] W, 2:332.

laws relating to the leper, the Nazarite, and the redemption of lands—all these, and many more had a deep and important meaning beyond their outward appearance: each, in their place, pointed to "the Lamb of God who was to take away the sins of the world" (John 1:29), derived their efficacy *from him*, and received their full accomplishment *in him*.[14]

Indeed "Christ is the end of the Law, the sum of the Prophets, the completion of the promises, the scope of the types and ceremonies, and the great object of the whole Old Testament dispensation."[15]

One of the best extended illustrations of Christ's presence in the Old Testament is found in Newton's two-volume book *Messiah: Fifty Expository Discourses, On the Series of Scriptural Passages Which Form the Subject of the Celebrated Oratorio of Handel*, a series of fifty sermons preached in 1784 and 1785, which follow Handel's biblical citations in sermon form. When the two-volume collection was sent to press the next year, Newton, then sixty years old, called it "my most important publication" (and added, "it will probably be my last").

Messiah is a significant achievement, designed to confront what Newton perceived to be the dangerous spirit of the age: attending performances of the oratorio as a mere act of entertainment devoid of any necessary spiritual value. (Having attended modern performances of *Messiah* in places like the National Cathedral in Washington, DC, I resonate with Newton's sentiment. One wonders how many in the crowded seats are beholding the glory of Christ in the lyrics.) Newton clearly felt this tension, saw the popularity of the oratorio, and delivered his fifty Christ-exalting sermons to capitalize on the wide popularity of the piece to make the glory of Christ as explicit as possible. Not surprisingly the sermons are joy-filled, God-centered, and Christ-exulting.[16] And yet, of the sixty-three biblical passages that comprise the libretto, thirty-six are taken from the Old Testament. For the series, Newton invested much prayer and preparation in preaching Christ from the Old Testament.

A Sermon Worth Preaching

Preaching fifty consecutive sermons on the glory of Christ is ambitious, but not impossible, given the inexhaustible subject of the person and

---

[14] *W*, 2:333.
[15] *W*, 2:339.
[16] By sheer keyword frequency, *God* appears 1,097 times. Terms for the person of Christ (*Jesus, Christ, Saviour, Lamb*) appear 583 times. Terms for the work of Christ (*cross, crucifixion, atonement, blood, gospel*) appear 573 times. Other prominent terms include *joy, happiness*, and *rejoicing* (373), *glory* (311), and *grace* (173).

work of Christ. In fact, "it is not worth while to preach unless we preach Christ and him crucified."[17] Such a Christ is all-sufficient for every sermon, because he is all-sufficient, and the all-sufficient answer for every need in life:

> It is thus the Scriptures, to help the weakness of our apprehensions, testify of Christ, under the threefold view of Prophet, Priest, and King of his people. These are his principal and leading characters, which include and imply the rest; for the time would fail to speak of him, as he is declared to be their Head, Husband, Root, Foundation, Sun, Shield, Shepherd, Lawgiver, Exemplar, and Forerunner. In brief, there is hardly any comfortable relation, or useful office, amongst men; hardly any object in the visible creation, which either displays beauty, or produces benefit, but what is applied in the word of God, to illustrate the excellence and sufficiency of the Lord Jesus Christ. The intent of all is, that we may learn to trust him, and delight to serve him; for these must go together.[18]

Christ should be in our thoughts and our delights as we enjoy creation, as we dwell on the people we depend on daily, and of course as we study the Old and New Testaments.

Of the Christian who searches the Bible with sincerity, diligence, humility, and prayer in order to discover and enjoy Christ, Newton wrote:

> He is happy in life; for the word of God is to him as a "fountain of living water." He shall be happy in death; the promises of his God shall support him through that dark valley: and he shall be happy forever in the presence and love of him for whose sake he now searches the Scripture; "whom having not seen," yet, from the testimony there given of him, "he loves; in whom, though now he sees him not, yet, believing, he rejoices with joy unspeakable and full of glory" (1 Pet. 1:8).[19]

As we pursue the glory of Christ in Scripture, we discover God's will for our lives. God "guides and directs his people, by affording them, in answer to prayer, the light of his Holy Spirit, which enables them to understand and to love the Scriptures." By loving the Bible we behold Christ, and by beholding Christ we take hold of power for all outlets of the Christian life. Newton wrote of this biblical empowering of Christians:

---

[17] *Letters* (Bull 1847), 207.
[18] *W*, 2:349–50.
[19] *W*, 2:337.

The word of God dwells richly in them, is a preservative from error, a light to their feet, and a spring of strength and consolation. By treasuring up the doctrines, precepts, promises, examples, and exhortations of Scripture, in their minds, and daily comparing themselves with the rule by which they walk, they grow into an habitual frame of spiritual wisdom, and acquire a gracious taste, which enables them to judge of right and wrong with a degree of readiness and certainty, as a musical ear judges of sounds.[20]

Awareness of Scripture tunes our inclinations so that we can make small decisions of obedience every day.

John Newton's Bible Reading Plan

So how do we best read the Bible? Newton's advice is clear and simple:

I know not a better rule of reading the Scripture, than to read it through from beginning to end; and, when we have finished it once, to begin it again. We shall meet with many passages which we can make little improvement of, but not so many in the second reading as in the first, and fewer in the third than in the second.[21]

Guided Bible-reading plans may be additionally useful, but his main point is important. Rereading the Bible over and over will help you make sense of Scripture. And reviewing Scripture over and over will help you see more of Christ. To see Christ on every page requires a familiarity with the entire Bible, a point Newton makes in one hymn:

Precious Bible! what a treasure
Does the word of God afford!
All I want for life or pleasure,
FOOD and MED'CINE, SHIELD and SWORD:
    Let the world account me poor,
    Having this I need no more.

FOOD to which the world's a stranger,
Here my hungry soul enjoys;
Of excess there is no danger,

---

[20] *W*, 1:329–31.
[21] *W*, 6:418.

Though it fills, it never cloys:
On a dying Christ I feed,
He is meat and drink indeed![22]

All Bible study, done rightly, is a feast upon Christ and him crucified.

The Other Books

Newton was self-educated and loved to read both the Bible and other books. By highlighting the value of Scripture, he sounds an appropriate warning: "There are *silver* books; and a very few *golden* books: but I have one book worth more than all, called the Bible; and that is a book of *bank-notes*."[23] In other books, even books by Christians, "a mixture of human infirmity is inseparable from the best human composition; but in the fountain the truth is unmixed."[24] The value of the Bible (for those with eyes to see) is incalculable and inexhaustible. Foolish is the sinner who neglects the infallible Bible for fallible books or simply neglects Scripture, a common tendency for Christians and a trend Newton lamented in his own life. "There is no right knowledge of God where the Bible is not known."[25]

> Alas, how much time have I lost and wasted, which, had I been wise, I should have devoted to reading and studying the Bible! But my evil heart obstructs the dictates of my judgment, I often feel a reluctance to read this book of books, and a disposition to hew out broken cisterns which afford me no water, while the fountain of living waters are close within my reach.[26]

Bible neglect is an ethical lapse, and a gold mine untapped.

But as long as we are not reading other books *instead of* Scripture, there is a proper place for reading books *alongside* Scripture. If we have time for only one book, let that be Scripture. In reading "human authors," especially theologians, Newton suggests reading books like eating an apple—eat what's good, toss the rest.[27] In speaking of building a library, Newton commends Bunyan's *Pilgrim's Progress* and Augustine's *Confessions*, along with spiritual biographies of faithful saints in previous centuries.[28] New-

---

[22] W, 3:528.
[23] W, 1:108.
[24] W, 6:416.
[25] W, 4:79.
[26] W, 6:418–19.
[27] *Letters* (Coffin), 88.
[28] W, 6:211–12.

ton gives priority "to those books that can say something to me about Jesus, or give me some directions towards stirring me up to faith and communion with him."[29] If you are looking to prioritize books in your busy life, put the priority on books that disclose the beauty of Christ and warm your affections toward him. True knowledge, true learning, will make sin *more hateful* and Jesus *more precious* to the soul.[30] Books that achieve this end should find priority in our libraries.[31]

Likewise, Newton was drawn to letters by their heartwarming potential. He admits to having more interest in reading personal letters over books, which often have the opposite effect.

> I get more warmth and light sometimes by a letter from a plain person who loves the Lord Jesus, though perhaps a servant maid, than from some whole volumes put forth by learned doctors. I speak this not out of disrespect either to doctors or learning; but there is a coldness creeping into the churches, of which I would warn my friends as earnestly as of a fire that was breaking out next door.[32]

Newton felt the winds of a dangerous gospel winter, and he was concerned that icy theology in frigid theology books would chill Christian zeal in local churches. Rather, maintaining a warm and affectionate zeal for the gospel of Jesus Christ requires care in choosing the books we read.

Newton seems convinced that a reader who is marked by sincerity, diligence, humility, and prayer will be quite busy reading the Bible. "Books and letters written in a proper spirit, may, if the Lord is pleased to smile upon them, have their use; but an awakened mind that thirsts after the Savior, and seeks wisdom by reading and praying over the scripture, has little occasion for a library of human writings."[33] While Newton did read a number of Christian books (and enjoyed some occasional Shakespeare), his priority of reading Scripture is unmistakable.

Beholding in a Mirror

John Newton's devotion to Scripture is of course tied directly to his conviction that beholding the glory of Christ transforms the Christian life. "The

---

[29] *Letters* (Clunie), 167–68.
[30] W, 2:113–14.
[31] See Tony Reinke, *Lit! A Christian Guide to Reading Books* (Wheaton, IL: Crossway, 2011), 93–107.
[32] *Letters* (Clunie), 10.
[33] W, 6:416.

more we read of his person, offices, power, love, doctrine, life, and death, the more our hearts will cleave to him: we shall, by insensible degrees, be transformed into his spirit."[34] Taking his cue from 2 Corinthians 3:18 and 4:6, Newton describes how, in direct proportion to our view of Christ's glory, we are given life and progressively changed into Christ's image, from glory to glory.[35] "They say, whoever looked at the Gorgon was transformed into a stone—such are the effects of sin. But, oh! For such a sight of Jesus in the glass of the gospel, as might transform my heart from stone to be a heart all over love to him who has loved me."[36] The glass of the gospel is Scripture.

Christ's glory, beheld in the Word, awakens new spiritual affections. The Christian desires to "live and feed upon the precious promises, John 14:16, 17, 26; and 16:13–15. There is no teacher like Jesus, who by his Holy Spirit reveals himself in his word to the understanding and affections of his children. When we behold his glory in the Gospel glass, we are changed into the same image. Then our hearts melt, our eyes flow, and our stammering tongues are unloosed."[37] "In proportion as we grow in the knowledge of Jesus we shall grow in grace."[38] "Even now, when we contemplate his glory as shining in the glass of the Gospel, we feel ourselves, in some measure, transformed into the same image."[39] "In ourselves we are all darkness, confusion, and misery; but in him there is a sufficiency of wisdom, grace, and peace suited to all our wants. May we ever behold his glory in the glass of the Gospel, till we are changed into the same image from glory to glory."[40] Such transformation happens incrementally as we gradually see more and more of Christ's glory in Scripture.

> It is thus by looking to Jesus, that the believer is enlightened and strengthened, and grows in grace and sanctification, according to that passage of St. Paul, "We all with open face," or unveiled face, "beholding as in a glass the glory of the Lord, are changed into the same image, from glory to glory, as by the Spirit of the Lord" (2 Cor. 3:18). The word of God is a glass in which the goodness and beauty of the Lord Jesus are manifested to the eye of faith by the light of the Holy Spirit. In this wonderful glass the

---

[34] W, 2:354.
[35] W, 2:380.
[36] Letters (Bull 1847), 132.
[37] W, 2:99.
[38] Letters (Taylor), 265.
[39] Letters (Bull 1869), 50.
[40] Letters (Clunie), 185.

whole object is not seen at once, but every view we take strengthens the sight to discover something not perceived before: and the prospect is not only affecting, but transforming; by beholding we are gradually formed into the resemblance of him whom we see, admire, and love.[41]

The Christian life centers on Christ, the Bible centers on Christ, and therefore we must center our Bible interpretation on Christ. "If men have not eyes to see what is taught of the person, offices and saving work of Christ, even the Scripture is a sealed book to them, and with the Word of God in their hands and in their mouth, they stumble like the blind at noonday."[42] The glory of Christ is the hermeneutical key to understanding the entire Bible (Luke 24:27). Such a key is hidden from the "wise" and given to the childlike (Matt. 11:25–27; 1 Cor. 1:18–31).[43]

With this key in hand, Bible reading is a lifelong discipline we never outgrow. By this discipline we daily search for more of Christ in Scripture, to see more of his glory and to enjoy, by faith, more of that "joy that is inexpressible and filled with glory" (1 Pet. 1:8). By this, God generates new affections in our lives to expel our sinful affections. As Cowper so poignantly penned in a hymn,

One view of Jesus as he is,
Will strike all sin forever dead. (1 John 3:2)[44]

Our ultimate hope for eternity is the same pattern for mortifying sin today—we look at Jesus. The glory of Christ, hunted for in our daily Bible reading, is the instrument of our sanctification and the cradle of our greatest delights.

The Best Advice

Given the fundamental nature of this conclusion, what implications follow for Christian communicators, songwriters, authors, and pastors? It would seem that the aim of all ministry, the essence of all true sermons, the theme behind all Christian books, and the choruses of all worship tracks should all be the same: putting on display the magnificent beauty

[41] W, 2:487.
[42] John Newton, *365 Days with Newton*, ed. Marylynn Rouse (Leominster, UK: Day One, 2006), 48.
[43] W, 2:374–76.
[44] W, 3:637.

of Christ.[45] This aim can be accomplished from the Wisdom Literature and the Psalms in the Old Testament, or it may be reached through the Gospels and the Epistles in the New. If the glory of Christ is the hermeneutical key to all of Scripture, every Christian communicator is called to achieve this same end in laboring to faithfully and creatively articulate and promote the glory of Christ.

Newton's highest aim in ministry was to point people to Christ, and he did it by building confidence in Scripture. This was his best advice.

> The best advice I can send, or the best wish I can form for you, is, that you may have an abiding and experimental sense of those words of the apostle, which are just now upon my mind,—"LOOKING UNTO JESUS." The duty, the privilege, the safety, the unspeakable happiness, of a believer, are all comprised in that one sentence. Let us first pray that the eyes of our faith and understanding may be opened and strengthened; and then let us fix our whole regard upon him.
>
> But how are we to behold him? I answer, *in the glass of his written word*; there he is represented to us in a variety of views; the wicked world can see no form nor comeliness in the portraiture he has given of himself; yet, blessed be God, there are those who can "behold his glory as the glory of the only begotten Son of God, full of grace and truth"; and while they behold it, they find themselves, "changed into the same image, from glory to glory," by the transforming influence of his Spirit.
>
> In vain we oppose reasonings, and arguments, and resolutions, to beat down our corruptions, and to silence our fears; but a believing view of Jesus does the business.
>
> When heavy trials in life are appointed us, and we are called to give up, or perhaps to pluck out, a right eye, it is an easy matter for a stander-by to say, "Be comforted"; and it is as useless as easy;—but a view of Jesus by faith comes home to the point. When we can fix our thoughts upon him, as laying aside all his honors, and submitting, for our sakes, to drink off the bitter cup of the wrath of God to the very dregs; and when we further consider, that he who thus suffered in our nature, who knows and sympathizes with all our weakness, is now the Supreme Disposer of all that concerns us, that he numbers the very hairs of our heads, appoints every trial

---

[45] Spurgeon: "There may be times when church government is to be discussed, and peculiar doctrines are to be vindicated. God forbid that we should silence any part of truth: but the main work of the ministry—its every day work—is just exhibiting Christ" (*The New Park Street Pulpit Sermons*, vol. 3 [London: 1857], 369). Newton was once asked what makes effective preaching? "Effect, I believe," he responded, "has been produced in my preaching by a solemn determination to bring forth Jesus Christ as the great subject in all my discourses" (*Eclectic*, 20).

we meet with in number, weight, and measure, and will suffer nothing to befall us but what shall contribute to our good—this view, I say, is a medicine suited to the disease, and powerfully reconciles us unto every cross.

So when a sense of sin prevails, and the tempter is permitted to assault us with dark and dreadful suggestions, it is easy for us to say, "Be not afraid"; but those who have tried, well know that looking to Jesus is the only and sure remedy in this case;—if we can get a sight of him by faith, as he once hung between the two thieves, and as he now pleads within the veil, then we can defy sin and Satan, and give our challenge in the apostle's words, "Who is he that condemneth? It is Christ that died, yea, rather, that is risen again; who also maketh intercession for us" (Rom. 8:34).

Again, are we almost afraid of being swallowed up by our many restless enemies? Or, are we almost weary of our long pilgrimage through such a thorny, tedious, barren wilderness? A sight of Jesus, as Stephen saw him, crowned with glory, yet noticing all the sufferings of his poor servants, and just ready to receive them to himself, and make them partakers of his everlasting joy, this will raise the spirits, and restore strength; this will animate us to hold on, and to hold out; this will do it, and nothing but this can.

So, if obedience be the thing in question, looking unto Jesus is the object that melts the soul into love and gratitude, and those who greatly love, and are greatly obliged, find obedience easy. When Jesus is upon our thoughts, either in his humbled or his exalted state, either as bleeding on the cross, or as worshipped in our nature by all the host of heaven, then we can ask the apostle's question with a becoming disdain, "Shall we continue in sin that grace may abound?" God forbid. What! Shall I sin against my Lord, my Love, my Friend, who once died for my sins, and now lives and reigns on my behalf; who supports, and leads, and guides, and feeds me every day? God forbid. No; rather I would wish for a thousand hands and eyes, and feet, and tongues, for ten thousand lives, that I might devote them all to his service: he should have all then; and surely he shall have all now! Alas, that in spite of myself, there still remains something that resists his will! But I long and pray for its destruction; and I see a day coming when my wish shall be accomplished, and I shall be wholly and forever the Lord's.

I am your affectionate servant.
John Newton[46]

---

[46] *W*, 6:4–6. Italics and paragraph breaks mine.

CHAPTER 11

BATTLING INSECURITY

Even while the Christian walks through this life by faith, the stability under his feet ebbs and shifts with the personal assurance in his soul. Questions of security and assurance pose some of the most seismic challenges to the joyful and faithful Christian life, and no question unsettles the Christian more than this one: Can I be certain I am a genuine Christian?

We humans are as unstable as water, Newton often said, and the waves and shifting subterranean flows of dark doubts and insecurities tug at us like riptides. Playing off these doubts, Satan further attempts to frighten us by raising all sorts of doubts about God—whether he simply tolerates us in his family, whether he really loves us, or whether he simply remains unimpressed by us. These doubts are painful, but like Peter's faith in walking across water to Jesus, the Christian's faith will be tested to remain focused on Christ.

Growing Assurance

In a key letter to his longtime friend Hannah Wilberforce (the aunt of William), Newton addresses the topic of assurance most succinctly. In first addressing indwelling sin, he writes that grief over the remaining evil in the Christian's heart is appropriate, but it must never "rob us of the honor, comfort, and joy" of what Scripture tells us about the person, offices, and grace of Jesus (Ps. 23:1; Song 5:16; Isa. 54:5; Jer. 23:5; Matt. 1:21–23; John 15:1, 15; 1 Cor. 1:30; 1 John 2:1).[1] He commends Mrs. Wilberforce to

---

[1] W, 2:175.

read Psalm 89:15–18 (what he titles "The Believer's Triumph") because, "though they [believers] are nothing in themselves, yet having all in Jesus, they may rejoice in his name all the day."[2] Over the backdrop of praising Christ, Newton offers this concise summary of assurance:

> The joy of the Lord is the strength of his people: whereas unbelief makes our hands hang down, and our knees feeble, dispirits ourselves, and discourages others; and though it steals upon us under a semblance of humility, it is indeed the very essence of pride. By inward and outward exercises the Lord is promoting the best desire of your heart, and answering your daily prayers. Would you have assurance? The true solid assurance is to be obtained no other way. When young Christians are greatly comforted with the Lord's love and presence, their doubts and fears are for that season at an end. But this is not assurance; so soon as the Lord hides his face they are troubled, and ready to question the very foundation of hope.
>
> Assurance grows by repeated conflict, by our repeated experimental proof of the Lord's power and goodness to save; when we have been brought very low and helped, sorely wounded and healed, cast down and raised again, have given up all hope, and been suddenly snatched from danger, and placed in safety; and when these things have been repeated to us and in us a thousand times over, we begin to learn to trust simply to the word and power of God, beyond and against appearances: and this trust, when habitual and strong, bears the name of assurance; for even assurance has degrees.
>
> You have good reason, madam, to suppose, that the love of the best Christian to an unseen Savior is far short of what it ought to be. If your heart be like mine, and you examine your love to Christ by the warmth and frequency of your emotions towards him, you will often be in a sad suspense whether or not you love him at all. The best mark to judge, and which he has given us for that purpose, is to inquire if his word and will have a prevailing, governing influence upon our lives and temper. If we love him, we do endeavor to keep his commandments: and it will hold the other way; if we have a desire to please him, we undoubtedly love him. Obedience is the best test; and when, amidst all our imperfections, we can humbly appeal concerning the sincerity of our views, this is a mercy for which we ought to be greatly thankful. He that has brought us to will, will likewise enable us to do, according to his good pleasure.

---

[2] W, 2:175–76.

> I doubt not but the Lord whom you love, and on whom you depend, will lead you in a sure way, and establish and strengthen and settle you in his love and grace. Indeed he has done great things for you already. The Lord is your Shepherd; a comprehensive word. The sheep can do nothing for themselves: the Shepherd must guide, guard, feed, heal, recover. Well for us that our Shepherd is the Lord Almighty. If his power, care, compassion, fullness, were not infinite, the poor sheep would be forsaken, starved, and worried. But we have a Shepherd full of care, full of kindness, full of power, who has said, I will seek that which was lost, and bind up that which was broken, and bring again that which was driven away, and will strengthen that which was sick.[3]

Here in this letter to Mrs. Wilberforce, Newton builds several key points of assurance, each worthy of brief explanation.

1. *Trials provide the resistance for faith to be exercised and the need for God's deliverance to be manifested, without which genuine faith would be difficult to see.* All throughout his works Newton assumes that assurance is the product of God's deliverance manifested in our lives a thousand times over. "Experience and observation may convince us, that, however rational and easy this assurance may seem in theory, it is ordinarily unattainable in practice, without passing through a train of previous exercises and conflicts."[4] Thus, the deepest assurances are often reserved for the oldest and most wise Christians. "In mercy he [God] has frequently stirred up my nest, shaken me in it, and forced me to fly to him, when I should otherwise have dropped into sleep and security"—a false security.[5] We are prone to wander, and trials stir us from spiritual laziness. False securities are exposed as frauds, we discover again our weaknesses, and we call out for deliverance from our self, our sin, our idols, and our false securities. This self-emptying is a critical process in learning assurance.

So rather than grounding assurance on intense self-examination, or in the felt presence of God, Newton grounds it in the repeated deliverances of God in the life of the Christian (external). "He has delivered, he does deliver, and I trust he will yet deliver. My whole history has been a series of marvelous mercies."[6] This series of marvelous mercies—deliverance from trials and sin and temptations—is the key ground for genuine assurance in

---

[3] *W*, 2:176–77.
[4] *W*, 6:466.
[5] *Letters* (Taylor), 76.
[6] *Letters* (Taylor), 269.

the Christian life. "By trials our graces are proved, exercised, and strength-ened, and the power and goodness of the Lord towards us are more mani-fested and glorified."[7] In years of trials and in thousands of struggles we see the delivering grace of God in our lives, and our assurance grows.

2. *If we love Christ, we will obey him* (John 14:15–24; 1 John 5:1–5). We may try to live off our experiences of joyful communion with Christ, but there will be no true assurance where there's a lack of genuine obedience to Christ. Any so-called assurance and confidence that remain unscathed by seasons of willful sin and backsliding are "vain confidence and presumption."[8] We can expect living faith to exhibit life, and life will be manifested in degrees of love, holiness, and overcoming the world. More on this later.

3. *Indwelling sin remains in the Christian, therefore genuine obedience is not perfection* (Rom. 7:15–20; Gal. 5:17). Living faith will evidence itself in obedience, but a principle of disobedience will remain deeply rooted in the heart of even the most sincere and genuine Christian. Assurance is not the eradication of indwelling sin, but the honest and humbled aware-ness of it. This too comes by hard experience. "We cannot be safely trusted with assurance till we have that knowledge of the evil and deceitfulness of our hearts, which can be acquired only by painful, repeated experience."[9] Young believers are prone to trust themselves, like Peter, too confident in their own powers and pledges (Matt. 26:33). By experience we face our sins; we are humbled by our limitations and weaknesses, emptied of all self-confidence, and fitted for genuine assurance.

4. *Assurance and brokenness for sin are consistent* (1 John 2:1–6). Chris-tian assurance cannot wait until indwelling sin is eradicated from the heart, but a broken spirit and sorrow for sin evidence a living faith just as moments of genuine obedience (Pss. 34:18; 51:17). The remaining deprav-ity in our hearts and sorrow over our sins are no hindrances to assurance.

5. *Willful sin inescapably erodes assurance; indwelling sin does not.* New-ton is careful to maintain a distinction between *indwelling sin* and *willful sin*. Willful sin is committed in light of full knowledge of its evil, and yet with willful continuance of the disobedience (Num. 15:22–31; Heb. 10:26). Perhaps it's easier to explain willful sins as a string of interlocking sins.

The boldest biblical example of willful sin by a believer is King David's lustful longing for a bathing woman, which became his act of adultery,

---

[7] *Letters* (Taylor), 114.
[8] *W*, 2:598.
[9] *W*, 6:471.

which led to his murderous attempt to cover it all up (2 Sam. 11). Indulging his lustful eyes on the beautiful woman lured him into more sin. This example is rather dramatic, but the principle applies to every sinner. Willful sin is often manifested as a string of iniquities committed by a sinner who cherishes sin more than Christ, an idolatry leading to deeper and darker sins or into an ingrained habitual pattern of sin in one area (like pornography). To preserve our willful sin we must attempt to hide it from God and lie about it to ourselves and others. Under this cover of deceit, willful sin corrodes the conscience until the power of the Holy Spirit breaks into our lives, bringing conviction and sincere repentance (2 Samuel 12). Willful sin cannot otherwise be stopped because it has captured the consent of our will. Such sin will necessarily erode any sense of assurance (Rom. 8:13).

> If our faith was strong, and our dependence upon the Savior simple, nothing would break our peace but *willful sin*. There is sin mingled with our prayers, our preaching, our every thing; but if it has not the consent of our wills, though it should lay us low in the dust before the Lord, it need not interrupt our confidence in him, or our communion with him, unless we give way to unbelief (1 John 2:1).[10]

6. *Personal assurance is not to be confused with affections and emotions that wax and wane throughout life.* Young converts are especially susceptible to confusing seasons of spiritual comfort with assurance. It is possible to experience warm affections and yet have weak faith, so that when the feelings and affections subside, the fears and insecurities return.[11]

> But strong faith, and the effect of it, an abiding persuasion of our acceptance in the Beloved, and of our final perseverance in grace, are not necessarily connected with sensible comfort. A strong faith can trust God in the dark, and say with Job, "Though he slay me, yet will I trust in him" (Job 13:15).[12]

The consistent simmering of warm affections is not the measure of our assurance.

7. *Personal assurance can thrive in darkness.* Because it cannot be measured by the consistency of our affections, our assurance can be strong

---

[10] *Letters* (Coffin), 152–53.
[11] *W*, 6:467.
[12] *W*, 6:467.

and settled even in seasons of spiritual depression, seasons of discipline, or seasons when God chooses to hide his face from us and "suspend his influence."[13] If we think of assurance in terms of warm emotions, "such an assurance we may possess and lose several times in the same day. . . . But the true faith of assurance is to trust God in the dark," a confidence found in the light of Christ's death and resurrection.[14] If we are armed with this understanding, even periods of painful discipline in our lives can assure us of God's particular love (Heb. 12:3–11).

8. *Assurance is not essential to the existence of faith.* Again, progress toward assurance is gradual, learned by a thousand conflicts, and rarely given fully to new converts. Faith begins small. What doubting Christians need "is not some new principle which they have not yet received, but only a stronger degree of that faith which they already possess."[15] This growth in grace happens over time in trials and in spiritual battles, and in marvelous mercies of deliverance. Insecurities and doubts that remain in the Christian are due to an underdeveloped faith, a weak faith, *not* to the absence of faith.

9. *Unbelief erodes assurance because assurance is robust faith.* When our trust in Christ declines, our assurance takes the hit. "Assurance is the essence of faith; that is, it springs from true faith, and can grow upon no other root. Faith likewise is the *measure* of assurance. While faith is weak (our Lord compares it, in its first principle, to a grain of mustard seed) assurance cannot be strong."[16] Thus, the temptations toward unbelief should be firmly resisted: "Rejoice in Christ Jesus, and resist every temptation to doubt your interest in his love, as you would resist a temptation to adultery or murder."[17]

> This inability to take God at his word, should not be merely lamented as an infirmity, but watched, and prayed, and fought against as a great sin. A great sin indeed it is; the very root of our apostasy, from which every other sin proceeds. It often deceives us under the guise of humility, as though it would be presumption, in such sinners as we are, to believe the

---

[13] W, 6:467–68.
[14] *Letters* (Coffin), 102.
[15] W, 2:586–87.
[16] W, 6:465. This is key for Newton: "Some good writers speak of faith of reliance, faith of adherence, faith of assurance, direct and reflex acts of faith, etc.; but these are not Scriptural modes of expression, nor do they appear to me to throw light upon the subject, but rather to increase the perplexity of plain people, who are apt to imagine these are so many different kinds of faith. The Scripture mentions only two kinds; 'a living and a dead faith'" (W, 2:587).
[17] W, 6:178.

declarations of the God of truth. Many serious people, who are burdened with a sense of other sins, leave this radical evil out of the list. They rather indulge it, and think they ought not to believe, till they can find a warrant from marks and evidences within themselves.[18]

Unbelief, as manifested in a sulky, sad, dreary Christian profession, is not humility but a manifestation of pride.

10. *Personal assurance rests not on escalating personal reformation, but on increasing confidence in the saving power of Jesus Christ for sinners like us.* It is true that without the evidence of holiness there can be no assurance (Rom. 8:13; Heb. 12:14). For assurance to be real, "there must be an alteration in yourselves."[19] But this holiness, and its increase, is the evidence of a living faith in Christ. "We may well mourn that our love to the Lord is so faint and wavering; but oh, what a cause of joy to know that his love to us is infinite and unchangeable! Our attainment in sanctification is weak and our progress slow; but our justification is perfect, and our hope sure."[20] Assurance does not rest on the confidence we have in our personal reform, but rests on the confidence we have in our justification in Christ.

> Desirable and precious as sanctification is, it is not, I trust it will never be, the ground of my hope. Nor, were I as sinless as an angel in glory, could I have a better ground of hope than I have at present. For acceptance, I rely simply, wholly, and solely, upon the obedience unto death of my surety. Jesus is my righteousness, my life, and my salvation.[21]

11. *Personal assurance is objectively grounded in the Christ revealed in Scripture.* The Christian does not wait for a voice from heaven or for some "sudden impulse" to bring assurance. The lack of assurance results from "inattention to his revealed word."[22] "Assurance is the result of a competent spiritual knowledge of the person and work of Christ as revealed in the Gospel, and a consciousness of dependence on him and his work alone for salvation."[23]

> When our knowledge is so far increased as to overpower the objections arising from inward corruptions, defects of obedience, unbelieving fears,

---

[18] *W*, 6:468.
[19] *W*, 2:532.
[20] *Letters* (Bull 1869), 80.
[21] *W*, 6:340.
[22] *W*, 2:590.
[23] *W*, 2:593.

and the temptations of Satan; when we can cut them short with that question of the Apostle, "Who is he that condemneth? It is Christ that died" (Rom 8:34), assurance follows of course.[24]

12. *Assurance is the ground of joy.* We do not measure our assurance by our joy, but for true joy to flourish we must experience some level of assurance. While assurance

is not absolutely necessary to our safety, it is exceedingly needful to make us unwearied, cheerful, and evangelical, in a course of holy obedience; to the exertion of all our powers and faculties in the service of him who has loved us, and washed us from our sins in his own blood; and to give us courage to endure and surmount the many difficulties and oppositions which we are sure to meet with in the course of our profession.[25]

13. *Such an assurance brings humility and kindness with it.* "Whoever doubts or disbelieves the *leading truths* of the gospel is not very fit to be a preacher; but a man who has never felt doubts or shakings respecting *his own interest* in them, is not likely to be the most acceptable and useful preacher to a congregation."[26] Pastors, and any Christians, who deal honestly with the evils within remain confident in Christ. Experienced in wrestling with their own doubts, they will display humility and kindness to others.

Faith, Holiness, and Assurance

The Christian life is compromised by two errors: the error of wrongly assuming that salvation is earned through works, and the error of failing to appreciate works as the fruit of faith.[27] "Let us neither confound, nor divide what God has joined—faith and holiness."[28] True faith is married to holiness, and true faith must evidence itself in fruits of *gospel holiness*. To one minister Newton explained how fluctuating affections, the person and work of Christ, Scripture, depression, and assurance all interrelate.

To be sure, faith may be said to be weak when it cannot depend simply upon the work and promise of the Savior, without expecting some ex-

[24] *W*, 2:594.
[25] *W*, 2:597.
[26] *Letters* (Coffin), 98.
[27] *W*, 6:406.
[28] *Letters* (Jones), 43.

traordinary manifestations to confirm its warrant. But this weakness we are all liable to. When we are lively and comfortable in our frames; that is, when we see or feel, *then we believe*. But though such comfortable manifestations are very desirable, they are not the scriptural evidences of faith, which may be true and even strong without them. The object of faith is Christ, as living, dying, rising, reigning, interceding, for sinners. The warrant to believe is the word of God, "This is my beloved son, hear him" (Matt. 17:5). "Him that cometh to me, I will in *no wise* cast out" (John 6:37). "He is able to save to the uttermost" (Heb. 7:25). The proper *act of faith* is to receive these testimonies and to cast ourselves on this Savior, without regarding any thing in ourselves, but a consciousness that we are unworthy, helpless sinners, and that we are willing and desirous to be saved in this way of God's appointment. The best evidences *that we believe*, are a broken spirit, obedience to the Lord's precepts, submission to his will, and love to his cause and people. Our frames and sensible feelings are like the weather, changeable, and equally out of our power. [Some Christians are] affected by low spirits, or what we call nervous disorders; and these I well know are sufficient to hide comfort from us—yea, in many cases, to plunge a strong believer into a state of despair for a season. Thus it is with my dear friend Cowper, who has been miserable, and to his own apprehension, forsaken of God, for many years; though for many years before he was a burning and a shining light, full of alacrity in the Lord's service and rejoicing in the sunshine of his presence.[29]

Make no mistake, living faith evidences itself—faith *works*, faith *purifies*, and faith *overcomes* (Acts 15:9; Gal. 5:6; 1 John 5:4). Living faith is active faith. It

purifies the heart from the love and practice of sin; it works by love to the Lord Jesus Christ, his ordinances, ways, and people; and it enables the professor to overcome the world, to stand fast against its frowns, and to resist the more pleasing but not less dangerous influence of its smiles. Each of these effects is beyond the power, and contrary to the inclination, of the natural man.[30]

This is why Newton can say that true faith will evidence itself in a broken spirit, obedience to the Lord, submission to God's will, and love toward God's cause and people. These evidences authenticate faith. Where there

---

[29] *Letters* (Coffin), 91–92, and *Letters* (Bull 1869), 386–87.
[30] *W*, 2:586.

are no works there is no living faith, and where there is no living faith there can be no genuine assurance.

Jesus Alone, My Everything

Newton is eager to stress obedience and holiness as evidences of faith, so long as we are first convinced that our salvation is based not *on our faith* but in the *object of our faith*, Jesus Christ. As modern theologian D. A. Carson puts it, "The assurance that we are accepted by Almighty God is tied not to the intensity of our faith or to the consistency of our faith or to the purity of our faith, but to the object of our faith."[31] Newton would heartily agree. And the object of our faith (Christ) is also the Author of our faith and the Finisher of our faith, a High Priest who saves "to the uttermost" (Heb. 7:25). In this phrase, which Newton treasured, we find a Christ who triumphs over every difficulty, supplies every need, delivers every necessity, and will "save to the uttermost in defiance of all our sins, fears, and enemies!"[32] "That word *uttermost* includes all that can be said: take an estimate of sins, temptations, difficulties, fears, and backslidings of every kind, still the word *uttermost* goes beyond them all."[33]

In the end, Newton can write:

> If I am saved, (I trust I shall,) it will be freely and absolutely, in a way of sovereignty; with a *non obstante* [notwithstanding] to a thousand things which should seem, humanly speaking, to make salvation next door to impossible. But when I am beaten from everything else, it still remains true that Christ has died, that he now lives and reigns, that "he is able to save to the UTTERMOST" (Heb. 7:25), and that he has said, "Him that cometh I will in NO WISE cast out" (John 6:37). In NO WISE and to the UT-TERMOST are great words, they have an extensive signification, and take in all varieties of cases, characters, and circumstances. Upon such unlim-ited sovereign promises I cast my anchor, and they hold me, otherwise I should be the sport of winds and waves. Dr. [Isaac] Watts' motto shall be mine, it is big enough for him, me, you, and for thousands that approve it, *In uno Jesu omnia* [In Jesus alone is my everything]. In him I have an offering, an altar, a temple, a priest, a sun, a shield, a savior, a shepherd, a hiding place, a resting place, food, medicine, riches, honor, wisdom, righteousness, holiness, in short, everything.[34]

---

[31] D. A. Carson, *Basics for Believers: An Exposition of Philippians* (Grand Rapids: Baker, 1996), 41.
[32] *W*, 6:147.
[33] *W*, 6:66.
[34] *Letters* (Bull 1847), 191–92.

In Jesus we find everything we need to sustain our confidence in him.

The Best Test

As we grow more convinced that Jesus alone is our everything, so also grows the fruit of genuine faith (obedience). True obedience and faith in Christ grow concurrently. Thus, Newton can say the sincerity of our faith is measured by obedience.

All manner of external religious conformity can be faked, making genuine and heartfelt obedience (the fruit of gospel simplicity and sincerity) the best mark of a living faith and a true love for Christ. We noted this in the opening letter of this chapter. Newton makes the point in two letters, written almost thirty years apart:

> If we love him, we do endeavor to keep his commandments: and it will hold the other way; if we have a desire to please him, we undoubtedly love him. *Obedience is the best test*; and when, amidst all our imperfections, we can humbly appeal concerning the sincerity of our views, this is a mercy for which we ought to be greatly thankful.[35]

> *Obedience is the best test* of sincerity; feelings are various, transient, and often deceitful; but a broken, humble spirit, and an upright walk, evidence the finger of God; other things may be and are often counterfeited.[36]

In comparing Paul and James on works (Rom. 3:20–28; James 2:14–24), Newton writes:

> The sum is; The one declares that nothing renders us acceptable to God but faith in the Lord Jesus Christ: the other, that such a faith, when true and genuine, is not solitary, but accompanied with every good work. The one speaks of the justification of our persons—this is by faith only; the other of the justification of our profession—this is by faith not alone, but working by love, and producing obedience.[37]

A faith in God resulting in no life change is a demonic faith (James 2:19). Faith *without works* is a dead faith. Faith *with works* is a living faith.

Personal holiness is the product of a genuine conviction of the

---

[35] W, 2:177. Italics mine.
[36] *Letters* (Coffin), 132. Italics mine.
[37] W, 2:555.

sufficiency of Christ, a delight in God, and a hatred for sin. These fruits are
the products of a living faith and are impossible to counterfeit. The most
beautiful appearances of holiness unaccompanied by true faith in Christ
"may be safely rejected as counterfeits," just as, on the other hand, a profession of faith that fails to evidence the fruits of gospel holiness is "dead, de-
lusory, and destructive."[38] As clear as Newton is on the limitations posed by
our indwelling sin, he is also clear that living faith must exert itself on the
whole of our lives. Dead faith produces no obedience, and the absence of
obedience is proof of a heart yet enslaved to the world, the flesh, and Satan.[39]

Newton loved to preach the free grace of God in Christ, but he admitted
that even Satan will preach on free grace "when he finds people willing to
believe the notion as an excuse and a cloak for idleness."[40] Rather, where
the gospel of free grace truly prevails, "the practical duties of Christianity
have flourished in the same proportion."[41] Free grace, when twisted to excuse spiritual laziness and disobedience, is demonic. This meant Newton
could freely and openly denounce the disobedience he noticed in the lives
of his congregation. In one sermon on James 2:26, he proclaimed, "When I
tell you, that without holiness no man shall see the Lord with comfort [Heb.
12:14], and that you must break off from your vain company and evil prac-
tices, if you expect or desire to be saved, you know that I speak the truth;
and your looks often testify that you feel the force of it."[42] Turning from evil
is an evidence of living faith. Continuing in open sin is an indictment of
dead faith. Are you willing to leave your sins because you love Christ? Such
a question is a litmus test of faith. Living in willful sin casts doubt on the
sincerity of faith, and such doubt erodes assurance.

Sabotaging Assurance

As we have seen, genuine faith in its mustard-seed size does not bring
much assurance with it. For the Christian, especially when faith is weak,
three hindrances undercut our assurance: *insincerity, indolence,* and *misapprehensions.*

Insincerity is a lack of gospel simplicity, "a secret cleaving of the will

---

[38] W, 3:232.
[39] W, 2:560.
[40] *Letters* (Bull 1869), 64. Elsewhere the phrase "believe the notion" is transcribed "receive the notion," more accurate to Newton's original letter (*Letters* [Clunie], 139).
[41] W, 3:33.
[42] W, 2:562.

to evil," a double-mindedness (James 1:8), so there is a "kind of halting between two opinions; so that while the desire and prayer of the soul seems expressed against all sin universally, there is still an allowed reserve of something, inconsistent with light received."[43] The simplicity of dependence upon God alone is missing. There remains an attachment to some idolatrous security, a clutching to some power or worldly comfort. This double-mindedness erodes assurance.

Indolence is when a Christian becomes lazy in making his Christian calling and election certain (2 Pet. 1:10). Indolent Christians

> go on for months or years in a complaining, unsettled state; and deservedly, because they are not earnest in seeking, asking, waiting, knocking at the gate of wisdom, and at the Throne of Grace, for that blessing which the Lord has promised to those who persevere in wrestling prayer, and will take no denial.[44]

God has intended for daily Bible reading and prayer, the Lord's Table, and membership and fellowship in the local church as disciplines to cultivate our faith and assurance. In this way, "the path of duty is the path of safety."[45] And when these medicinal duties are neglected by our laziness, assurance erodes.

Misapprehensions, or wrong assumptions about assurance, have a similar eroding effect. Newton confronted many of these errors, including the assumption that assurance is unattainable in this life, or that assurance is measured by our daily joy in God, or that full assurance arrives in a moment of awakening, or that assurance must be fully experienced from the initial stages of faith, or that assurance arrives only with the eradication of indwelling sin. All these wrong ideas will deteriorate assurance.

> If inherent sanctification, or a considerable increase of it, is considered as the proper ground of assurance, those who are most humble, sincere, and desirous of being conformed to the will of God, will be the most perplexed and discouraged in their search after it. For they of all others will be the least satisfied with themselves, and have the quickest sense of the innumerable defilements and defects, which the Scripture assures us are inseparable from our best tempers and best actions.[46]

---

[43] *W*, 2:591.
[44] *W*, 2:591–92.
[45] *Letters* (Jones), 71.
[46] *W*, 2:592–93.

Full Assurance . . . in Christ

If obedience is a mark of genuine faith leading to assurance, how do we respond to our sins when we commit them? Again, deep sorrow for sin is quite consistent with genuine faith and assurance. In sorrow for sin, we look to Christ. In one of Newton's favorite little books, Puritan Thomas Wilcox (1622–1687) writes, "Thou complainest much of thyself. Doth thy sin make thee look more at Christ, less at thyself? That is right, else complaining is but hypocrisy. To be looking at duties, graces, enlargements, when thou shouldst be looking at Christ, that is pitiful."[47] The goal of our sanctification is not to adore obedience, but to despise our indwelling sin and worship Jesus Christ.

Newton's letters place little emphasis on intense self-examination in personal assurance. Self-examination was certainly a part of his own devotional life, but the close study he made of his own heart (and the viper colonies of sin he found lurking there) only made him decreasingly confident in himself as the years passed. Newton's backstory had become famous: a troubled teenager, a blaspheming adult, then a slave in Africa, a slave trader, then a pastor. He was a chief of sinners, "snatched, by a miracle, from sinking into the ocean and into hell," delivered from the "most hardened degrees of profaneness and Atheism," and later called to gospel ministry. And yet Newton never presumed his own preservation into the future based upon this backstory or his conversion, but he continued to pray "that I may be preserved humble, watchful, faithful, and dependent."[48] Newton's amazing testimony and his own assurance in Christ did not make him indolent or lazy or careless (a danger equally serious as legalism).[49]

The closer Newton investigated himself, the less impressed he became. At age thirty-one he wrote, "I am, by grace, kept from such sins as would dishonor my calling openly, and stumble my brethren; but the wickedness of my heart is amazing."[50] Newton then names specific sins of pride, ingratitude, and insensibility. He is specific because he is familiar with his sins. In the prime of his ministry Newton admitted, "My best service is defective, my all is defiled, my heart is deceitful and desperately wicked, my every power is disordered and depraved, so that my services and duties,

---

[47] Thomas Wilcox, *A Choice Drop of Honey from the Rock Christ; or, A Short Word of Advice to All Saints and Sinners* (London, 1757), 10. Newton commends the book (*Letters* [Clunie], 54).
[48] *Letters* (Jones), 69.
[49] *W*, 6:44. Quite the opposite. Newton's daily rehearsal of his testimony worked in him a profound humility (*Letters* [Bull 1847], 279).
[50] *Letters* (Jones), 21.

my preaching and my prayers are sufficient to ruin me, if the Lord should enter into judgment."[51] Newton would not grow more impressed with himself over time. Fittingly, his final recorded words were said in the present tense: "I am a great sinner." Honesty about sin is a painful discovery, but it's also an essential discovery if we are to embrace the all-sufficiency of Christ.

The Paradox of Assurance

For a sinner like Newton—weak as water and chief of sinners—the only stable foundation for assurance was Christ. "Assurance is the result of a competent spiritual knowledge of the person and work of Christ as revealed in the Gospel, and a consciousness of dependence on him and his work alone for salvation."[52] Throughout his works, Newton labored to communicate this point. "May the Lord turn our mourning into joy, or rather teach us the apostle's experience, to be sorrowful, yet always rejoicing; delighting in him, and loathing ourselves for all our abominations."[53] This is the heart of Newton's assurance. Yes, we obey. But we find our spiritual strength to obey not by looking within ourselves, but by looking to Christ (Eph. 6:10; 2 Tim. 2:1).

> The everlasting love of God; the unspeakable merits of Christ's righteousness; and the absolute freeness of the Gospel promises—these form the threefold cord by which my soul maintains a hold of that which is within the veil (Heb. 6:19). Sin, Satan, and unbelief, often attempt to make me let go and cast away my confidence, but as yet they have not prevailed; no thanks to me, who am weaker than water: but I am wonderfully kept by the mighty power of God, who is pleased to take my part, and therefore I trust in him that they never shall prevail against me.[54]

> As the sun can only be seen by its own light, and diffuses that light by which other objects are clearly perceived; so Christ crucified is the sun in the system of revealed truth; and the right knowledge of the doctrine of his cross satisfies the inquiring mind, proves itself to be the one thing needful, and the only thing necessary to silence the objections of unbelief and pride, and to afford a sure ground for solid and abiding hope.[55]

---

[51] *Letters* (Bull 1869), 195.
[52] *W*, 2:593.
[53] *Letters* (Bull 1847), 139.
[54] *W*, 6:20.
[55] *W*, 6:470.

Yes, we obey, but God doesn't need our service, for "we cannot properly *serve* him who is all-sufficient."[56] Our service is wholly dependent on him. Therefore, "we can have no security from gifts, labors, services, or past experiences; but that from first to last our only safety is in the power, compassion, and faithfulness of our great Redeemer."[57] We have hope because we are united to Christ. Apart from Christ we are dead (John 15:5). "We are never more safe, never have more reason to expect the Lord's help, than when we are most sensible that we can do nothing without him."[58] This is the paradox of assurance.

Emanating Spark to Eternal Flame

The full assurance of faith is confidence in our all-sufficient Christ and his preservation of our sinful, powerless souls.

> Only he who made the world can either make a Christian, or support and carry on his own work (2 Cor. 4:6). A thirst after God as our portion; a delight in Jesus, as the only way and door; a renunciation of self and of the world, so far as it is opposite to the spirit of the Gospel: these, and the like fruits of that grace which bringeth salvation, are not only beyond the power of our fallen nature, but contrary to its tendency; so that we can have no desires of this kind till they are given us from above.[59]

Salvation is all of grace (2 Tim. 1:9), and in light of the free grace of the gospel, Paul can be certain of God's preserving power in his life (2 Tim. 1:12). This conviction came late in Paul's life and required years to develop, and it developed into an assurance grounded on three realities: (1) a knowledge of Christ as the object of Paul's faith, (2) a confidence that his own sinful soul has been entrusted to Christ, and (3) a confidence in Christ's ability, willingness, and faithfulness to secure and preserve his soul to the end of the ages.[60]

To build his friend's confidence in Christ, Newton turned to a variety of metaphors. "A little grace, a spark of true love to God, a grain of living faith, though small as a mustard-seed, is worth a thousand worlds. One draught of the water of life gives interest in, and earnest of, the whole

---

[56] *Letters* (Taylor), 46.
[57] *Letters* (Bull 1869), 413.
[58] *W*, 2:146.
[59] *W*, 2:14–15.
[60] *W*, 2:590.

fountain."[61] The gospel is medicine—it began a healing work in the believer that will not be thwarted.

> My medicine enlightens the understanding, softens the heart, and gives a realizing of what the Scriptures declare of the glorious person, the wonderful love, the bitter sufferings, of the Savior, and the necessity and efficacy of his death and agonies upon the Cross. When these things are understood by the teachings of the Holy Spirit, (whose influence is always afforded to those that take the medicine) the cure is already begun; all the rest will follow, and the patient recovers apace; though there are sometimes transient relapses, and a spice of the old disorder will hand about them, until they are removed to the pure air of a better world.[62]

Assurance is finally rooted in the unthwartable work of God and the presence of the Holy Spirit in our lives (Rom. 8:16; 1 John 3:24; 4:13). "The love I bear him is but a faint and feeble spark, but it is an emanation from himself; he kindled it, and he keeps it alive; and because it is his work, I trust many waters shall not quench it."[63] Once the believer is united to Christ, the sap of Christ's life begins surging through his spiritual veins by the Spirit of Christ. It will not stop. It cannot stop. It is an emanating spark that will grow into an eternal flame (Phil. 1:6).

---

[61] *W*, 2:175.
[62] Letters (Jay), 320.
[63] *W*, 1:644. In full: "I know that I am a child, because he teaches me to say, Abba, Father. I know that I am *his*, because he has enabled me to choose him for *mine*. For such a choice and desire could never have taken place in my heart, if he had not placed it there himself. By nature I was too blind to know him, too proud to trust him, too obstinate to serve him, too base-minded to love him. The enmity I was filled with against his government, righteousness, and grace, was too strong to be subdued by any power but his own. The love I bear him is but a faint and feeble spark, but it is an emanation from himself; he kindled it, and he keeps it alive; and because it is his work, I trust many waters shall not quench it."

CHAPTER 12

VICTORY OVER SPIRITUAL WEARINESS

This fallen world weighs people down under a thousand possible worries and woes, and Christians are not exempt. In earlier chapters we explored Newton's counsel to Christians suffering from long-term spiritual ailments: depression, personal trials, physical suffering, and chronic disabilities. In this chapter we focus on Newton's counsel to believers bearing spiritual weariness from the day-to-day ups and downs of the Christian experience.

John Newton was quick to diagnose his own soul weariness. Though he lamented it, he also recognized that his experience prepared him to mentor his Christian brothers and sisters.[1] Which explains why he had so much to say on the topic. His counsel can be divided into four levels: the three common causes of spiritual weariness, and the one main root feeding all our spiritual weariness.

Wearied by Broken Cisterns

First, the Christian soul is wearied when we wrongly seek our joy in broken cisterns. In biblical times, a cistern was something like a primitive water tank carved from underground rock in the shape of a giant wine bottle. The small, ground-level opening to the cistern was normally fed by rainwater,

---

[1] "Some of our afflictions perhaps befall us for the sake of our people, that we may be reminded and enabled to speak their feelings, by what we feel ourselves. In this way the tongue of the learned is acquired and skill to speak a word in season to the weary" (*Letters* [Ryland], 192). See also *W*, 1:665.

usually the runoff from nearby roofs and streets. Needless to say, cistern water could be quite disgusting, and many cisterns were leaky to begin with. If the cisterns walls were not maintained with fresh coats of mortar, water would drain through the rock walls and back into the ground, leaving in many cases an empty cavern good for little more than a dry holding cell to throw local prisoners (e.g., Joseph in Gen. 37:18–24). Even if the water was contained, cistern water was likely to be putrid, but often this was the only good option for year-round water. But when a freshwater spring offered water, a cistern was a wretched alternative. And so, evil is pictured in Scripture as a thirsty soul turning away from a freshwater fountain of living water (God) to drink from a broken and polluted cistern (idolatry) in the hunt for spiritual life and joy (Jer. 2:13). The soul becomes anemic and wearied when its thirst turns away from God, the only source of abiding joy, and toward a leaky holding tank of self-sufficiency.[2]

Spiritual *weariness* and spiritual *thirstiness* are two metaphors for the same needs in the human soul. Only in Jesus will the weary and thirsty sinner find rest (Matt. 11:28) and slaked thirst (John 7:37). Jesus puts no qualification or limitation or price on the offer; the only condition is a *felt* weariness and a *felt* dehydration: "The Spirit and the Bride say, 'Come.' And let the one who hears say, 'Come.' And let the one who is thirsty come; let the one who desires take the water of life without price" (Rev. 22:17).

In a sermon, Newton addressed those who

> spend your money for that which is not bread,
>   and your labor for that which does not satisfy. (Isa. 55:2)

"While you are pursuing the wealth or honors of this world, or wasting your time and strength in the indulgence of sensual appetites, and look no higher, are you, indeed, happy and satisfied?" he asked. Apart from Christ, the soul is thrown into bedlam, tossed from empty promise to empty pleasure, from one empty cistern to another—a spiritual vortex dehydrating and dizzying the soul. "Are you not often, at least sometimes, like children in the dark," he asks, "afraid of being alone; unable to support the reflections which are forced upon you in a solitary hour, when you have nothing to amuse you?" Worldly comforts are powerless to support or encourage your soul. The cisterns are empty. Peace is out of reach. There is only one

---

[2] W, 4:75–76, 165–66.

Friend who can "comfort you, in all seasons, and under all circumstances; whose favor is better than life."[3]

Tragically, the same broken cisterns of worldly wealth, honor, and prestige allure those who have already tasted living water. "They are to be pitied, who, if they are at some times happy in the Lord, can at other times be happy without him, and rejoice in broken cisterns, when their spirits are at a distance from the Fountain of living waters."[4] And yet this is a tragic irony of the Christian life. We *know* only the freshwater of Christ will satisfy our souls, and yet we still seek our pleasures in broken cisterns, in good things made *ultimate* things.

This happens in relationships. Newton warned one newlywed couple not to find their ultimate happiness in each other. Newlyweds begin their union in prosperous bliss, a blessing from the Lord, but their wedded bliss is no replacement for Christ. Companionship becomes a broken-cistern idol when prized more than Christ. Modern readers may struggle to immediately grasp Newton's concern, but it was a warning he reiterated throughout his ministry.[5] When your personal security and chief comforts rest on the shoulders of your spouse, you have made your husband or wife into an idol and put him or her under a weight of expectancy no fallen human can support. God will graciously expose this idolatry through marital conflict, or in the sickness or mortality of the spouse. This explains why Newton could earnestly warn the blissful newlyweds by writing: "Alas! the deceitfulness of our hearts, in a time of prosperity, exposes us to the greatest of evils, to wander from the fountain of living waters, and to sit down by broken cisterns."[6] Such wandering may not feel like it in the moment, but transferring the ultimate security and satisfaction of your life to a new spouse is an abuse of God's gift, and it will dehydrate and dizzy your own soul.

We were created with Christ-sized thirsts for pleasure, and our gifts and successes and relationships and worldly pleasures and securities are but broken cisterns that cannot fill the void.[7] He is the one Spouse who can satisfy our souls. "We are prone (at least I may speak for myself) to forsake the fountain of living waters, and to hew out broken cisterns. Instead of

---

[3] *W*, 4:165–68.
[4] *W*, 1:455.
[5] For examples of one reader who struggles to understand Newton's point, see Aitken, 105, 141, 195–96, 256, 335. For examples of a reader who understands the gravity of Newton's concern, see Timothy Keller's sermons "Marriage Supper of the Lamb" (October 13, 1991) and "The First Wedding Day" (January 4, 2009).
[6] *W*, 6:132.
[7] *Letters* (Bull 1869), 201–2.

receiving him, I am often looking in myself for something to enable me to do without him."[8] For the Christian to avoid this soul weariness and dehydration, Christ must reign in his proper place—his central place—in our lives. The Christian can and should aim to live toward this: "a delight in the Lord's all-sufficiency, to be satisfied in him as our present and eternal portion." Such a soul "is not at leisure to take or to seek satisfaction in any thing but what has a known subserviency to this leading taste."[9]

As we have seen, this delight in Christ's all-sufficiency grows as we prioritize our study of Scripture.[10] In Scripture we behold Christ, whose glory and beauty and love is the all-satisfying center of the Christian life and the fountain of living waters to satiate the soul. "Oh, how happy is it to know the Lord, the Fountain of living waters!" Newton once wrote. "For every other acquisition without him will prove a broken cistern."[11] That last sentence is key. Soul weariness is not avoided by dismissing good gifts; rather, it's avoided by properly placing Christ as the ultimate gift. "Cisterns must be broken, but the fountain of living waters is always full and always flowing."[12]

Wearied by Legalism

Second, soul weariness washes over the souls of Christians who seek to ground their security before God in personal righteousness and obedience. In the gospel message, Christ offers to sinners a spectrum of freedoms and spiritual comforts that

> includes a freedom from the forebodings and distressing accusations of a guilty conscience; from the long and fruitless struggle between the will and the judgment; from the condemning power of the law; from the tyranny of irregular and inconsistent appetites; and from the dominion of pride and self, which makes us unhappy in ourselves, and hated and despised by others.[13]

The gospel justifies the Christian and satisfies all of God's righteousness

---

[8] W, 6:74–75.
[9] W, 1:454–55.
[10] W, 2:337; 3:609.
[11] W, 6:260.
[12] *Letters* (Bull 1869), 325.
[13] W, 4:168–73.

for our eternal happiness. We saw this point in the last chapter, on battling insecurity. Here we look at the weariness produced by this legalism.

Gospel amnesia is again the problem. We too quickly forget the liberating power of Christ and the gospel, and we grow spiritually weary by the drudgery. "I find a vast difference between my judgment and my experience," Newton wrote.

> I am invited to take the water of life *freely*, yet often discouraged, because I have nothing wherewith to pay for it. If I am at times favored with some liberty from evils, it rather gives me a more favorable opinion of myself, than increases my admiration of the Lord's goodness to so unworthy a creature. And when the returning tide of my corruptions convinces me that *I am still the same*, an unbelieving legal spirit would urge me to conclude that the Lord is changed: at least, I feel a weariness. [14]

Legalism clings to false securities (like works), is blinded to small progresses in personal growth, and turns us *away* from the all-sufficient Christ, not *toward* him as our Savior and solution. As we grow weary of ourselves, legalism pushes us to think of God as a grumpy master who is never happy with us, never pleased, always frowning over our lives.

This soul-wearying legalism is the special design of Satan, and he works his subtle art in believers' spiritual disciplines. "If he cannot make them omit praying, he will repeatedly endeavor to weary them by working upon the legality which cleaves so close to the heart. Satan is a hard task-master, when he interferes in the performance of our spiritual duties." [15] What a scam! Legalistic tendencies, plus disappointment with ourselves, plus hard thoughts of God are a recipe for weariness—and Satan knows it. His recipe drives us *away* from God exactly when we need him most. The true gospel speaks to powerless sinners and teaches us to renounce all self-sufficiency before God and to find in Christ our full sufficiency. [16]

If Christ were to supply 95 percent of our salvation, we would then remain 100 percent hopeless under the wearying load of our sin. The mirage of our sufficiency blinds us to amazing grace, we lose sight of Christ's glory, and clouds darken our souls, leaving us weary under the heavy weight of self-righteous manure. Christ's all-sufficiency alleviates this weight. Christ

---

[14] *W*, 1:447.
[15] *W*, 1:235.
[16] *Letters* (Bull 1869), 256.

is our full and complete answer to God's law and holiness, and he is the grounds of God's favor in us. United to Christ we are adopted into God's family, a status unchanged by any conditions within us. Newton was fond of Paul's testimony: "I count all things but loss for the excellency of the knowledge of Christ Jesus my Lord: for whom I have suffered the loss of all things, and do count them but dung, that I may win Christ" (Phil. 3:8 KJV). Christ flushes the burden of self-righteousness.

In other words, *justification* is essential to a healthy and joyful Christian life (e.g., 1 Cor. 6:11; Gal. 3:22–29; Phil. 3:1–11). To be justified in Christ—to be declared guiltless in God's sight on the basis of Christ's perfect life, substitutionary death, and victorious resurrection—and to have a conscious knowledge of this grace sunk deep into our hearts changes everything about the daily Christian life. "The right knowledge of this doctrine is a source of abiding joy; it likewise animates love, zeal, gratitude, and all the noblest powers of the soul, and produces a habit of cheerful and successful obedience to the whole will of God."[17] Legalism is weariness; justification is joy (Rom. 4:7–8; 5:1–11).

Justified *in Christ* and united *to Christ*, we discover both the purpose of obedience and the power for obedience. And we find that obedience to our Creator is perfect freedom. *Perfect freedom* was a phrase Newton adopted from the Anglican liturgy, a "beautiful expression," and one he used often to talk about joyful Christian obedience. If legalism wearies and justification liberates, then true obedience is *perfect freedom*. It is an obedience that flows from our identity in Christ. Newton said about preaching obedience, "If I wanted a man to fly I must contrive to find him wings; and thus, if I would successfully enforce moral *duties*, I must advance evangelical *motives*."[18] Christ gives wings to the Christian life, or to use another uplifting metaphor, the gospel is power.

My dear friend, may the great and glorious name of Jesus, be deeply engraved on your heart and mine, and on the hearts of all dear to us. Whether we consider him as our Surety, our Advocate, or our Lord, how precious should he be! His favor is life, his service is perfect freedom. The knowledge of him is safety, wisdom, and happiness. A discovery of the glory of God in his person fills the understanding with heavenly light, the affections with divine love, and unites the will to our proper good. How

[17] W, 4:526–27.
[18] W, 1:119.

many things utterly impossible to a man's natural strength, are practi-
cable and easy by the right application of mechanical powers! Without
them a stone of a few hundred weight is immoveable, but with them he
can raise a stone of many tons to the height of St. Paul's Cathedral. But
there are no powers comparable to those which are furnished by the gospel machine, if I may so speak.[19]

Wearied by Spiritual Battles

Our souls are wearied in a third way: by the ceaseless spiritual battles of the
Christian life. We battle the allurements of worldly idolatry, the wiles of Satan,
and the indwelling sins of our flesh. "The opposition between nature and
grace, flesh and spirit, renders the Christian life a state of constant warfare."[20]
The Christless sinner may feel very little or nothing of the spiritual battle inside the soul. In fact, this heavy burden of spiritual warfare felt in the soul is
a good sign of God's activity in us. "The Lord does not give us our arms and
regimentals only to strut about in, like the Beef-eaters at court," Newton said
of the ceremonial troops. "We must expect blows, yea sometimes wounds, but
the leaves of the tree of life are appointed for healing."[21] And the blows come,
sometimes with the force and frequency of a prizefighter in peak condition,
and these repeated blows will sometimes breed weariness. True to his pastoral
concern for the weary, Newton wrote a hymn about this type of weariness:

> A wicked world, and wicked heart,
>   With Satan now are join'd;
> Each acts a too successful part
>   In harassing my mind.
>
> In conflict with this threefold troop,
>   How weary, Lord, am I!
> Did not thy promise bear me up,
>   My soul must faint and die.

The singers of the hymn join a chorus of anguish in the battle of the Christian life. The world, remaining sin, and the Devil conspire in battle against
the Christian. The conflict with this "threefold troop" is wearying. The soul
is weighed down. There's only one hope.

---

[19] *Letters* (Bull 1847), 182–83; a point beautifully described in *W*, 4:232–33.
[20] *W*, 6:481. See also *Letters* (Bull 1869), 351; *Letters* (Coffin), 45.
[21] *Letters* (Ryland), 86.

But fighting in my Savior's strength,
   Though mighty are my foes,
I shall a conqu'ror be at length
   O'er all that can oppose.[22]

Here we find the solution for our spiritual weariness. United to Christ we find spiritual strength for the battle, and in his crucifixion we have the victory secured, but we are prone to forget both. When we fight in our own strength, we grow weary. When we fight with the weapons of the Lord, our joy cannot be extinguished.

But Satan remains our accuser and adversary, the god of this world, a serpent and roaring lion. His wiles and devices and darts aim at disrupting the Christian life. "He knows how to aggravate sin, to strengthen unbelief, to raise objections against the truth of the gospel, or to work upon the imagination, and to fill us with dark, uncomfortable, wild, or wicked thoughts." But "he is a conquered and a chained enemy: Jesus has conquered him, he has broken his power, and taken away his dominion, so far as concerns those who flee for refuge to the hope of the gospel. And Jesus holds him in a chain, and sets limits to his rage and malice, beyond which he cannot pass."[23] A conviction of Christ's sovereignty over Satan's influence in our life is essential to avoiding the weariness of spiritual battles.

Spiritual victory and rest are found in Christ alone. He purchased our rest and gave it to us freely. United to Christ we have all the benefits of his life, death, and ongoing intercession in our battles. All our spiritual needs are abundantly provided. In him we will be saved "in defiance of all the opposition of earth and hell," and saved not because of what we are. We are unstable, weak as water, bruised reeds and helpless infants. All spiritual victory we have is gifted to us. We put all our trust and hope for spiritual victory in him. And although we have battles to fight and spiritual weapons and armor to take up, yet, says Newton, "he will fight your battles, heal your wounds, refresh your fainting spirits, guide you by his counsel while here, and at last receive you to himself."[24] The battle against weariness is a battle against unbelief. To Captain Scott, a friend who lived many years in legalistic unbelief, Newton wrote of Christ:

----

[22] W, 3:541–42.
[23] W, 6:251–52.
[24] W, 2:477–78.

His blood, righteousness, intercession and unchangeable love, keep me from giving way to the conclusions which Satan and unbelief would sometimes force upon me. It is he who must do all things for me, by me, and in me. I long to live more above the influence of a legal spirit and an unbelieving heart.[25]

Spiritual warfare is not comfortable, but the victory is certain in Christ, and we are promised the battle will be over soon. "A few brushes more, and the King will say to us, Come near, and set your feet upon the necks of your enemies. Then the redeemed shall enter into the kingdom with songs of triumph, and shouts of everlasting joy, and sorrow and sighing shall flee away."[26] Here in the all-sufficiency of Christ we are protected from the weariness of spiritual warfare.

The Root of Our Weariness

In all these areas, Newton is eager to show us how weariness is all rooted in disregard for our all-sufficient Savior. Gospel forgetfulness is the diagnosis behind weary sinners chasing broken cisterns, behind weary legalists chasing self-righteousness, and behind weary Christians fighting spiritual battles out of their own reserves. Christ allows repeated disappointments and trials and losses in the Christian life, not to grieve and weary us, but to train us to treasure Christ above all else, and to find in him the solution to all our spiritual disillusionments.

But Newton presses deeper still. What feeds all these forms of weariness is a systemic infection of selfishness, a paradoxical and stinging lesson Newton discovered from studying his own heart. Self-satisfied sinners find Christ's all-sufficiency wearying! Here's how Newton says it:

I find that many of my complaints arise more from the spirit of self, than I was formerly aware of. Self, as well as Satan, can transform itself into an angel of light. To mourn over sin is right; but I do not always rightly mourn over it. Too often a part of my grief has been, a weariness of being so entirely dependent upon Jesus, of being continually indebted to him for fresh and multiplied forgiveness. I could have liked better to have some stock, ability, and power of my own, that I might do a little without him; that I might sometimes come before him as a saint, as a servant that

---

[25] *Letters* (Bull 1869), 146.
[26] *W*, 6:82–83.

has done his duty, and not perpetually as a poor worthless sinner. Oh, that I could be content with what is, and must be, my proper character; that I could live more simply upon the freeness and fullness of his grace![27]

Our high estimation of self pushes away Christ, and in pushing away Christ we grow weary. We are far too easily pleased with the dung of self-righteousness and self-sufficiency. The comforts of Christ in the gospel are offered only to those who are dissatisfied with themselves, poor sinners who live in need every day.

Self-righteousness has had a considerable hand in dictating many of my desires for an increase of comfort and spiritual strength. I have wanted some stock of my own. I have been wearied of being so perpetually beholden to him, necessitated to come to him always in the same strain, as a poor miserable sinner. I could have liked to have done something for myself in ordinary situations, and to have depended upon him chiefly upon extraordinary occasions. I have found indeed, that I could do nothing without his assistance, nor any thing even with it, but what I have reason to be ashamed of. If this had only humbled me, and led me to rejoice in his all-sufficiency, it would have been well. But it has often had a different effect, to make me sullen, angry, and discontented, as if it was not best and most desirable that he should have all the glory of his own work, and I should have nothing to boast of, but that in the Lord I have righteousness and strength. I am now learning to glory only in my infirmities that the power of Christ may rest upon me; to be content to be nothing that he may be all in all. But I find this a hard lesson; and when I seem to have made some proficiency, a slight turn in my spirit throws me back, and I have to begin all again.[28]

Newton displays pastoral perception of the subtlest sort. Those full of themselves are wearied by the fullness of Christ. This is the tragedy of a lost world, and it's a painful pill for Christians, but it's the kind of prescription that brings healing if we can turn from the lies that promise we will find our ultimate happiness and security in self-righteousness, self-power, and self-satisfaction in all its forms. This soul-wearying sickness can only be cured by turning to Christ, our daily all-sufficient treasure.

---

[27] W, 6:139.
[28] Letters (Ryland), 37.

Turning from Self—Refreshed in Christ

Here is Newton's point in all this. Our souls are wearied by chasing broken cisterns, by seeking security in legalism, by fighting spiritual battles from our own resources, and by neglecting our true dependence on Christ. What makes the Christian life wearisome is *me*. The crushing weight of weariness is not the yoke of Christ, but the lead-weight anvil of our still-uncrucified self, made heavier by our own unbelief and remaining pride. "Nothing in you that has not died will ever be raised from the dead," wrote C. S. Lewis. "Look for yourself, and you will find in the long run only hatred, loneliness, despair, rage, ruin, and decay. But look for Christ and you will find Him, and with Him everything else thrown in."[29] This was Newton's conclusion about soul weariness.

So God brings into our Christian lives repeated disappointments and trials and losses, not because he wants to grieve us and weary us, but because these are necessary lessons teaching us to treasure Christ above ourselves. By taking our eyes off Christ, our own spiritual inclinations become hazardous to us. We turn inward for sufficiency, we pursue broken cisterns of worldly joy, legalistic obedience, and self-sufficiency. The very things we pursue, if we were to get them, would be like pouring boiling water over our own heads.[30]

An "amen" to the doxology of Christ's sufficiency requires our genuinely humbled acknowledgment of our insufficiency. The two go together. As we explore in the next chapter, our securities and successes and comforts in the Christian life depend fully on Christ through a humbled self-awareness of our neediness and weakness.[31] "This is God's way: you are not called to buy, but to beg; not to be strong in yourself, but in the grace that is in Christ Jesus."[32] "I am the vine; you are the branches," says Jesus. "Whoever abides in me and I in him, he it is that bears much fruit, *for apart from me you can do nothing*" (John 15:5).

Newton leaves wearied souls with great hope. Although our neglect of Christ and our attraction to self-sufficiency is a serious disease (dis-ease of the most serious and wearying sort), it's a disease under treatment. "But though my disease is grievous, it is not desperate; I have a gracious and infallible Physician. I shall not die, but live, and declare the works of the Lord."[33]

---

[29] C. S. Lewis, *Mere Christianity* (1952; repr., San Francisco: HarperCollins, 2009), 227.
[30] *W*, 1:702.
[31] *W*, 1:645.
[32] *W*, 2:141.
[33] *W*, 1:448.

Our Infallible Physician, our Savior, our Christ, our Friend, will never leave us lost in the delusion of self-sufficiency. Christ has initiated in our souls the work of his Holy Spirit to make Christ look more excellent and more beautiful and more satisfying to our thirsty hearts. By forsaking the false promise of self-sufficiency, and by owning our own sinful weaknesses, we find a burden-relieving joy in Christ. In this discovery we find new relief for our soul's heavy disillusionment, for another part of the self has died.

CHAPTER 13

VICTORY OVER MR. SELF

In chapter 12 we began looking into the depths of our selfishness, but we have only rippled the surface. We need more time exploring these dark waters because the Christian's chief foe is not the world or the Devil, but the *self*. "Take care of self," wrote Newton.

> This is the worst enemy we have to deal with—self-will—self-wisdom—self-righteousness—self-seeking—self-dependence—self-boasting. It is a large family. I cannot reckon up all the branches; but they are all nearly related to Satan—they are all a sworn enemy to our peace. If we lie low, the Lord will raise us up; but if we will be something, his Arm will surely pull us down.[1]

"That monster Self has as many heads as Hydra, as many lives as a cat. It is more than twenty-five years since I hoped it was fast nailed to the cross, but alas it is alive still mixing with and spoiling every thing I do."[2]

Newton's favorite name for selfishness (particularly his own) was Mr. Self. In its many manifestations, Mr. Self is spiritual enemy number one to the Christian life, the universal idol. United to Christ, Christians are empowered to crucify selfishness in all its branches—sinful ambition, conceit, self-seeking, bitter jealousy, enmity, gossip, slander, strife, fits of anger, rivalries, dissensions, grumbling, divisions, envy, and the rest. Left unchecked, Mr. Self will stoke these interpersonal sins and stew disharmony.

---

[1] *Letters* (Clunie), 84.
[2] *Letters* (Ryland), 70.

"Why are we liable to anger, pride, positiveness [self-certainty], and other evil tempers but because we think too highly of ourselves and suppose we are not treated as we ought to be?"[3] Mr. Self is pushy. And when we gratify Mr. Self, we sell out for lesser pleasures.

Mr. Self Goes to Church

What makes all this so dangerous for the Christian life is that Mr. Self can veil himself in religion. He thrives in three denominations: the Pharisees, Sadducees, and Herodians.[4] All three of these denominations were well represented in Newton's time, and they still exist today.

The modern *Pharisee* is a guardian of the law, in love with his reputation for upholding exact conformity to all matters of external obedience, and quick to despise anyone who fails. "His heart rises with enmity at the grace of the Gospel, which he boldly charges with opening a door to licentiousness."[5] Free grace leads to willful sin, he says. But by rejecting free grace, all his fasting and prayers—and really every one of his religious activities—become the ornaments of his self-glory. He's a slave to his sin more than he knows. The modern Pharisees, "if not hypocrites in the very worst sense, yet deceived both themselves and others by a form of godliness, when they were, in effect, enslaved by their passions, and lived according to the corrupt rule of their own imaginations."[6] The modern Pharisee's religious zeal is dark, narrow, envious, and bitter. The gospel of free grace in Christ to unworthy lawbreakers stirs up enmity in his heart.

The modern *Sadducee* readily admits that God has spoken in the Bible, but arranges that revelation in varying degrees of importance as he sees fit. He reviews everything and "affixes, without hesitation, the epithets of absurd, inconsistent, and blasphemous, to whatever thwarts his pride, prejudice, and ignorance."[7] Whatever he finds in the Bible is measured by his own prejudice, and whatever fails to measure up to his approval gets discarded, like the resurrection from the dead (Matt. 22:23; Acts 23:8). Thus, the glorious revelation of the gospel is evaluated by the Sadducees, torn apart, and ultimately rejected because it fails to accord with his (so-called) reason.

The modern *Herodian* attempts to synthesize his friendship with the

[3] *Letters* (Bull 1869), 368.
[4] W, 3:37–41.
[5] W, 3:40.
[6] W, 3:37–38.
[7] W, 3:40.

world and friendship with Christ. His aims are split from the start. He fundamentally lacks gospel simplicity. The Herodian calls himself a moderate, avoids the excesses of overzealous Christians, but also manages to put a fair distance between himself and his Christian convictions in the public square. Because the numbers are on his side, he can easily blend in to the world by never making a scene over truth and error. The Herodian is a master of situational elasticity. He is very happy to be called religious and maybe even a Christian, but not in public. If you really pressed him, he would admit he finds the message of the gospel too demanding, too exclusive, and too dividing of him and his love of money and reputation. The Herodian harbors resentment toward the gospel, but he keeps it largely to himself.

The gospel confronts the selfishness of all three versions of Mr. Self. The freeness of the gospel to unworthy sinners offends the modern Pharisee's legalistic, self-righteous superiority (Matt. 9:11–13). The extravagant claims of the gospel in the death and resurrection of Christ offend the modern Sadducee's unwavering fidelity to only what constitutes intelligent human wisdom (1 Cor. 1:18–31). And the holistic, life-changing gospel offends the modern Herodian's double-minded balancing act (Matt. 10:34–39; 16:24–28; James 4:4). "The doctrines of free grace, faith, and spiritual obedience, were diametrically opposite to their inclinations," Newton writes.

> They must have parted with all they admired and loved if they had complied with him; but this is a sacrifice too great for any to make, who had not deeply felt and known their need of a Savior. These, on the contrary, were the whole, who saw no want of a physician, and therefore treated his offers with contempt.[8]

Mr. Self does not share glory.

Charles Simeon (1759–1836), a preacher and friend of Newton, reached a similar conclusion.

> Even in the things which have respect to religion, a carnal man will still feel no higher principle than *self*: self-seeking, self-pleasing, self-righteousness, and self-dependence, will be found at the root of all that he does in waiting upon God. He has no real delight in any religious

---
[8] W, 3:41.

exercise; and all his conformity to religious observances is a mere trib-
ute to *self*, rather than to God: it is a price paid for self-esteem, and for the
esteem of those around him.[9]

Mr. Self will pay this price. He likes to parade in religious observances.
In both his artificial humility and religious pageantry, Mr. Self keeps the
glory for himself.

By these examples you can see the perils of Mr. Self in the life of a genuine believer. Newton faced this danger, for example, when Mr. Self manifested himself in a pouty, mopey, dreary Calvinism. When Mr. Self wants to
call his pouting "religious humility," believers can call it by another name.
"The joy of the Lord is the strength of his people: whereas unbelief makes
our hands hang down, and our knees feeble, dispirits ourselves, and discourages others; and though it steals upon us under a semblance of humility, it is indeed the very essence of pride."[10] Mr. Self's artificial humility is
authentic arrogance. It is right to live aware of our total depravity and to
be emptied of spiritual self-confidence, but such emptiness should make
room for more joy and delight and happiness in the sovereign atoning work
of Jesus Christ. Thus, the truly humbled Calvinist should be among the
happiest people in the world.[11]

Reverend Self

Ministry leaders are particularly vulnerable to Mr. Self in the church. Self-
importance is the "great snare" of preachers, and over time Newton witnessed ministry envy in older pastors who wrongly built their identities
upon their gifts and successes rather than in the grace of Christ (recall
the gifts/grace distinction in chap. 4). Newton himself was aware of the
temptation and cherished for many decades one particular quote from New
England Puritan Cotton Mather (1663–1728): "My usefulness was the last
idol I was willing to part with, but the Lord has enabled me to give even this
up. I am now content to be laid aside, overlooked, neglected, and forgotten—only let his wise and holy will be done."[12]

---

[9] Charles Simeon, *Horae Homileticae*, vol. 15, *Romans* (London, 1833), 196.
[10] *W*, 2:176.
[11] A point well explained in one of Newton's favorite books, Andrew Fuller, *The Calvinistic and Socinian Systems Examined and Compared as to Their Moral Tendency*, chap. 13, in *The Complete Works of Andrew Fuller: Controversial Publications*, ed. Joseph Belcher, 3 vols. (Harrisonburg, VA: Sprinkle, 1988), 2:206–14.
[12] Source unknown. Newton cites the quote in two letters (*Letters* [Bull 1847], 295; *Letters* [Ryland], 380), but they read slightly differently, and in one case he appears to be recalling it from memory (fifty years after he first read it!). Without a doubt the quote sounds like Mather, a minister deeply concerned about

There's no security to be found in our gifts and usefulness. Yet we are tempted to build our identity by our gifts and usefulness. Failure to humble ourselves as insufficient sinners, failure to delight in Christ (the solid gold of *grace*), creates a self-sufficient minister who feeds off the candy of praise (the tinsel of his *gifts*). Such a man is headed for disillusionment, spiritual disaster, and jealous resentment toward emerging gifted ministers. Newton feared for his own soul here.

> I have known good men in advanced life garrulous, peevish, dogmatic, self-important, with some symptoms of jealousy, and perhaps envy, towards those who are upon the increase while they feel themselves decreasing. Do, my friend, pray earnestly that it may not be so with me, but that I may retire, if laid aside, like a thankful guest from a plentiful table, and may rejoice to see others coming forward to serve the Lord (I hope better and more successfully) when I can serve him no longer.[13]

Newton was hedging his future and asking for help against the inevitable influence of Reverend Self for a day coming when God would "disable" his public ministry, when his gifts would no longer be necessary for the church, when all that would be left is the grace of God (the solid gold of *grace*), his delight in Christ, and communion with God.

The common thread between fake Christianity (the Pharisee, Sadducee, and Herodian), the pouty "Calvinist," and the envious minister is selfishness. If selfishness didn't exist, distortions of Christianity wouldn't exist, self-absorption wouldn't exist, and jealousy in the church wouldn't exist. The gospel of the all-sufficiency of Christ is, at its core, a profound message that calls for denial of the self, conviction of the truth, death to the praise of the world, and a spirit of humility and joy—the very things Mr. Self opposes. "Beware of that worst of evils, spiritual pride," Newton writes. "Pray earnestly for a deep sense of your own insufficiency."[14] And

---

Christian usefulness and keenly aware of idolatry in such usefulness. To combat a tendency to be puffed up after his sermons appeared to be powerful or effective, Mather once wrote in his personal diary: "How *dangerous*, how *destructive*, an evil is this *pride* of mine! I provoke the God of Heaven to take away every one of those *idols*, which in my fond *pride* I dote upon; and if the Lord should now deprive me of my capacities and my opportunities [preaching], where am I, but in a horrid pit of most *unpittyable miseries!* Yea, let me remember, *pride* sooner than any thing will drive away the good Spirit of God from the heart of a poor creature. And if that should be my fate, Oh Lord have mercy!" (*Diary of Cotton Mather, 1681–1708*, Massachusetts Historical Society Collections [Boston, 1861], 17).

[13] *Letters* (Bull 1869), 314. For more on this related point, see *W*, 1:163–66; 2:390; 3:515–16; 5:77–78; 6:115–16, 127–28, 171–72; *Letters* (Bull 1869), 169, 313–14, 364; *Letters* (Campbell), 36–37; *Letters* (Bull 1847), 239, 255, 303.

[14] *W*, 6:31.

when we get a sense of our spiritual pride, when we're awakened to how Mr. Self taints all our best religious duty, and when we find our best offerings all polluted and stained by our pride, we turn to Christ.

Suffering by the Cheat

The tension between Mr. Self and Christ is probably best illustrated in the legalism plaguing the Christian life, something we looked at briefly in the last chapter, but now look at more closely in light of Mr. Self. Newton writes, "Most of our complaints are owing to unbelief, and the remainder of a legal spirit." The attempt by a Christian to appease God's wrath on the basis of personal obedience not only is a vain pursuit, but again, falsely casts God as a frowning, hard-to-please father and harsh taskmaster.[15] The "unbelieving believer," Newton calls him, is a believer who struggles with doubt for a lack of "a clear apprehension of the Lord's way of justifying the ungodly."[16] God does not justify the *partly broken*—he justifies the *ungodly* (Rom. 4:5). By muddying the gospel with the false notion that God justifies those who try to justify themselves, Mr. Self clouds over the all-sufficient righteousness of Christ (Phil. 3:2–11).

Mr. Self spoils the gospel. Wilcox writes:

> Christ is the mystery of the scripture; grace the mystery of Christ. Believing is the most wonderful thing in the world. Put any thing of thy own to it, and thou spoilest it; Christ will not so much as look at it for believing. When thou believest and comest to Christ, thou must leave behind thee thine own righteousness, and bring nothing but sin. (O that is hard!) Leave behind all thy holiness, sanctification, duties, humblings, etc., and bring nothing but thy wants and miseries, else Christ is not fit for thee, nor thou for Christ. Christ will be a pure Redeemer and Mediator, and thou must be an undone sinner, or Christ and thou will never agree. It is the hardest thing in the world to take Christ alone for righteousness: that is, to acknowledge him Christ. Join any thing of thine own, and thou un-Christ him.[17]

By his self-righteousness, Mr. Self "un-Christs" Christ. And if Christ came to save sinners, we cannot expect a self-healing. It's a contradiction that

---

[15] W, 2:141.
[16] W, 2:566–67.
[17] Thomas Wilcox, *A Choice Drop of Honey from the Rock Christ; or, A Short Word of Advice to All Saints and Sinners* (London, 1757), 7–8.

unravels the whole coming to Christ. As Wilcox writes, "Every day thy self-sufficiency must be destroyed."[18] Every day Mr. Self's self-sufficiency and self-righteousness must be dethroned. Every day the gospel must silence the boasting of Mr. Self (Rom. 3:27).

The hardest thing in the world is to take Christ *alone* for salvation and then to return to Christ *alone* every day of the Christian life. To illustrate the power of Mr. Self, Newton regularly addresses his own legalistic tendencies.

> I have often detected unbelief in my own heart, muffled up, and disguised in the mask of humility, when, indeed, all the pretenses to humility have been founded in a secret desire of self, to be something, and to have something of its own. I find this mistake deeply rooted in my heart; it is not yet removed, though I hope it is weakened. I have suffered by the cheat a thousand times.[19]

There's the key. The cheat—Mr. Self—desires glory, and that's the root of legalism. Legalism is an attempt at self-atonement for the purpose of self-worship and self-glory. Legalism is an attempt *to be something* apart from Christ.

Low Thoughts, High Thoughts

As if a blindfold were dropping from our eyes, the more aware we become of our insufficiency, the more aware we become of the all-sufficiency in Christ. At the same time, our lives are unburdened from so many layers of pressures and strain and weariness that accumulate with years of serving the self. This was key to everything Newton believed to be true about the Christian life: "Could I truly know myself to be nothing, I should then cordially rejoice that Jesus is all in all."[20] All throughout his works these two realities are directly connected. As our self-valuation is emptied, Christ's glory weighs heavier in our lives. "Through grace, I can say, that, as I never saw more of my own vileness, so, I think, I never saw Jesus more precious and desirable, or was more clearly sensible of the vanity of every thing without him, than I have of late."[21] Now we arrive at the heart of Newton's definition of personal holiness in the Christian life.

---

[18] Ibid., 12.
[19] *Letters* (Jones), 63–64. See also *W*, 1:444–48 and Newton's poem "The Kite" (*W*, 3:669–70).
[20] *Letters* (Ryland), 70.
[21] *W*, 6:42; see also 6:58.

We launched this flight across the pastoral counsel of Newton by addressing the all-sufficiency of Christ, and now we begin our final descent by looking at the utter insufficiency of self. These are intentional bookends. Newton contrasts Mr. Self with Christ because the more of Christ we want, the more of Mr. Self we must deny. Consistently, Newton holds this maxim: "I am persuaded a broken and a contrite spirit, a conviction of our vileness and nothingness, connected with a cordial acceptance of Jesus as revealed in the Gospel, is the highest attainment we can reach in this life."[22] These two convictions are inseparably linked. "As Jesus rises more glorious in the eye of faith, self is in the same degree depressed and renounced; and when we certainly see that there is no safety or stability but in his name, we as certainly feel that we expect them from him, and from him only."[23] At the name of Jesus, our idol of self must fall like Dagon.[24]

Such evacuating of Mr. Self requires decades of wisdom. "Depend upon it," says Newton, "if you walk closely with God forty years, you will at the end of that time have a much lower opinion of yourself than you have now."[25] With that awareness as his seventieth birthday approached, Newton could write a friend: "I hope to die like the thief upon the cross. I have no hope, no comfort in myself."[26]

On Controversy (and Mr. Self)

One of Newton's celebrated letters addresses how Mr. Self operates in theological debate. In the late 1760s and 1770s, Calvinists and Arminians were locked in a heated and public dispute.[27] Newton wrote a letter titled "On Controversy" and had it published in the Calvinistic *Gospel Magazine* in 1771. The magazine was growing increasingly hostile to Arminian evangelists like John Wesley.[28] The letter was Newton's first of many for the magazine, and as was his custom, he signed off under the pseudonym Omicron, the Greek letter for the little *o* (o), modest in comparison to the great *O*, omega (Ω). But from the tone and character of the letter, his alias was quickly decrypted.

---

[22] *W*, 1:676.
[23] *W*, 2:596.
[24] *W*, 3:335.
[25] *Letters* (Bull 1869), 389. See also *Letters* (Coffin), 95. Indeed, at age sixty-seven, Newton testified, "I am little aware of what is yet in my heart" (*Letters* [Bull 1847], 261).
[26] *Letters* (Bull 1847), 282. See also *W*, 4:436.
[27] See *Letters* (Ryland), 57–60.
[28] At the time, John Wesley called *Gospel Magazine* "that Monthly Medley of truth and error, sound Words and Blasphemy, trumped up as a vehicle to convey Calvinism and slander the nation" (Hindmarsh, 249).

First, Newton wrote, before you engage in debate, you must take heed of your opponent. He is an eternal creature. If he is not a Christian, he is lost, and he warrants your deepest pity, kindness, and prayers. And you would be just as hopeless and hardened to the truth as he if God had not acted on your soul first. If, however, your theological opponent is a genuine Christian, think about your future together in heaven. This point was deeply rooted in the large, generous heart of Anglican John Newton, who was fond of saying that he loved anyone who loved Christ, whether they be Anglican, Presbyterian, Baptist, Independent, Congregationalist, Episcopalian, Methodist, Moravian, or Quaker. "If they love the Lord Jesus Christ in sincerity, I care not a button by what name they are called, nor to what party they are joined. They are as my mother, and my sisters, and my brethren." He meant it. Indebted to all parties for something, Newton was "as Calvinistic as need be," but also a "speckled Calvinist," one who wore a coat of many colors stitched together from the best of every party. He longed for the last trumpet when all denominational walls would fall like the walls of Jericho, and at that point, he advised, your opponent will then become "dearer to you than the nearest friend you have upon earth is to you now," and "though you may find it necessary to oppose his errors, view him personally as a kindred soul, with whom you are to be happy in Christ forever."[29]

Second, Newton wrote, pay careful attention to the tone of your writing. The humbling theology of Calvinism is undermined by embittered, angry, and scornful words. Calvinism, rightly understood, breaks us, and that should be clear to others. More on this in a moment.

Finally, Newton maintained, defending the faith is a necessary work, but fraught with many dangers. Writers of controversy are often hurt by it. Their own self-importance flourishes, or they "imbibe an angry contentious spirit," or they get distracted from feeding their souls on the food of first importance—Christ, and him crucified (1 Cor. 15:3). "What will it profit a man," Newton asks, "if he gains his cause, and silences his adversary, if at the same time he loses that humble, tender frame of spirit in which the Lord delights, and to which the promise of his presence is made!"[30] Such is the loss endangering those engaged in controversy.

In this letter, Newton addresses Mr. Self. When theological controversy

---

[29] *W*, 1:269. For a sampling of Newton on denominational contention, see *W*, 1:352–56; 2:97–99, 234–35, 238–41, 391; 3:258–59; 4:422–23; 5:41–42; 6:198–200, 231–33, 278–79; *Letters* (Bull 1847), 20, 25, 58, 214; *Letters* (Bull 1869), 43–44, 121–22, 304–5, 323–24; *Letters* (Ryland), 47–48, 65, 134, 143, 295, 318, 323–24, 342–45, 370.
[30] *W*, 1:273.

gets hot, Mr. Self likes to take the microphone. Controversy presses the question, has your Calvinism humbled you?

> There is a principle of self, which disposes us to despise those who differ from us; and we are often under its influence, when we think we are only shewing a becoming zeal in the cause of God. I readily believe that the leading points of Arminianism spring from, and are nourished by, the pride of the human heart; but I should be glad if the reverse was always true; and that to embrace what are called the Calvinistic doctrines was an infallible token of an humble mind.
>
> I think I have known some Arminians—that is, persons who, for want of clearer light, have been afraid of receiving the doctrines of free grace—who yet have given evidence that their hearts were in a degree humbled before the Lord. And I am afraid there are Calvinists, who, while they account it a proof of their humility that they are willing in words to debase the creature, and to give all the glory of salvation to the Lord, yet know not what manner of spirit they are of. Whatever it be that makes us trust in ourselves that we are comparatively wise or good, so as to treat those with contempt who do not subscribe to our doctrines, or follow our party, is a proof and fruit of a self-righteous spirit.
>
> Self-righteousness can feed upon doctrines, as well as upon works; and a man may have the heart of a Pharisee, while his head is stored with orthodox notions of the unworthiness of the creature and the riches of free grace. Yea, I would add, the best of men are not wholly free from this leaven; and therefore are too apt to be pleased with such representations as hold up our adversaries to ridicule, and by consequence flatter our own superior judgments.
>
> Controversies, for the most part, are so managed as to indulge rather than to repress this wrong disposition; and therefore, generally speaking, they are productive of little good. They provoke those whom they should convince, and puff up those whom they should edify.[31]

The challenge for the Calvinist is to engage in controversy with purity, peace, and gentleness. To lack these, to act selfishly in debate, is

> like the dead fly in the pot of ointment, [it will] spoil the savor and efficacy of our labors. If we act in a wrong spirit, we shall bring little glory to God, do little good to our fellow-creatures, and procure neither honor nor

---

[31] W, 1:272–73. Newton: "I have learned the unprofitableness of controversy. If God had not interposed, and Job and his friends had lived to this day, they would have disputed till now" (Eclectic, 211–12).

comfort to ourselves. If you can be content with showing your wit, and gaining the laugh on your side, you have an easy task; but I hope you have a far nobler aim, and that, sensible of the solemn importance of gospel truths, and the compassion due to the souls of men, you would rather be a means of removing prejudices in a single instance, than obtain the empty applause of thousands.[32]

Mr. Self loves the ovations.

Contending for the truth must be done generously, with a broken spirit and a contrite heart (Ps. 51:17; Jude 3). Such a spirit is fitting a Calvinist, who believes and defends the biblical truths behind TULIP—total depravity, unconditional election, limited atonement, irresistible grace, and perseverance of the saints. "Calvinists should be the meekest and most patient of all men."[33] The gospel has come for the poor, the brokenhearted, the captives, the sick, and the blind. Thus, Newton can say, "I believe it not more impossible to find a humble Arminian, than a proud and self-sufficient Calvinist."[34]

Mr. Self can sound a lot like a self-righteous Pharisee while he thinks he's doing a fine job defending Calvinist orthodoxy.

My All in All

Newton employed many illustrations in his letters to help his friends prune Mr. Self from their lives, including this lengthy but illuminating excerpt:

The evil principle of self lies deep, and spreads wide into many branches— self-will, self-wisdom, self-dependence, self-seeking, self-righteousness; one or other of these abominations are continually sprouting up from the poisonous root within, and defiling our experiences; and the heavenly Husbandman, whose love is engaged to make us fruitful, and whose wisdom chooses the best means, sees when and how far it is necessary to use the pruning-knife, to cut off the growth, and prevent the increase of these weeds, that the plants of his grace may flourish in our souls. This is the reason why we are so often afflicted and disappointed both in temporals and spirituals. A tendency to rest in creature comforts often deprives us of what we might otherwise enjoy. And a tendency to rest our souls on something received rather than on the unsearchable riches and fullness of

---

[32] *W*, 1:274.
[33] *Letters* (Campbell), 150.
[34] *Letters* (Ryland), 15.

Christ, brings us into many a dark distressing frame of mind, which might be avoided if we knew how to live by faith in the Son of God. O that from a heart-felt knowledge of who Jesus is, and what he has done, we could at all times, and in all circumstances, say with the apostle, "I have all and abound—I have learnt to be content; yea, doubtless, I count all things loss and dung for the excellency of the knowledge of Christ Jesus my Lord!"

Was it as easy to do as to say, I should be happy, for the Lord has shown me how true peace is to be possessed, even by a simple reliance on his all-sufficiency and love, living upon his free grace, and sure mediation, and receiving strength continually from him suited to the occasions of every hour. O the happiness to eat his flesh, to drink his blood, to contemplate his glory, his faithfulness, his power, and the near relation he stands in to his poor children! Here is a fund of consolation suited to every case.

The man who drinks deep at these streams will not thirst after other waters. When we behold Jesus and his love by the eye of faith, we may, with the Prophet of old, sit down by a barren fig tree and a failing crop, and still rejoice in the God of our salvation. I say, to talk of this is easy, but I find the experience of it not so easily maintained. With respect to this life of faith, I may say as Paul in another place, I delight in it after the inner man; but when I would enjoy this good, evil is often present with me—I have not yet attained; but blessed be God I am pressing after it, and I hope, through grace, he is, according to his promise, drawing me nearer to himself. I hope I do gain a more abiding sense of my own utter vileness, depravity, and helplessness; and that in consequence of this, the name of Jesus is sweeter to my soul, as I find I cannot without him take a single step, nor enjoy one glimpse of comfort. My heart's desire is to love him more and more; to live still more entirely upon him, and to him, that he may be, as he well deserves, MY ALL IN ALL.[35]

Here is where the battle against self-will, self-wisdom, self-dependence, self-seeking, and self-righteousness must be waged. By God's grace, our lives must be pruned of Mr. Self to thrive off the all-sufficient and all-satisfying presence of Christ. This is the only way to find true self-control.

One Pushback

Before closing this chapter I'll offer one critique. For all his proper debasing of Mr. Self, I'm left wondering if Newton properly accented God's *delight*

---

[35] *Letters* (Clunie), 15–18.

over his redeemed children (Isa. 62:3–5; 65:17–19; Zeph. 3:17). Scripture tells us that God's children are *known* by him, *loved* by him, *delighted in* by him, and *rejoiced over* by him (Ps. 41:11; Jer. 1:5; 1 Cor. 8:3; Gal. 4:9; 2 Tim. 2:19; Heb. 12:6). Christ has redeemed sinners in order to reclaim his delight in the men, women, and children he created (Prov. 8:31). Yet divine delight in the redeemed is a regrettably rare theme in Newton's letters, sermons, and hymns. Occasionally he will affectionately speak of the Christian as "the apple of God's eye" (Deut. 32:10; Zech. 2:8). But this theme is infrequent and could have played a much larger role in his pastoral theology.

We see the glory of God shining in the face of Jesus Christ in Newton's writing. But in Christ, God's smile is also directed back at us, and in Newton this theme is missing. In justification, all of God's adopted and justified children are given the unconditional life-giving smile of God (Pss. 4:6; 16:11; 17:15; 21:6–7; Zeph. 3:17). Yet for Newton God's smile is mostly a circumstantial reality in the Christian life, a periodic comfort or felt affection that breaks into our lives, something to be measured by our subjective senses, but never the permanent possession of the redeemed. The abiding objective delight of God in his justified and adopted children would have helped balance out how our willful disobedience grieves God (chaps. 5 and 11), but this would be left to a later Anglican hymn writer to press home:

> Think what Spirit dwells within thee;
> 　what a Father's smile is thine;
> What a Savior died to win thee,
> 　child of heaven, shouldst thou repine?[36]

Closely related to God's delight is the Calvinist doctrine of *limited atonement* (or *definite atonement*), which claims that God set his free eternal love on his elect by name and accomplished their particular redemption in the cross.[37] This love of God for his chosen people is spontaneous and free, and it has no prior cause—he sets his love on his children *because he loves them* (Deut. 7:7–8). He loves us *because he loves us*.[38] He loves us because of who he is, not because of what we are.[39] Divine election is not conditioned

---

[36] Henry Francis Lyte (1793–1847), "Jesus, I My Cross Have Taken" (1833).
[37] Rightly so, Newton did not appreciate the label "limited" atonement (W, 4:193–95).
[38] See Thomas Manton, *The Complete Works of Thomas Manton*, vol. 2 (London, 1871), 340–41. See also Thomas Brooks, *The Complete Works of Thomas Brooks*, 6 vols. (Edinburgh, 1867), 2:40; 6:415.
[39] Leon Morris, *The Epistle to the Romans*, The Pillar New Testament Commentary (Grand Rapids: Eerdmans, 1988), 224.

by our self-righteousness, and Newton knows this well.[40] While he appears to be a five-point Calvinist in creed, yet (possibly for evangelistic reasons) when speaking of the extent of the atonement, Newton chooses the language of God's love in the sacrifice and the *general offer* of his Son to all sinners, over the particular love of God for certain sinners (*definite atonement*). For Newton, God's extensive love for sinners in Christ is sufficient to pay the sins of a thousand worlds, and is freely offered to all sinners for the taking. All of this is (gloriously) true, but Newton fails to stress the atonement as proof of God's particular love for each of his children. In his desire to see many sinners come to Christ, and possibly his desire to avoid becoming the centerpiece in theological debate, Newton's ministry remains vague on definite atonement.[41] Yet the doctrine offers impermeable assurance for all who truly believe in Christ. God, by his own initiative, has set *on me* an unbreakable and particular love.[42]

Here in these two related themes—God's smile over his children and Christ's definite atonement on their behalf—Newton missed two opportunities to apply gospel grace to broken lives. These two opportunities would have helped prevent genuine believers battling against Mr. Self from becoming overly introspective or condemning. These themes would have helped Newton make a clearer distinction between the *self* (Mr. Self, the flesh that must die) and the *selfhood* of the particular new-creation saint whose name was graven on God's hands in eternity past, adopted and redeemed by the blood of Christ, and rejoiced over in heaven by loud singing of angels and the triune God.

Nevertheless, in our secular, postmodern society—where personal meaning is sought in self-actualization and self-defined autonomy apart from a Creator, and where self-seeking and self-absorption and self-

---

[40] Newton affirms in a favorite story he liked to tell: "As some preachers near Olney dwelt on the doctrine of predestination, an old woman said, 'Ah! I have long settled that point: for, if God had not chosen me before I was born, I am sure he would have seen nothing in me to have chosen me for afterwards'" (*W*, 1:105). Charles Spurgeon enjoyed retelling this humorous story in the pulpit.

[41] See Hindmarsh, 162–66.

[42] John Piper: "When we preach, we long for our people to feel loved with the fullness of God's love for them. The Arminian and Amyraldian way of thinking make this experience difficult, if not impossible. They obscure the truth that it was precisely the distinguishing 'great love' of God (Eph. 2:4), expressed in the death of Christ, by which God brings his elect to life and gives them faith. Both views make it harder for the children of God to read Galatians 2:20 with the personal sweetness God intended: 'I have been crucified with Christ. It is no longer I who live, but Christ who lives in me. And the life I now live in the flesh I live by faith in the Son of God, *who loved me and gave himself for me*.' He loved *me*. He gave himself for *me*. The preciousness of this personal love is muted where it is seen as an instance of the same love that Christ has for those who finally perish. It is not the same" ("My Glory I Will Not Give to Another: Preaching the Fullness of Definite Atonement to the Glory of God," in *From Heaven He Came and Sought Her: Definite Atonement in Historical, Biblical, Theological, and Pastoral Perspective*, ed. David Gibson and Jonathan Gibson [Wheaton, IL: Crossway, 2013], 635).

glorification are no longer condemned as expressions of evil, and where the contours of gender and personhood are modified and re-created by plastic surgeons under the direction of unchecked hunches and inclinations of the sovereign self—this desire to exterminate Mr. Self is shockingly relevant. Newton is right about the severity of self-will, self-wisdom, self-righteousness, self-seeking, self-dependence, and self-boasting. Every day the thorns of self-sufficiency must be cut off and cast away. Self and selfishness—all the works of Mr. Self—are our greatest enemy and the cause of our greatest self-inflicted wounds. We will be happiest when Mr. Self gets finally evicted, because then, and only then, will we be freed to fully experience Christ in his all-satisfying glory.

CHAPTER 14

TO DIE IS GAIN

To begin this book, I introduced a summary of John Newton's theology of the Christian life, and throughout the book I have unpacked it. Looking again at the summary will help us retrace the steps we have covered. (Chapters are noted in parentheses.) John Newton's vision for the Christian life centers on the all-sufficiency of Jesus Christ (1, 2). Awakened to Christ by the new birth, and united to Christ by faith, the Christian passes through various stages of maturity in this life (7) as he or she beholds and delights in Christ's glory in Scripture (3, 10). All along the pilgrimage of the Christian life—through the darkest personal trials (9), and despite indwelling sin (5) and various character flaws (8)—Christ's glory is beheld and treasured (2, 3), resulting in tastes of eternal joy, growing security (11), and progressive victory over the self (12, 13), the world, and the Devil— a victory manifested in self-emptying and other-loving obedience (6), and ultimately in a life aimed at pleasing God alone (4).

The chapters in this book were carefully chosen for their value in displaying the heart of Newton's theology of the Christian life. Much more could be said about Newton on a number of other themes, like spiritual warfare, the role of Christian friendship and fellowship, the spiritual temptations of ministry, the importance of church unity, the discerning of God's will for our lives, the value of a disciplined prayer life, the common pitfalls of marriage, and so on.

But for all the details (and sub-details), Newton's theology of the Christian life can be boiled down to one main point: to live *is Christ*

(Phil. 1:21). "None but Christ" is Newton's motto, and it's the best advice Newton has to offer. That three-word phrase "looking unto Jesus" (Heb. 12:2) frames the believer's duty, privilege, safety, and happiness. The Christian life is all about Christ. And while we find ourselves rising to worship and praise him here, most of our days pass in muffled, mumbled, stammering attempts at worship. We find it impossible to maintain a level of praise that matches his worth. The remaining sin within dulls our worship. When we feel our hearts growing cold, and we lament our chilled worship, we look again to the brazen serpent of the glory of Christ. He is the solution. United to Christ, and looking to Christ, we are tethered to his victory.

By the brilliant glory of Christ, our souls have been recreated, invigorated, and transformed.

> And we all, with unveiled face, beholding the glory of the Lord, are being transformed into the same image from one degree of glory to another. . . . For God, who said, "Let light shine out of darkness," has shone in our hearts to give the light of the knowledge of the glory of God in the face of Jesus Christ. (2 Cor. 3:18; 4:6)

Our hope can rest only in this all-sufficient Christ. He is everything— our all-sufficient Shepherd, Husband, Prophet, Priest, King, and Friend; our Lord and Savior, Head, and Root; our Meat, Drink, Medicine, and Strength; our Hope and Foundation; our Sun and Shield; our Example and Forerunner; our Wisdom and Righteousness; our Sanctification and Redemption; our Life and Way and End. *In uno Jesu omnia*—in Christ alone is our everything!

The moment we behold Christ in his full glory, we immediately experience Christlike conformity within us, and the full joy and delight of the presence of Christ all around us. "The forerunners of death are indeed often painful and formidable; but death itself, what is it to a believer but to shut our eyes upon pain, grief, and temptation, to open them the next moment in the presence of God and the Lamb!"[1] To live *is Christ*, but to die *is gain*, because in death we get more of Christ as we commune with him face-to-face, free from all the sinful limitations that now diminish his beauty in our lives (Phil. 1:21–23). "O the excellency of the knowledge of Christ! It

---

[1] *Letters* (Jones), 82.

will be growing upon us through time, yea, I believe through eternity."[2] An unending discovery into the all-sufficiency of Christ makes death a win-win for us.

Christ's worth stands in sharp contrast to worldliness. To live for wealth or sexual sin or any pleasure or security or comfort of this world will make our dying pure loss. But to live *in*, *with*, and *for* Christ makes dying pure gain. Death proves to be Christ-centered gain only for the one who is Christ-centered in this life. Newton was aware of this, he sought to live it himself, and his pen was tirelessly employed to help his friends learn to live in the light and grace of Christ's radiant all-sufficiency, and to develop an appetite for the day when all the redeemed "unite in one song of endless praise to the Lamb that was slain."[3]

I Am What I Am

Until that day of greatest gain, all the world's a stage, all the creation's a theater, and all the Christian's life is a dress rehearsal for glory.[4] As we live out the Christian life in this great cosmic theo-drama, we return to our tasks and vocations and callings under the watchful care of our Infallible Physician. We are still desperately sick, but he is a perfect doctor who has taken up our cause and will not rest until the cure is finished.

To explain the riddle of the Christian life in all its shortcomings and its hopes, John Newton penned what has possibly become the most famous sermon outline in church history. He had been asked to preach a little homily in the home of a friend, which he happily obliged. He chose for his text 1 Corinthians 15:10: "But by the grace of God I am what I am." All that remains of Newton's living-room message is an outline, written

---

[2] W, 1:640.

[3] W, 4:560.

[4] Newton: "The motto of Drury Lane play-house holds forth a lesson which I fear is seldom duly attended to by those who frequent it—*Totus mundus agit histrionem* [the whole world plays the actor]. Human life is a drama, in which every man has a part, higher or lower, to perform. But the far greater number think it a reality, and are not aware how fast the plot is hastening to the catastrophe, and how soon the curtain will fall. Then the external distinctions, upon which some prided themselves as if properly their own, will cease, and all the actors will stand upon a level, and be judged according to their works. The question will not be, 'What part we performed?' but 'How we performed it?' The Lord grant that we may find mercy of the Lord in that day! It will be an awful day to many who were admired and envied while upon earth. Alas! For the rich, the gay, the wise (as they are called), the busy, and the mighty, who strutted for a while in borrowed plumes, lived without God in the world, regardless of their Maker, and instead of employing their talents in his service, perverted them for the ruin of themselves and their connections, as far as their influence could reach" (Letters [Wilberforce], 105–6). This life is a prep school, writes Newton: "We are now at school, learning to sing the song of redeeming love, and, ere long, we shall be translated to sing it before the throne" (*Letters* [Bull 1847], 129).

down by a nameless note taker in attendance. Over time, the sermon outline morphed and merged into this remarkably concise summary of the Christian life on earth:

> I am not what I *ought to be*. Ah! how imperfect and deficient. Not what I *might be*, considering my privileges and opportunities. Not what I *wish to be*. God, who knows my heart, knows I wish to be like him. I am not what I *hope to be*; ere long to drop this clay tabernacle, to be like him and see him as he is. Not what I *once was*, a child of sin, and slave of the devil. Though not all these, not what I *ought to be*, not what I *might be*, not what I *wish or hope to be*, and not what I *once was*, I think I can truly say with the apostle, "By the grace of God I am *what I am*" (1 Cor. 15:10).[5]

The parallels and contrasts within Newton's statement become clearer when decorated with visual cues to highlight corresponding clauses:

I am not what I ought to be.
Ah! how imperfect and deficient.

Not what I might be,
considering my privileges and opportunities.

Not what I wish to be.
God, who knows my heart, knows I wish to be like him.

I am not what I hope to be;
ere long to drop this clay tabernacle, to be like him and see him as he is.

Not what I once was,
a child of sin, and slave of the devil.

---

[5] My paragraph blends the two published versions of what Newton reportedly said. First, from this version: "I am not what I *ought* to be! Ah! how imperfect and deficient!—I am not what I *wish* to be! I 'abhor what is evil,' and I would 'cleave to what is good!'—I am not what I *hope* to be!—Soon, soon, I shall put off mortality: and with mortality all sin and imperfection! Yet though I am not what I *ought* to be, nor what I *wish* to be, nor what I *hope* to be, I can truly say, I am not what I *once* was—a slave to sin and Satan; and I can heartily join with the Apostle, and acknowledge; *By the grace of God I am what I am!*" (*The Christian Spectator*, vol. 3 [1821], 186). The second version apparently conforms more closely to Newton's original sermon outline. It reads: "1. I am not what I ought to be. Ah! how imperfect and deficient. 2. Not what I might be, considering my privileges and opportunities. 3. Not what I wish to be. God, who knows my heart, knows I wish to be like him. 4. I am not what I hope to be; ere long to drop this clay tabernacle, to be like him and see him as he is. 5. Not what I once was, a child of sin, and slave of the devil. Though not all these, not what I ought to be, not what I might be, not what I wish or hope to be, and not what I once was, I think I can truly say with the apostle, 'By the grace of God I am what I am' (1 Cor. 15:10)" (*Letters* [Bull 1869], 400).

Though not all these,

> not what I ought to be,
> not what I might be,
> not what I wish or hope to be, and
> not what I once was,

I think I can truly say with the apostle,

"By the grace of God I am what I am."[6]

"That's invaluable," says D. A. Carson of Newton's summary. "It understands Christian sanctification in one pithy statement better than anything I know."[7] All of the rather complex dynamics of the Christian life converge here—regret over sin and lost opportunities, desire for holiness, hope for future transformation, praise for salvation, and gratitude for abundant grace.

Newton was keenly aware of his faults and failures, but he was more aware of Christ's perfections and beauties. "My poor story would soon be much worse, did not he support, restrain, and watch over me every minute."[8] And Newton knew his story was not over. He anticipated a glorious reunion with Christ, when he would be changed into perfect conformity. In his hymn "Amazing Grace" Newton offers corporate language to describe God's converting and sustaining grace. In this sermon outline, Newton offers corporate language to describe the Christian's present status.

As modern Christians, we live with this same awareness: we are not what we ought to be, not what we could be, and not what we hope to be, but still we are not what we once were. And when we confess this, we pronounce a confession echoed by our spiritual ancestors. Their race is over, and we find ourselves in the middle of a divine drama looking forward in hope. Wrote Newton, "I am not what I would be; but there is a period coming, when I shall be so, yea, more than my heart can conceive. I hope to see Jesus, to be like him, and be with him forever."[9] The whole Christian life advances by footsteps of faith in forward progress toward beatific vision.

---

[6] Thanks to Justin Taylor for the visual formatting.
[7] Audio lecture, "Preaching and Biblical, Systematic, Historical, and Pastoral Theology, Part 3A" (October 7, 2010), 21:25–33.
[8] W, 1:626.
[9] W, 6:133.

To Live Is Christ

To close this study I sign off with a farewell from Newton. He was left with space at the bottom of one letter, and as was his custom, he liked to "fill up the paper," which he often did by penning words about his precious Christ. In one such letter, with space for one final paragraph on the page, Newton dipped his pen and offered to a friend this closing benediction:

> Let me commend you and yours to the grace and care of our Lord Jesus. They that dwell under the shadow of his wings shall be safe. His service is perfect freedom; in his favor is life. May his name be precious to your heart! And may you have such increasing knowledge of his person, character, and offices, that beholding his glory in the gospel glass, you may be more changed into his image, drink into his spirit, and be more conformable to him. The highest desire I can form for myself, or my friends, is, that he may live in us, we may live to him, and for him, and shine as lights in a dark world. To view him by faith, as living, dying, rising, reigning, interceding, and governing for us, will furnish us with such views, prospects, motives, and encouragements, as will enable us to endure any cross, to overcome all opposition, to withstand temptation, and to run in the way of his commandments with an enlarged heart. And yet a little while, and he will put an end to our conflicts and fears, and take us home to be with him forever. Thus, by the power of his blood, and the word of his testimony, we shall be made more than conquerors, and in the end obtain the crown of life, which the Lord hath promised to them that love him.
>
> I am sincerely,
> Your very affectionate and obliged
> Friend and servant,
>
> JOHN NEWTON.[10]

---

[10] *Letters* (Taylor), 44–45.

ACKNOWLEDGMENTS

Over the years I've grown keenly aware that a book does not happen apart from the fountain of all grace, Jesus Christ, who sustains me and provides an army of friends (old and new) to support my work.

From the start, this project required the foresight and vision of editors Justin Taylor and Stephen Nichols. I'm honored to work with these men, to contribute to their outstanding series, and to be writing again for Crossway. Speaking of the team at Crossway, this book benefited from the aesthetic touch of Josh Dennis and his design team, the promotional skill of James Kinnard and his marketing team, and the wise and judicious work of Thom Notaro, my editor and writing coach. The staff at Crossway displays professionalism at every stage of publishing.

This book required friends around the world to sift old libraries in search of rare books from the eighteenth century. To Jon Vickery (Kelowna, BC), Eric Frazier (The Library of Congress), Dan Johnson (Oxford, UK), and Adam Winters (James P. Boyce Centennial Library), thank you for your labors, and (in the most desperate cases) your page-by-page iPad camera pictures!

Through this book project I met new friends who have long studied the life and writings of Newton, and who offered to help edit my book and help me cut through a lot of speculations and urban myths surrounding his life. Without the edits of Grant Gordon (Aurora, ON) and Marylynn Rouse of The John Newton Project (Stratford on Avon, UK), this book would have been more exciting, but less accurate.

This book benefitted in many ways from my friends and colleagues at Desiring God, from the boost of encouragement generated when John Piper eagerly agreed to write the foreword, to the painstaking copyediting work of Bryan DeWire, and the fellowship of Josh Etter, David Mathis, Jonathan Parnell, Marshall Segal, Stefan Green, Jon Bloom, and Scott Anderson.

But most of all, this book benefitted from a committed companion behind the scenes, Karalee, who first became my editor, then my friend, and eventually my wife. On this our sixteenth anniversary, you remain my best friend and my most valuable editor. When I set out to write an entire book focused on the Christ-centeredness of the Christian life through the eyes of Newton, I knew it would require much time and many prayers. You graciously released me and prayed and edited this project to the finish line. To you—my right hand—I promise my life and dedicate this book. I love you!

GENERAL INDEX

new life, 143
Newton, John
  call to pastoral ministry, 21–22
  Christ-centeredness of, 30–31
  conversion of, 35
  epileptic seizure of, 180
  faced personal sins directly, 111
  great trial of, 203–4
  imagination of, 72–73
  imprisoned in West Africa, 179
  letters of, 22–25, 29, 31, 166, 180
  as pastor, 16, 120, 135
  sailing days of, 21
  self-evaluation as chief of sinners,
    36, 109
  as theologian, 25–27
  theology of, 265
  use of metaphors, 15–16, 41
  voluntary imprisonment of, 107
nonfiction imagination, 74–75, 88

oak tree metaphor, 141–42, 158
obedience, 101–3, 104, 129, 147,
  155–56, 222, 229–30, 242
Olney, 22, 23, 39, 141, 158
Omicron (pseudonym), 23, 256
ordinary to-dos of life, 169

Packer, J. I., 15, 25
"parlor preaching," 28n28
Pascal, Blaise, 129
pastoral surgery, 16
patience, 158
Paul
  on apostolic ministry, 92–93
  on assurance, 234
  on the cross, 70
  self-evaluation as chief of sinners,
    108–9
perfect freedom, 242
perseverance, 120
personal types, 208
Pharisees, 250–51, 253
philosophers's stone, 169

Phipps, William E., 21, 34n2
Pilgrim's Progress, The (Bunyan), 28,
  212
Piper, John, 138n11, 190–91n42, 262
Plantane Island, 179–80
pleasure, and duty, 132
politics, 171–75
postmodern society, 262
prayer, 114, 183–84, 205
  in approaching Scripture, 207–8
pride, 84–85, 87, 119, 122n52, 232,
  247, 254
priest, Jesus Christ as, 56–58
prince and pauper analogy, 134–36
private sin, 146–47
profanity, 193
promises, 189
prophecies, in the Old Testament, 208
prophet, Jesus Christ as, 55–56
propitiation, 62
Prudens (character flaw), 164–66, 176
punctuality, 166–67
purity of heart, 101

Querulus (character flaw), 171–76

reading books, 212–13
reconciliation, 60
redemption, extent of, 116
regeneration, 68
relative types, 208
"respectable" sins, 176–78
Riccaltoun, Robert, 25, 154
Roman Catholics, 26n19
Rouse, Marylynn, 37n10

Sadducees, 250–51, 253
sanctification, 70–72, 75, 131, 133,
  137–39, 146, 225, 232, 269
  as clash of competing affections,
    154–55
  and daily Bible reading, 215
Satan, lies of, 192–94
scaffolding metaphor, 41–42

SCRIPTURE INDEX

WISDOM FROM THE PAST FOR LIFE IN THE PRESENT

Other volumes in the Theologians on the Christian Life series

AUGUSTINE

BAVINCK

BONHOEFFER

CALVIN

EDWARDS

LUTHER

OWEN

PACKER

SCHAEFFER

WARFIELD

WESLEY

Visit
crossway.org/TOCL
for more
information.